HOT HOUSE PEOPLE

American-born broadcaster and journalist Jane Walmsley joined Capital Radio when it first went on the air in 1973 as a producer. She won several awards for her radio documentaries and news programmes and became head of documentaries before moving to BBC Television. She co-presented the BBC TV series *Out of Court* and later co-presented Yorkshire Television's documentary series *First Tuesday*. She now runs her own independent television production company for which she produced and presented the documentary series *Hot House People* for Channel 4 Television.

She writes regular features for *Company* magazine and is the author of one previous book *Brit-Think Ameri-Think: A Transatlantic Survival Guide*. She is married and has one daughter.

Jonathan Margolis is a senior feature writer with *The Mail on Sunday*. He is the co-author with Roger Cross of *The Yorkshire Ripper* published by Granada.

HOT HOUSE PEOPLE

Can We Create Super Human Beings?

Jane Walmsley
and
Jonathan Margolis

A *Pan Original*
Pan Books
London, Sydney and Auckland

The television series Hot House People was produced for
Channel 4 Television by Jane Walmsley Productions Ltd.

First published 1987 by Pan Books Ltd,
Cavaye Place, London SW10 9PG
9 8 7 6 5 4 3 2 1
Copyright © Jane Walmsley and Jonathan Margolis 1987
ISBN 0 330 29954 9
Printed and bound in Great Britain by
Richard Clay Ltd

This book is sold subject to the condition that it
shall not, by way of trade or otherwise, be lent, re-sold,
hired out, or otherwise circulated without the publisher's prior
consent in any form of binding or cover other than that in which
it is published and without a similar condition including this
condition being imposed on the subsequent purchaser

Contents

Introduction

The idea of 'hot housing' – enhancing the mental and physical faculties of 'average people' – is familiar to any reader of science fiction. It now appears that recent developments in a range of fields (such as education and biogenetics) may soon combine to turn fantasies into possibilities. Already, isolated attempts are being made to 'upgrade' the human stock. Experiments tend to concentrate on people at extreme ends of the age scale – and the results are significant.

Such research is controversial, frightening . . . and rather thrilling. The two major questions being asked are:

1. Assuming that IQ is a legitimate measurement of intelligence (many would argue that it isn't), is it inborn and *constant* throughout life – or can it be systematically increased?
2. Is lifespan genetically predetermined – or can it be extended?

Other questions also arise. Are smarter people *better* people – whether they're young or old? Have we the power – indeed, the duty – to improve upon nature? Should the rate at which young children learn be deliberately intensified and speeded up? Should the elderly be actively encouraged to exercise their minds and preserve their bodies in the wider social interest? Is America overreacting to the challenges of life at the turn of the millennium, and doing too much? Is Britain failing to anticipate trends, and doing too little? Are large-scale attempts at 'social engineering' now legitimate and even necessary?

This book invites readers to look into the future, and consider the Brave New World. What progress has been made so far? How close are scientists to understanding – perhaps manipulating – the natural development of minds and bodies? Who, and where, are the 'hot house' people? And where is the dividing line between adventurous but legitimate experiment and intrusive lunacy?

Hot housing people – both mentally and physically, in order to create the best human beings possible – has been a preoccupation for centuries. Plato had much to say about the intellectual and physical training of the best and the brightest. In more recent years, Hitler's 'Master Race' theories put the concept in bad repute. Between the extremes, there have existed a wide range of experiments – educational, epistemological, and biological. Many of the most recent efforts are chronicled here.

Today hot housing has fresh relevance. This book seeks to catch both scientific and social developments in full flood and to document an astounding and timely story. Many scientists and educators seem to agree that we stand on the threshold of great discoveries. For example, advances in biogenetic research mean that soon it may be possible for pregnant women to determine and choose not only the sex of their children, but other features as well, such as the colour of hair and eyes. A firm in Chicago is now working on a technique which will allow newly-conceived embryos to be washed from the womb, and genetically 'reprogrammed' for certain physical characteristics. This could one day extend to greater intelligence.

Meanwhile, better understanding of cognitive development and how very young children acquire knowledge, is helping educators to design large-scale teaching programmes which seem capable of raising the achievement levels of entire generations.

At the other end of the age scale much attention is now being paid to the quality of life available to the elderly. Both Britain and America have declining birthrates and ageing populations; this is sometimes refered to as the 'Greying Trend'. It is an oft-quoted figure that, by the year 2,000, nearly one fifth of the populations of both countries will be aged sixty five or over. Naturally enough, such a social shift has wide implications. Unless the elderly can be helped to lead lives which are healthy and active – mentally as well as physically – the social burden will be increasingly difficult to sustain.

Much expert opinion maintains that we stand on the brink of a breakthrough in geronotological research. Scientists can now artificially, and demonstrably, extend lifespan in certain animals, notably mice and rats. Many argue that there is potential application to human beings; one noted California doctor is testing his theories on himself. More importantly, latest research is at last providing endocrinologists with clues to the mystery of cell reproduction. Once this is fully under-stood, it may be possible to delay cell death, and so to prevent much of the disease and deterioration associated with old age. There are predictions of a new hot house human lifespan, lasting 110 to 120 years.

In Britain and America, systematic hot housing of children may soon be regarded more as a necessity than an educational luxury. The age of 'Star Wars' and microchip technology demands a new breed of scientist, capable of a level of creative and abstract thought never before required. Where will such people come from? Where, and how, are they being trained? It may be that the 'Cold War' is about to give way to a 'war of intelligence', in which the ultimate weapon is the human brain, and the implications are as far-reaching as nuclear power. Prince Charles was probably quite prescient in suggesting that 'Britain is being left behind in the technological race – and is in grave danger of becoming a fourth-rate power'.

There is also a more ordinary, yet crucial, dimension to the debate about hot housing. Few need reminding of the present concern in Britain for the young, the disaffected, the unemployed and the unemployable and the resulting horror of recent inner-city riots. It has long been a point of received wisdom that education is the only long-term solution to complex social problems. So, questions must be asked: why has education failed these youngsters so far? Would they have been different people – smarter, better, happier – if they had been approached and taught in a different fashion early in life? Is it too late to help, or can we hot house them now?

The research on which this book is based was carried out for a four-part *Channel 4* documentary series between 1985 and 1987. The more we pursued the lines of enquiry, the more extensive – even panoramic – the subject became. Like most issues connected with education, health, and human potential, it touches on politics, philosophy and social concerns in the widest (and most controversial) sense. The reader looking for expert theories and conclusive arguments on such matters should look elsewhere. These are beyond our qualifications or ambitions. Instead, what the book aims to be is a documentary report on *work in progress* on accelerated rearing of the young, and extending the active lifespan of the elderly. Perhaps more questions are raised than answered . . . but that is often the outcome of looking at unfinished experiments, or presenting the opposing sides of unresolved scientific and ethical debates.

We have resisted the temptation to indulge in too many flights of fancy – tempting though these are. For instance, can we envisage a time when rivalry between nations will no longer be commercial, or strategic, but cerebral? Will third world countries try to leap the north/south divide in a single step by hot housing a whole generation of young people? Can we imagine the impact of groups of super-people, whose intellect and potential for achievement far exceeds our own? Or is it all just hokum?

One aspect of our research which struck us is that far more ambitious research and experiment is under way in the USA, Japan, and even in parts of the third world such as Venezuela, than in Britain. Does this imply a prudent caution or even scepticism in the British scientific and educational establishment, or a lack of foresight which could cost the country dear in future?

The book starts with a look at one of the most vigorous areas of debate and experiment: at what age should the stimulation and education of children begin, and examines the work of several organizations in America which espouse hot housing from earliest infancy, (in one case, from *before* birth). We also take note of the growing enthusiasm amongst parents (especially mothers) to take on a new rôle as educators themselves and how their considerable energies are being mobilized in the interests of producing 'better babies'. The rôle of parents in a more extreme form is documented in *Chapter 3*, with a look at a series of fascinating case studies of individual parents who, for a variety of personal reasons, deliberately set out to make their children geniuses. Do such projects work? Or are they simply a means by which parents can live vicariously through their offspring? Are they a special form of parental cruelty? The evidence seems to suggest that they are not.

Chapter 4 looks at the broader context of the role of hot housing in providing educational compensation for the disadvantaged – from poor backgrounds, from poor countries. If hot housing works (and it does) for special cases, where objectives are narrowly focused (for example, in the cases of young gymnasts, chess players, violin virtuosos or ballerinas), can it work for whole sectors of society at the general level?

Conventional wisdom has it that hot housing children to create genius denies them their childhood, causes unhappiness, and produces human wrecks more often than it creates successful achievers. However *Chapters 5* and *6* contain abundant evidence that hot housed children can be (and usually are) both happy and successful. Unsettling though the thought may be, they also turn out to be wealthy – with adult incomes of around four times the national average, according to one USA statistic.

Chapter 7 wades into the mysterious (and, for many, frightening) waters of biogenetic experiment. Secrecy surrounds much of the work going on in this field. Many scientists are wary of talking to journalists for fear of the backlash of hostile public opinion. It is now well within the ability of geneticists to engineer a wide range of mutations in animals: to clone preferred characteristics, or to fuse embryos, thus eliminating the uncertainties of even the most sophisticated selective breeding. Much of the bona fide research in this area has welcome application in eliminating defects in human babies, but where should the line be drawn between improving lives, and 'programming' model babies?

The same underlying issues are carried through in the second half of the book. The genetics of ageing, the advances in understanding the rôle of diet, health, and stimulation are all central to the increasing preoccupation with improving the quality of life while extending its length. These are examined in *Chapter* 9. 'Use it or lose it' is the catchphaase of many researchers and counsellors whose work is devoted to arresting physical and mental decline in the elderly, and *Chapter 10* explores the ways in which our natural assumptions about life-expectancy are being seriously challenged. For life's true trenchermen, the dietary regime at California's Pritikin Institute for Longevity will lack the fun of a Maxim's menu, but there is convincing evidence that it can postpone arterial deterioration, and add extra years of active life.

A final note – wherever possible throughout this book, we have tried to use the language of 'human achievement' rather than IQ, a concept which has had a chequered history since the Stanford-Binet IQ test was first used as a tool by Professor Terman of Stanford University in 1916, and which has been in and out of favour with researchers, educators and sociologists ever since. For those who are interested, we begin with a capsule history of the yo-yo-like progress of the principle of the Intelligence Quotient.

1

Intelligence: The Great Debate

Who are You Calling Stupid, Stupid?

It used to be said that the worst way to insult a man was to cast aspersions on his virility and his driving. Times have changed a little. Machismo is regarded in many quarters as strictly for gorillas. Similarly, the simpering, subservient woman is, in most people's ideal world, an anachronism. As for driving, it is perfectly acceptable not to do it at all, or not to do it very well.

Intelligence is another matter entirely. This is surely the last frontier in insult. There is no circumstance anywhere in the world, in any social group, where it is OK to tell someone that he is not very bright. In Germany, it is an arrestable offence to point to another person's head, and so suggest that he or she is stupid.

Everyone says that intelligence is what separates us from animals — yet we have an ambivalent attitude to it. In Britain and America, populist politicians often make great issue of being straight, accessible, uncomplicated 'regular guys' . . . yet few have so far ventured to frankly advertise themselves as unintelligent. When Princess Diana announced recently that she was 'as thick as a plank', she was breaking relatively new ground in public life. She, on the other hand, does not have to worry about being reelected. Ronald Reagan's initial appeal was as a plain man, a non-intellectual; but his apparent slip into mental frailty has been met with international alarm.

Cleverness in this political context is seen to be the enemy, the province of sharp-suited city lawyers and their ilk. Being an ordinary, sensible type is the sound thing, and it is certainly pretty sharp of our politicians to exploit it. Princess Diana will certainly have succeeded in making the public believe she is honest.

More than half the world's population may profess to be devoted to the teachings and ideals of 'good' gods, and to value good people, but on a day-to-day level, intelligence seems to be the most important (or, at least, the most emotive) human characteristic — far and away more so than any notion of goodness, niceness, humanity or worth. There is little doubt that if you are good but stupid, you will draw the short straw in life; neither the meek nor the dim have so far managed to inherit the Earth. The world wide popularity of evil and con-niving J. R. Ewing in the TV soap opera *Dallas* provides some evidence of this attraction of canny infamy. You can call almost anyone — your spouse, your boss, your friend — mean or ruthless. Call them stupid and you could be in serious trouble.

The sensitivity of the subject explains why it causes the academic and the political world quite extraordinary anxiety. We have, or so it is argued, only the crudest most inaccurate and blunt method of measuring and quantifying intelligence, which is the very thing we value above all other aspects of ourselves.

IQ Bashing

In 1916, the American psychologist Lewis Terman published the first standardized intelligence test and called it the IQ — intelligence quotient. The Stanford-Binet test (Terman was the professor of psychology and education at Stanford University; Alfred Binet was the French founder of intelligence testing, back in 1905) signified intelligence by a score on which the 'average' person of any age had an IQ of 100. Terman saw his work as an attempt to recognize the importance to society of identifying intellectually-gifted children and providing them early in life with exceptional educational opportunities. Human potential, he believed, was being missed.

He and his supporters felt passionately that despite the fact that people were poor they were not necessarily dim; it was a very American and democratic-spirited idea. It also ran contrary to current feeling about cleverness. Genius was often regarded as a mere step from lunacy, from an overdeveloped brain, which was a very dangerous thing to have. It was to take Professor Terman until 1921 to disprove this; he showed (in a study that we will look at later in this book) that intelligence was more often than not accompanied not only by creativity, but, more significantly, by *happiness*. He also knew that an oversupply of *information* could all too easily be mistaken for intelligence.

IQ testing has, in the intervening years since 1916 and Terman's book *The Measurement of Intelligence*, been on shaky ground. Now, however, it is beginning to move back into favour amongst many psychologists, not because it is a particularly *good* measure of intelligence, but because it remains the best such measure there is.

Many in the intelligence testing debate had forgotten that the IQ test was once seen as a great social advance, making it possible to prove that poor children also had talent, and could rise above their economic circumstances to succeed despite their background. (Such an argument of course formed part of the equally controversial notion that intelligence is inherited from one's parents rather than absorbed from the social and economic background of one's upbringing.) However thousands of people, particularly children, have suffered grievously, literally had their lives ruined, at the hands of IQ testers. An immense amount of talent has gone unrecognized. Whole races have been publicly written off.

Racists were given powerful ammunition by the work of psychologists in the 1950s and '60s who apparently discovered that black people were not as 'clever' as white or yellow people. Then, some time later, a generation of students grew up learning how the black people had simply been asked the wrong questions. There were fundamental social and political questions raised by the issue. What started as a scientific investigation became, quite rightly, a debate on economics, morals, town planning – virtually whatever you chose. In the end, the 'anti'-black theory looked rather ridiculous, worn and tired. The blacks gained just a little respect, and the IQ testing lobby lost a great deal of public and media credibility.

As a random example of the genre of IQ-knocking the London *News Chronicle* in the 1950s reported triumphantly 'Little Sally Trounces the IQ Expert'. Nine-year-old Sally had taken an intelligence test before an Education Department child guidance expert in Sydney. He had pronounced her 'mentally backward'. Her parents were worried and distressed. Then they found a report Sally had written on the man who tested her. She headed the report 'Description of Testing Person'. 'Tired appearance, rubbing of eyes, taking glasses on and off . . . not placing hand over the mouth while yawning . . . Flopped into chair, which should not be done (sign of bad manners) . . . Book thrown from chair to desk (lazy) . . . While reading from card, he had his head in the drawer looking for a rubber. Not paying attention . . . not an interested or talkable type . . . ' Sally's damning personality test on her examiner continued. The New South Wales Education Department hastily destroyed their official's report. Yet how many parents would have had the nerve to storm back to the Education Department as Sally's did?

By 1974 IQ tests were, despite both intellectual and populist derision (Einstein and Churchill, as everyone knew by now, were dunces at school), becoming more pervasive. In company recruitment, particularly, an intelligence test (sometimes disguised as a 'personality' test) was common practice. Yet at the same time, IQ was routinely being referred to as a gigantic fraud. Teachers and parents were warned against its 'brutal pessimism' by Professor Leon Kamin, the Princeton University psychologist, in his book *The Science and Politics of IQ*. It is highly intriguing that the phrase 'brutal pessimism' belongs, not to a modern critic of IQ testing, but to the man who invented the tests in 1905, the French psychologist, Alfred Binet.

'Some recent philosophers,' Binet declared, 'have given their moral support to the idea that the intelligence of an individual is a fixed quantity – a quantity which one cannot augment. We must protest and react against this brutal pessimism.' Binet's warning was largely ignored in the heyday of IQ tests. Public figures still occasionally speak of curtailing the ability of the 'genetically inferior' to reproduce. Kamin, however, convincingly made the point that what IQ tests tested in the main was one's ability to do IQ tests.

To demonstrate their legendary fallibility he cited the example of First World War US Army recruits, who were asked whether the nickname for the Brooklyn Nationals was 'The Giants', 'The Orioles', 'The Superbas' or 'The Indians'. Kamin remarked wryly: 'The Italian or Hebrew immigrant who could not answer such questions was thereby shown to have defective genes.' In another test from the same era, fourteen-year-olds were asked to explain this: 'My neighbour has been having queer visitors. First a doctor came to his house, then a lawyer, then a minister. What do you think happened there?' The official answer to this conundrum was 'a death'. One child failed with the following wrong answer, 'Somebody was sick, the lawyer wanted his money, and the minister came to see how he was.'

The anecdotes raise many questions today. Being flippant it is possible to wonder if the minds setting such questions were entirely sound. On the other hand, it could be argued that 'a death' *is* the correct answer to the second riddle. It may be that it is an answer entirely based on a particular culture and time-locked at a particular moment in history, but to most people it was probably the correct answer. The alternative answers may be very imaginative and ingenious, but there is a direct clearness, brevity and logic to 'a death' that is hard to knock. It is certainly not incorrect. As for the Brooklyn Nationals, it *might* be argued that, at that time, a recruit who knew the answer was marginally more suitable than one who did not. One would have to be palpably stupid to say that this was an intelligence test, but it might have been quite useful to the US Army at the time.

Too many experts had concluded, said Professor Kamin, that between eighty and eight-five per cent of intelligence was inherited from one's parents. They were committed to the view, he said that 'those on the bottom are genetically inferior victims of their own immutable defects. The consequence has been that the IQ test has served as an instrument of oppression against the poor dressed in the trappings of science rather than politics . . . The poor, the foreign born and the racial minorities were shown to be born stupid. The under-privileged are today demonstrated to be ineducable – a message as soothing to the public purse as to the public conscience.'

Kamin went on to demolish the reputation of Sir Cyril Burt, Professor of Psychology at University College London from 1931 to 1950. Sir Cyril, in his day, was a highly respected British government advisor on education. In 1938 he assisted the Spens report, advising the government that intelligence was 'an innate, all-round ability'. The report was the foundation of the 1944 Education Act, and the creation of three grades of school for those different 'innate' abilities. Later in the 1960s Burt was an influential figure in the Black Paper group which said that modern education methods were eroding intellectual standards.

Burt was eager to prove that the major portion of IQ was inherited. It was controversial stuff, but only when it was used in America by Professor Arthur Jensen of Berkeley to show that black people inherited inferior intelligence was it more seriously questioned. Deeper investigation of the Burt research by Professor Kamin suggested that the British scientist must have started with his conclusions and then worked backwards. Still more investigation of what was now standard textbook material showed that he had, in fact, faked large tracts of his evidence; whole experiments and even research assistants had simply never existed, such had been Burt's anxiety to prove his point.

Sir Cyril Burt's subsequently discredited research on twins was seen at the time as important evidence in support of IQ tests. In apparently proving that separated twins had the same intelligence Burt had ignored the way they were brought up in their separate homes. It was, at the very least, a classic example of what psychologists call 'The Experimentor Effect' – the way an experimentor invariably comes up with the results he intended to find in order to prove the theory he had before he started work. Some extreme theories have even suggested that there was a darker purpose to Burt's shenanigans, perhaps some shady deal with 'The Establishment' to put down the lower orders. Perhaps an Establishment figure like Burt needed no deal or shady agreement, but just did what he thought right and necessary. Just what is it about intelligence and heredity, the conspiracy theorists would argue, that could make a man of Burt's reputation and stature do something so transparently wrong?

'What does it matter,' Kamin asked, 'if fifty or eighty-five per cent of intelligence is inherited?' The important question was: 'What do you *do* when you have decided how much is inherited?' Most fundamentally, perhaps, is the question of whether IQ is constant or can be changed in a person; in other words, whatever intelligence is, and wherever it comes from, can it – can *people* – be improved?

General thinking was that however much IQ was inherited, it was surely wrong to do nothing to help children who score low marks on IQ tests. Parents and teachers could still develop a child's brain power. At the same time Professor Denis Stott of Guelph University in Canada, one of the world's leading authorities on learning difficulties, lambasted IQ tests in his book, *The Parent as Teacher*. He said the tests had little more validity than 'black magic and witchcraft'. They deluded children into believing that they are stupid, when they were really suffering from a learning block which could be removed. But the tests could often lead children to 'act stupid' for the rest of their lives.

I Don't Know What It Is, But I like It

For all this, when it comes to assessing minds, we have nothing else; we produce machines whose every capability we know and can test, yet have no method of discovering in a satisfactory way what our own bodies – the machines we should know best – can achieve. The IQ test, the best method we have of measuring minds, is analogous to one of those small inspection hatches which enable us to peer into the working parts of a machine. What we see through the hatch is meaningful, but inadequate. The IQ test tells us something, as it is bound to do. It is indeed quite difficult for a stupid person to do well, although a person stupid in most social ways, as even enthusiasts for IQ acknowledge, can 'show' high intelligence. It is very easy indeed for a bright person like Sally in Sydney to do disastrously. And however contemptuous of IQ tests most of us would be if found to have a low score, few would complain if found to be at genius level. In that respect, a sceptic would say, IQ tests are a little like horoscopes!

What, after all is intelligence? There is little support for the existence of such a quality in any all-round sense, except for the fact that we all feel we can sense it when we see it. It is possible to be very negative on this subject. The extraordinary intelligence of some Aborigine tribesmen in their environment would go down as a poor performance in Manhattan. Eskimo brilliance does not play well in Barnsley. It is a shame if these problems lead to a defeatist attitude, where one is so confused by the various forms of intelligence and the apparent impossibility of quantifying them accurately, that hands are thrown up and the entire notion discarded as vaguely nasty and fascist.

We all know, or like to think we know, of brilliant mathematicians who can barely read, accomplished physicists who cannot speak articulately and fine writers capable of getting hopelessly lost on their way to the bathroom. Professor Hans Eysenck of the Institute of Psychiatry at the Maudsley Hospital in South London believes he has differentiated three types of intelligence. The Professor, who weathered the international storm produced by his espousal of the 'underachieving blacks' theory in the 1960s and '70s, is a middle European, a writer on intelligence for many years before he made himself something of a bogeyman. 'I never said black individuals were stupid,' he insists now. 'I simply said that if black people as a whole were assessed by IQ standards, they would be likely to score lower than a corresponding group of white people.'

Eysenck says the first type of intelligence is the biological intelligence produced by the brain, 'that makes us different from a pig or whatever'; then there is the ability measured by IQ, which is the *underlying* ability tempered by such social factors as education ('we are always sidetracked,' he says); thirdly, there is what Eysenck calls 'social intelligence'.

That is to say, our ability to use our God-given intelligence in society for earning a living and for doing all sorts of things to be successful and so on. This is much more complex than IQ and is much more complex than the fundamental biological intelligence because it takes into account personality, motivation, even drinking habits. If you are drunk you are not going to use your intelligence very well.

What determines intelligence for Eysenck? Social intelligence, he concludes, is influenced by too many factors to go into. 'IQ testing', Eysenck explains, 'was originally introduced in order to give people who were relatively unsuccessful in life or in school because of their social background a better chance to show their innate ability, particularly in England, where the original test was introduced to give children in some of the bad schools a chance to go to university or get a better education – and they were very successful in that. IQ is a very reliable and extremely valuable and predictive measurement that we can use to great advantage in education. When these IQ tests were discontinued, purely for political reasons, the proportion of working class children who went to university went down accordingly.'

There are three crucial points that could be used against the Professor here. Firstly, the decline in the numbers of working class children going to university coincides not only with the decline of IQ testing in schools, but also with the western economic recession; economically poor school leavers from the early 1970s onwards tended to look for jobs rather than 'waste time' in further education. Secondly, in British universities in the early 1970s it was exceedingly common to find students who had failed the '11 plus' IQ-based selection procedure and only got into higher education because they were pushed by parents who knew them better than IQ testers. The third point is that it is not certain that the proportion of working class students has gone down. Other reliable research suggests the proportion of working to middle class university entrants has simply not changed since the IQ testing days, and that the overall increase in the number of students in further education is accounted for by the tendency of middle class parents to encourage their daughters to go to university rather than to finishing schools.

However, biological intelligence, says Eysenck, 'is almost certainly, almost completely, determined by genetic factors, unless you injure the central nervous system. IQ on the other hand, he goes on, 'is to quite a considerable extent determined by education, temperament and so on. But even that is very largely, say to the extent of seventy per cent, something like that – it can't be very accurate – determined by genetic factors.'

It was in a letter to *The Times* in London, following a lengthy inter-expert correspondence in 1976, that Dr Alice Heim, the distinguished Cambridge psychologist, perhaps most crisply summed up this aspect of the debate. 'The spate of writing pro and con the IQ being hereditarily determined, and the erudite bandying about of precise figures such as "eighty-five (or sixty) per cent inherited" are ludicrous,' she wrote.

> Indeed, their perpetration would be inexplicable were it not for the rôle played by politics. The preoccupation of the left wing with extreme environmentalism and of the right wing with heritability is never stated – both sides claiming to be interactionists – but this preoccupation largely accounts for the axe-grinding dogmatism of the protagonists.
>
> Relevant facts are as follows: (i) intelligence, however defined, is complex and multiply-determined; (ii) heredity and environment cannot be separated since the two interact from the time of conception. (This holds true even of identical twins); (iii) their interaction is not necessarily constant.
>
> It is thus meaningless to divide intelligence into percentage parts, some attributable to environment and some to heredity. The exercise would not be attempted in the absence of ulterior motive.

Dr Edward Zigler, the Yale University child expert has a particularly balanced view of the pros and cons of IQ testing. He was head of the US Department of Child Development in the Nixon era and one of the founding fathers of Project Head Start, of which more in Chapter 4.

I believe that IQ has been too worshipped by some, and too maligned by others as a good standard measurement, [Zigler says]. It is probably the most important measure that pyschologists have ever come up with. It means more than any other measurement that we know about. I also think that it's probably much less open to environmental impact than a lot of other measures. [And Dr Zigler adds with wisdom] Nobody's going to argue that a low IQ is better than a high IQ.

Perhaps it is best to ignore the fact that they are called 'intelligence' tests – the meaning of the word intelligence itself is fuzzy and ill-defined – and regard them as tests of something else. Then they can be seen in a quite different light. If professionals are required in the west – doctors, lawyers, architects, and television producers, with quick-thinking, but relatively narrow minded, unoriginal, accepting minds, good at formal 'cognitive' tasks, well versed in the assumptions of middle class, white culture (by which nothing more fancy or ethereal is meant than sheer knowledge of customs, such as when a lawyer or a minister might visit a house) the IQ test is a better predictor than any other. If something else is being sought (like Nobel laureates, Picassos and Mozarts, creators of 'Star Wars' technology, microchips or a new generation of Toyotas) – and that is much of the theme of this book – we had better invent a new measure.

Alternative tests of intelligence have been devised and eagerly, if briefly, seized upon by those intent on putting a figure on accomplishment. Culturally 'neutral' tests come and go without setting the world alight. IQ and similar tests, apart from being criticized as class and race-biased are also said to discriminate against women. Itzhak Rosenbloom, Director of Heled, the Jerusalem Foundation for the Gifted Child, which works with 300 children from kindergarten age to fourteen, says: 'We have about fifteen to seventeen pupils in a group, about one fifth of them girls. This is because the tests are not sex-fair. The wheel that squeaks gets the oil, so the gifted girls still get less attention than the boys, less than they deserve and need. And it is easier to get measurable answers from boys, whereas girls often work on what can only be called a higher level, with a wider instinctive humanity in their responses. This is something we hope to get more generally recognized.'

In Vancouver, on the west coast of Canada, Professor Geraldine Schwartz, president of the International Foundation of Learning, has a stimulating and unusual personal criterion for intelligence. According to Professor Schwartz, 'The smartest people are the people who can use humour and appreciate humour. That, to me, is intelligence at the very highest level, so high that it cannot be defined or explained. It's that different way of looking at things, of seeing things . . . If you want to know if a person is super-intelligent,' continues the professor, who runs a school called the Vancouver Learning Centre, 'just have a look at the humour they use. It's not something measured by tests.'

There isn't anything more I can teach this child!

An amusing case of competing intelligence tests, indeed of competing definitions of intelligence, came to light early in 1987 with the rise to fame in California of ten-year-old Adragon Eastwood DeMello. Adragon Eastwood (so named because he was distantly related to the actor Clint Eastwood and was born in the Chinese Year of the Dragon) was already an 'A' student, well up on Dean's honour roll at Cabrillo College in the beach town of Aptos, near San Francisco. He was a computer wizard, a maths genius, a published poet and playwright and, said his father Augustine (a writer and flamenco guitarist), a genius who he hoped would win a Nobel Prize by the time he was sixteen. Mr DeMello claimed that his son's IQ was between 200 and 225, but that anyway, there was no IQ test that could accurately assess his intelligence.

Adragon was always special, said his father. 'My son is probably the most gifted scholar this century has ever seen,' he told the US media. He said 'Hello' at seven weeks, mastered chess and geometry at two and a half, was learning Greek, physics and philosophy at four, and was studying geology and geophysics at six. At eight, he was writing computer programmes. The party was spoiled a little, however, by Mr Lewis Keizer, a former teacher of Adragon at the Popper-Keizer School, an institution for gifted children in Santa Cruz, where Adragon was a student for eight months in 1985.

'The only way he could perform was when his father sat in the classroom next to him,' said Keizer. 'From a very young age, his father has trained him like a monkey.' He added than when *he* put the boy through 'the standard tests' for children of his age, he finished near the bottom of the class. Perhaps Mr Keizer was displaying nothing more than sour grapes, because his standard tests had failed their biggest test. Adragon's teachers at Cabrillo certainly rated him highly. 'Although his dad could have helped him, he has done remarkable work for me alone in my class,' said his English teacher Steve Hanley. 'He is extremely bright, less sophisticated and complex than my other students . . . for example, he doesn't know much about death or sex.'

One of the more original methods of measuring intelligence, and what might have been a revolutionary key to misunderstanding the nature of the human mind, was a controversial IQ machine invented by a Canadian psychologist, Dr John Ertl, in the early 1970s. Dr Ertl generously admitted his device was 'not designed to measure all-round intelligence', and the tag 'IQ machine' was not strictly his, but that of the American media.

The 'neural efficiency analyser,' which was used experimentally by a Maryland school board and was tested by the US Naval Academy at Annapolis, measured brainwaves and was conceived as a method of shedding intelligence testing from the stigma of being overly biased towards specific cultural influences. Electrodes attached to the subject's head measured the speed of reactions to changes in a light, lighted numbers and moving lines on an oscilloscope, Dr Ertl's tests seemed to suggest there was a relationship between a person's 'neural efficiency' and the amount he would score on conventional IQ tests. Dr Mone Buchsbaum of the National Institute of Mental Health in Washington was sceptical, however. He explained that while one 'smart' person might pay attention to the testing, another might sit in front of the machine and think his own thoughts. Another might succeed in combining attentiveness with other thoughts.

Of course, *discovering* what the brain is capable of achieving and simply measuring it are slightly different concepts. Perhaps our mechanistic view of the mental as well as the physical world is the problem here. Let us assume that unknown abilities can be discovered lurking in us; let us accept (as many researchers and writers do) that many or all of our children are potential Leonardo da Vincis. Why do we then need to go and put a figure on their performance? Do we rate the Mona Lisa on a scale of one to ten? (Paradoxically, in fact, you might say that we do: the performance rating in this case is called 'the price').

Yet *rating* intelligence and accomplishment continues to grow in popularity. Fashionable now in some of the more minor American universities is what has become known as 'the value-added approach', continual testing and the placing of hard numbers on what a student has *learned*. 'If I'm going to invest four years of my life,' said one student at Northeast Missouri State University, 'I want to know if I'm benefitting from it.' This university pioneered the idea, but it is now spreading under names such as 'assessment' and 'accountability', and its mechanistic appeal particularly attracts politicians who want to be able to tell people just what they are getting for their tax dollars. Missouri has ordered all State colleges to start accountability tests by the fall of 1987. Tennessee already distributes cash to colleges based on test results; Arkansas and Colorado are considering it.

It is almost true to say the potential of the human brain is unlimited, yet most of the species are happy, proud even to rely on using just a fraction of their ability, just as long as they can put a number (the price?) on what they *know* they have.

But consider for a moment, the very useful *innate* abilities that lie unused in our brains. It has long been considered, for example, that in drowning cases, brain death occurs within six minutes of the heart stopping. Yet thanks largely to the work of Flight Surgeon Martin J. Nemiroff of the US coastguard, it is now standard practice to assume an apparently dead body can be revived to full health, without any brain damage, after as long as half an hour or even forty minutes of drowning even in icy water. Nemiroff's theory was that cold water can preserve as well as destroy life by triggering a response known in whales, porpoises and seals as Mammalian Diving Reflex. MDR occurs when facial submersion in water below seventy degrees F sets off a response which shuts down blood supply to the skin and muscles to conserve oxygen in the brain.

A case reported by the London *Sunday Times* in 1975 put this theory decisively to the test. An eighteen-year-old youth had driven off a country road into ten feet of ice-covered water. The car filled with water, the youth inhaled and lost consciousness. The car was lifted thirty eight minutes later. Ambulancemen began to wrap the corpse ready for the morgue when a belch was heard. During the twenty minute drive to the hospital, resuscitation had no effect. At the hospital, there was found to be no sign of life in the youth. It took Nemiroff forty minutes to get to him. Thirteen hours of continuous resuscitation later, having been moved to a better-equipped university hospital, the youth awoke, hearing his distraught mother bemoaning his reckless driving, and gave her a 'two finger salute'. He went on to achieve A grades at college.

A British doctor, Edmund Hey, of Newcastle University, noted a similar phenomenon in babies surviving as long as a week without food or water in the ruins of an earthquake-stricken Mexico City hospital in 1985. 'If babies' temperatures drop, then they will go into a state of torpor or semi-hibernation,' he observed.

If such an ability, unused in ninety nine per cent of the population but waiting to be used if necessary, exists in the brain, one can only imagine what else is there, lying dormant.

2

Hot Housing: is it Ever too Early to Start?

'I wouldn't be surprised if, instead of holding up a mirror for a mother to see her baby's head emerging, we don't hold up a flashcard saying, "Hello".' – quoted from an eminent paediatrician in Vogue magazine.

'The problem in America,' said Californian Augustine DeMello in January 1987, speaking of his son Adragon Eastwood DeMello, the genius, 'is that giftedness is not easily recognized or even dealt with.' Some observers outside the USA, might say that giftedness seems rather *too* readily recognized there today. But then given the emotive importance of intelligence, it is not surprising that parents in the most prosperous society the world has ever known should be all too ready to identify the seeds of brilliance in their children. Prosperity is notoriously hard to keep up, and genius, though it has its problems, is still a first class meal ticket.

This is not to deny, however, that American prosperity and comfort have provided the best conditions so far in history for the extraordinary abilities of young children to be brought to the surface. Adragon DeMello will count himself lucky, if he does turn out to be something special, to have been brought up in the US. With the possible exception of the Eastern bloc countries, he is more likely to do well there than anywhere else. No one will laugh at him for being clever, and ambitious.

The likes of Adragon, who seem almost inexplicably to have

come into the world with giftedness in their mental baggage, would be very satisfying evidence to the early IQ theorists that most intelligence is inherited from our parents. Genius, with the secure promise of power, wealth and happiness that this quality carries is, in this attractive vision, seen as one of life's wonderful surprises. If you do not happen to possess it yourself, there might be a little recessive cleverness gene about, so your children or their children just might inherit it.

And if – a big if – you do not make genius level by accident, there is no reason in the 'can do' society why brilliance cannot be created or, put more baldly, bought. The idea leads inexorably to the very democratic, very American idea that the humblest member of society can be a genius, a president, a big wheel. Awkward questions concerning how, in the real world, the force of economics can stunt growth and destroy ability – the kind of stuff that a carping critic (particularly a socialist) might bring up – are naturally set to one side in this idealistic vision.

It is because of the stimulating American blend of open-mindedness, optimism and ambition that it is here that hot housing – enhancing the mental and physical faculties of 'average' people – has become one of the biggest educational issue of the late twentieth century. A belief in the concept of hot housing is a definitive statement on the 'nurture' side of the eternal 'nature versus nurture' debate.

Hot housing is what might be called 'supernurture', and it is significant that the American 1960s project Head Start (of which more later) was aimed by the liberal and civil rights lobbies at 'disadvantaged' children, who might have been written off as factory-fodder by those who believe the poor are poor because they are stupid, and ergo that their children must also be stupid.

If you accept that hot housing is a technique that works, or at least has an effect on children, (and it seems that it does, think only of such areas of endeavour as chess and athletics) the question immediately arises, at what stage in a child's life should these techniques be applied? Education experts are divided on the issue. The American 'Head Start' project postulated that children should be given a boost shortly before school age. But that was quickly judged to be too late in life; it has now become accepted widely that the age of three is an important deadline in a child's development, since by that time, he has acquired some seventy-five per cent of his adult language ability. Now a whole generation of angst-ridden parents has grown up in the USA believing that unless children start some kind of accelerated learning well before the age of three, those Harvard application forms might just as well be torn up. In England, the concept is immortalized in a thriving new chain of what are essentially toyshops. The shops' logo is a stylized toddler; they are called The Early Learning Centres.

The early-learning syndrome is naturally most demanding on parents. Professor Edward Zigler of Yale University goes so far as to say that if he had the choice of running an education programme for children or parents, he would concentrate on the parents. 'If you want to change children,' he points out, 'you have to change parents first.'

Beyond the fringe

Sometimes, the strategies of those intent on improving human performance go further than educating parents to stimulate their toddlers. Their natural, if unusual, premise is that education should begin in the womb. The idea may be a lot more acceptable morally than some of the ideas of genetic manipulation currently being explored. But why should the education of foetuses work? For one thing, the period of most rapid brain growth occurs while a child is still in the womb. For another, we know from watching unborn children through cameras in the womb that the foetus reacts far more to stimuli than was hitherto realized; the developing brain is obviously very active. California is the site, as we will see later, for what is termed a Pre-Natal University. And there are other intriguing examples of what *might* be evidence for the value of learning in the womb.

In the eighteenth century, a baby's mind was regarded as a void which parents were required to fill, and quickly, if they had ambition. Samuel Johnson's friend Mrs Hester Thrale made sure that her two-year-old daughter Queenie, 'knew her nine figures and the simplest combinations of them; but none beyond a hundred; all the Heathen Deities and the signs of the Zodiac in Watts' verses.' In 1800, it was not unknown for intensively coached boys to get into prestigious universities in their early teens. In the late nineteenth century an influential paediatrician called Pritchard wrote that the right information should be fed into the infant mind early, otherwise a neurotic baby would be produced, 'as irreversibly ruined as a telephone exchange would be if the lines were tangled, the numbers muddled and the operators themselves mentally deranged'.

Hot housing children in the new millenium West, which is to say for all practical purposes *now*, may be in most of our eyes a middle class gimmick, even a dangerous gamble with mental health. But systematic hot housing may soon be regarded as a necessity as great as literacy in developing countries. This, after all, is the age of micro-electronics, of lasers, 'Star Wars' and the new bio-technology (which may well be the dominant technology by the turn of the 21st century). These, and the frightening, exhilarating rate at which some of the most fundamental laws of physics are being overturned by new thinking, demand a new breed of scientist, capable of a level of creative thought never before required. Indeed the kind of straight-line thinking genius the old IQ test was so good at discovering would likely be perplexed and alienated by some of the 'New Physics' – with its mind-bending disavowal of even such certainties as Newton's laws of motion, and its fantastically intriguing drawing together of such previously disparate strands of thinking as mathematics, philosophy, biology and chemistry.

Brain Wars

It is probably no exaggeration, and has formed a theme of our research into hot housing, to suggest that the developed nations in the next millenium will be engaged in a *war of intelligence*, from which the cleverest (rather than the strongest or bravest or most handsome) will emerge as winner. The 1957 launch of the Soviet Sputnik 1 may be seen in future histories as the opening shot in this war. Someday soon, the balance of *brain* power may give as much cause for concern as the balance of *nuclear* power.

Some nations are taking this challenge far more seriously than others. Britain worries about the brain drain but does little in the way of direct action. Japan, on the other hand, sets out as a matter of national policy to raise the level of the population's IQ and is now said to have the highest average IQ of any nation on earth.

The British 'thinking skills' teacher and writer Tony Buzan is horrified by Britain's complacency:

The major corporations in the world, especially the computer corporations, are spending hundreds of millions of dollars a year on training their personnel, because they know that as soon as the big brains come into their organization, the organization wins.

There are ten people in Silicon Valley, ten brains, if you will, who are monitored by the financial community. If there is even a rumour that one of those brains is going to go from company A to company B, the world's stockmarkets start to shift. They've realized that intelligence, the use of the brain is, if you like, the next quantum leap in evolution, and everybody is now jockeying for position to see who's going to win that war. One of the nice things about it is that it's a kind of war that everyone benefits from.

Of course there is no harm at all in questioning what victory in this new war would entail, indeed whether it would be worth the trouble. Remember the apocryphal tale of the black man in a remote colonial outpost who is discovered happily alseep under a tree by a westerner. 'Come on, man, get up, do something!' says the westerner. 'What should I do?' asks the man. 'Well,' replies the westerner, 'invent something, or start a business, make some money for yourself.' 'What would I do with the money?' asks the puzzled native. 'You could afford a holiday and to relax a bit for one thing,' comes the reply. 'That is to say,' smiles the wise chap, 'precisely what I was doing before you woke me up.'

It is a pleasing parable, but perhaps a romantic one. Is development really so bad? — not the development that produces acid rain, but the progress which provides clean water and eradicates smallpox. If we are to reject progress, it had better be from a position of knowledge and strength. It is currently fashionable to reject 'development', particularly industrial development, as a proper national goal. Equally, many of us from our privileged positons in the élites of the west feel it might be a good thing for the less fortunate in the world to spurn the material and environmental advantages we already have. 'Believe us,' we seem to be saying, 'we've been there, and it's hell.'

Indeed, some of it is; we seem in the west to be capable of producing more ridiculous rubbish in the name of progress than ever before. Early in 1987, American scientists reported, with what appeared to be some excitement, that they had developed an electric motor so small that it could get lost next to a fingernail. The reason for such an obscure invention? The rumour was that it was to be fitted in a new type of electrical, remote controlled insect, thousands of which might be set off to swarm across a battlefield. The insects could then crawl up a Soviet gun barrel and POW! Peaceful uses were also posited; imagine setting a swarm of friendly electrical insects off around your house to search out and clean every nook and cranny? The researchers soon spoiled the fun by announcing that the *real* use for the tiny motors would be in gryoscopes for extremely small guided missiles. The same team had developed a pair of scissors a fraction of a milimetre long. More garbage? The tool could be used to cut an individual optic nerve, and lead to whole eye transplants. Sneer at technological developments only with extreme caution!

Assuming that you think that little harm can come from intellectual competition and that much good may result, how should we, in practice, go about boosting the intelligence of our population? Are there any harmful side effects? 'Recipes for promoting intelligence in the next generation are as prolific as crank religious cults,' Christina Hardyment, author of *Dream Babies; Child Care From Locke to Spock* has observed. And even in its relative infancy, hot housing is being met by a small tidal wave of disapproval from educators and child care experts. In many cases, they seem to be more dismayed by ethical considerations, even issues of taste, raised by the ambition – often what appears to be the sheer desperation – of parents anxious for their children to clamber to 'the top' (whatever their particular top might be), than by a serious examination of the efficacy of the various methods of hot housing, or the need, real or imagined, for upping the standard of the next generation's abilities.

On a purely pragmatic level, there is little doubt that hot housing *works*. When objectives are narrowly focused, intensive training (beginning in early childhood) can make promising chess players into champions, ballerinas into primas, baby gymnasts into little Olga Korbuts. The world seems to accept the idea that prodigies who show signs of artistic or athletic talent should be identified and accelerated. It is far more equivocal about the treatment of those with *generally* fine minds. What do you do with kids who are just smart?

Any discussion of the value of hot housing seems to throw up three questions. (i) If you intervene and accelerate children already identified as gifted, do you make them into geniuses? Is that how nations should develop their own Einsteins? (ii) If you try it on 'average' children, can you make them *superior*? (iii) Perhaps most important of all – if you systematically hot house disadvantaged children, can you repair early social damage – or, better still, *prevent* it? A controversial hot housing guru in Philadelphia thinks he has the answer. Glenn Doman feels that *every* child should be programmed for genius. 'Yes,' he says in answer to critics, 'we *are* creating an 'élite' of children. And you know how many children we want in that élite? About a billion – because that's how many children there *are* in the world!' Start early enough, work hard enough, he tells his disciples (and, by 'hard' he means twenty-four hours a day) and *any* child can be a genius.

Re-Assemble Your Child

It is fitting that Philadelphia, the birthplace of the American Revolution, should be the city where Glenn Doman has established the now world-famous Institutes For the Achievement of Human Potential, or the Better Baby Institute, as it is more commonly called. Doman aims to create a new generation of what he calls 'renaissance children'. A romantic image of rebirth, freshness, wide-eyed, child-like curiosity pervades Doman's glossy brochure, entitled *The Better Baby*.

'You provide the Baby, we provide the Better' flows the copy inside. Several quotations from Doman are reproduced, and there can be little question that he is a considerable visionary and optimist.

Every child born has, at the moment of birth, a greater potential intelligence than Leonardo da Vinci ever *used* . . . the Magic is in the child . . . more than a quarter of a century ago, as a tiny band of us treated profoundly brain-injured children, we stumbled over the first clues as to how things might someday be for the well children, as well as the brain injured, and we remember the very night, or more accurately, the early morning hours, when we first dreamed the dream. Now they stand before us, better in the reality than in our most extravagant dream, and we know them for what they are – Renaissance children, children for all seasons.

Prominent like-minded grandees are similarly quoted. 'All children are born geniuses, and we spend the first six years of their lives degeniusing them.' (Buckminster Fuller). 'The difference between intelligence and an education is this – that intelligence will make you a good living.' (Charles Franklin Kettering). 'Feel the dignity of a child. Do not feel superior to him, for you are not.' (Robert Henri). 'Men fear thought as they fear nothing else on earth – more than ruin, more even than death.' (Bertrand Russell). There also appears this from Albert Einstein: 'It is, in fact, nothing short of a miracle that the modern methods of instruction have not yet entirely strangled the holy curiosity of inquiry.' Whether Einstein, the school dullard, would have approved and benefited as a boy from a Glenn Doman upbringing is an interesting point. Perhaps he would have done better in life?

So what is the Glenn Doman system for making a better baby? It would be unfair to distill Doman's prodigious output in a brief description, but it is best summed up, probably, as a programme of stimulation. Working with brain-damaged children, he became aware early of what is now quite familiar, the capacity of the brain to adapt and re-learn lost skills – to be reprogrammed. The stimulation required to effect improvements in such children could take months and years of intensely hard work by parents. Reprogramming by developing new pathways in the brain of a brain-damaged child is a strenuous, twenty four-hour effort. Adapting such routines to healthy children – reprogramming for genius – Doman discovered they could perform amazing feats; call it teaching, hot housing or systematic brainwashing (the technique is not dissimilar), tiny children (under three) could be trained or persuaded to read, do maths, perform well athletically and learn foreign languages.

Doman's famous and immensely successful books came along; *Teach Your Baby To Read* (complete with flashcards), *How To Multiply Your Baby's Intelligence, Teach Your Baby Math*, and, most aggravating to educationists, *How to Give Your Baby Encyclopaedic Knowledge*. ('Most kids are delighted,' says Doman, 'to know that the ferocious grizzly bear's proper scientific name is *Ursus Horribilis!* Especially do they love it when Mom or Dad makes a horribly grizzly bear face and pronounces the name with proper dread in the voice when teaching the Tenth Magnitude Program on the Bit "Grizzly Bear," by announcing that the grizzly bear is of the species *URSUS HORRIBILIS!!!*')

It is part of standard thinking today, of course, that robotic learning of such facts for their own sake is nothing better than worthless garbage, the very antithesis, paradoxically, of intelligent behaviour. Doman seems rather bravely to challenge all that. He maintains most controversially that 'a bit of intelligence is one bit of information', that building up an encyclopaedic knowledge will stimulate the brain to grow and lead to creative, original thought. Doman's funders have included the US Steel Corporation and Sony.

The hundreds of interested, ambitious parents at Doman's Better Baby courses learn how to stimulate their children and watch almost surreal performances of Doman-trained babies and toddlers solving equations, or naming a selection of paintings by Norman Rockwell. A four-year-old reads Portia's speech from *The Merchant of Venice*. 'What is forty plus fifty four?' asks a mother, laying out a selection of cards smothered in randomly placed red dots. A six-month-old baby crawls on his tummy and lands dribbling on the card with ninety four dots, ignoring those with ninety three or ninety five.

The difficulty for critics of Doman's methods and evangelical style is in explaining his success. It is extremely impressive to see an eighteen-month-old performing long division, a four-year-old all-American kid reading and speaking Japanese. It is very difficult, and rather churlish, to dismiss it all as 'party tricks'.

The Institutes, which have been in operation for thirty one years, provide on- and off-campus, (i.e. at home) study. Children from all over the world are enrolled in the off-campus programme, and small groups of children are taught in Doman's graceful mansion, behind a grey stone wall on a tree-lined avenue outside Philadelphia. A discreet black-on-white painted sign stands close to a brasher noticeboard: 'Parents are cordially invited to learn how to multiply their babies' intelligence'. A seven-day course ($400) in professional mothering — the Doman Institutes are for parents as well — is advertised in lettering whose size and style varies from line to line, giving it something of the look of a Victorian circus poster. Once on the 'campus', there are signs pointing to such facilities as the Better Baby Store. Approximately twenty five children attend Doman's school for geniuses, aged from birth to twelve. They walk around in navy uniforms, and rainbow-striped, sleeveless jumpers. They seem well-adjusted, friendly and open.

Building bigger brains is hard work. Outside the main building is the remarkable, if slightly comical sight of a woman crawling manically on all fours around a small racetrack behind her two young children. (Is this what they mean by 'in pursuit of genius'?) She loses no opportunity to teach. 'It's a beautiful sunny day,' she is shouting between puffs, S U N N Y D A Y THREE SIX NINE TWELVE FIFTEEN S U N N Y D A Y!' Doman's children are encouraged to crawl a mile each day in order to improve the 'cross referencing' ability of the brain while it is still growing. He believes that creeping helps to accelerate reading and thinking skills – one of the reasons why his hot house teaching usually takes place on the floor.

Hanging on a wall inside the building is a signed photograph of the married astronauts, Rhea Seddon and Robert 'Hoot' Gibson, flanking their little boy Paul; 'Thanks for making this a Better Baby!' reads the autograph. Letters of support from Jacqueline Onassis and Dwight D. Eisenhower are on prominent display. Glenn Doman, a kind-faced, grandfatherly man, white haired and bearded, is like Santa Claus with a mean line in oratory. He immediately makes it clear that he dislikes the phrase 'hot housing', which, throughout the hot housing world, seems to be regarded as a pejorative term. There is also near-universal bad reaction to the term 'super-baby', which, if they are to be believed, is the one thing all hot housing parents do *not* want.

The core of Doman's belief, which he expresses with evangelical zeal, is that just as muscle grows with exercise, the brain can grow simply by being used. Conversely, lack of use will cause it to lose its capacity. He believes that while the brain grows phenomenally between birth and six years, after six, its ability to take in information without effort virtually disappears. 'Most of the game is up by age three,' he asserts.

The clearest example of this is that there is no more difficult an act for an adult of an intellectual nature than to learn a foreign tongue – but to a child born in London tonight, English is a foreign tongue, no more, no less foreign than Swahili or Spanish. And then a miracle happens – he learns his language. If he lives in a bilingual household where two languages are spoken, he learns two languages without any effort at all. He will never be able to do that again without great effort.

Unhappily, in the United States, one begins school at six, when that capacity has just about gone. Happily, mothers have always been the best teachers since time began. [A theme to which

Doman warms: if hothousing is accepted as having any value, there is a knock-on effect on your perception of motherhood. A hothousing failure will be the mother's fault.] And by three years of age, we have been saying for thirty years, a child has learned more fact for fact than he will learn for the rest of his life.

As a first step towards creating a super-baby, Doman prescribes stimulation from immediately after birth by shining lights on and off in to the baby's eyes, making noises behind its head, even putting mustard on its tongue. The baby must then be familiarized with shapes by putting cards between the light and its eyes. Maths begins with red spots on cards, growing smaller and more numerous, so the baby learns by 'instant instinctual arithmetic'; a fascinating and well documented phenomenon. There are cases noted of people capable of 'counting' large numbers – in the hundreds – instinctively be recognition.

Doman's results must, even to a sceptic, be impressive on some level. Renaissance children of two are reading, composing music and poetry and displaying an encyclopaedic knowledge of maths and astronomy. The children are taught intensively – played with, shown flashcards, words, games, puzzles, numbers and patterns of objects, given simple exercises in association – from dawn to dusk. They have little 'free time' but even the babies appear to enjoy it, and bask in undivided adult attention. The people who work hardest of all are undoubtedly the parents.

The parents are re-educated to learn how to present material to their children, how to sustain interest and, where necessary, how to keep one step ahead of their budding geniuses. The programme does not appear to be the province solely of the aspirational middle class, either. Parenting seminars attract a fair number of local black mothers and fathers, several from some of the most blighted slums in the US. They too are convinced of the value of the 'Better Baby' method and use it at home. If they cannot afford the flashcards from the Better Baby

Stores (one on campus, one in downtown Philadelphia), they can make their own – according to careful instructions – by cutting up magazines. They appear to achieve the same results as more affluent parents. Though children have not been IQ-tested in any organized way, there is a certain amount of anecdotal evidence that such children adapt better if they move to new schools, and generally head for the top of the class.

The children at the Institutes' on-campus school are aged between four and twelve, but every one can read and write on entry. Six-year-olds can programme a computer and speak to it in three or four computer languages, hold a conversation in fluent Japanese (only one or two have Japanese parents) and play one or more musical instruments, peforming a snatch of music by almost any classical composer you care to name. Each student can also perform junior Olympic gymnastic routines and the four-year-olds can run from one to three miles non-stop.

Doman says that, in a sense, there is nothing new in his theories, and they do seem to have a pervasive home-iness.

> Individual parents have for ages instinctively understood this, and they have created the great geniuses of the world. I think we have spent our lives studying how the brain grows and that this was knowledge that didn't exist 300 years ago, but mothers have always known that tiny children would rather learn than do anything else in the world. Little children are so dumb that they think learning is a survival skill, and it is! Little things are in great danger – little squirrels, little rabbits – because they don't know enough yet, and so nature has made the brain capable of taking in staggering facts so they can survive. Children think learning is more fun than anything else, and it is a great shame that we sometimes talk them out of it. Genetics are rubbish. All children are born with the capacity for genius. From then on, they are the unadulterated product of what happens to them.
>
> Tiny children can learn absolutely anything that you can present to them in an honest and factual way. Then you do it with great love and affection and you teach them all there is to learn.

All we do to teach children at the Institutes, whether the objective is to make a paralysed child talk or a blind child see, or to make a child who begins as a well child extraordinary is to give him visual, auditory and tactile stimulation with increased frequency, intensity and duration.

His forty years of work have convinced him, unequivocally, that every child *can* be a genius. IQ? 'I think there is only one intelligence test, and that's every minute of every day. The children here play the violin, the same children do olympic routines, they read three languages, little red-headed girls with green eyes who read Japanese at five. All children are capable of doing everything, and we are not devoted to making Nobel prize winners or Olympic stars. We are devoted to giving children options, choices.'

Doman is perplexed by his detractors: 'It is the most astonishing thing I have ever heard that anybody should think it is bad to learn, bad to love children, bad to have families. I think the people who are saying it are going to die of terminal silliness.' What the experts in fact object to is that Doman has no proper data to back up his assertions. *He* is a genius, they say – a marketing genius. There are no IQ tests done on his subjects; he says the tests mean nothing, that what he creates is *competence*, for which, of course, there is no test. Doman's defence of his work on well children is engagingly simply – it works, and the kids are happy.

Don't Do It!

For all his hope and optimism about the human condition, what he says may be seen as profoundly depressing by those of us who are over six years old and were never signed up by Doman, or who have children that do not know Plato from Play Doh and show little sign of caring about it. So what do the experts say about the cultivation of such rare intellectual orchids?

'If you get hot housed, you end up being a rotten tomato – or at least a pallid tomato,' said Brian Sutton-Smith of the University of Pennsylvania at a 1985 symposium in Philadelphia (the venue was coincidental) called 'The Hot Housing of Young Children; So Much, So Soon'. The metaphor drew a laugh, according to the *New York Times*, from the 160 child development researchers, historians, educators, psychologists and child care professionals. The audience were reported as strongly anti-hot housing.

'There is a natural pace to the development of children,' said a research psychologist. 'When we hot house children we superimpose a learning environment in order to make them learn faster.' A Princeton educational research scientist Dr Irving Sigal, asked 'Where is it written that children have the natural urge to learn Japanese or Suzuki violin . . . You can get a horse to do half those things.' A devastating effect of hot housing, he said, is what a child 'comes to believe about himself'.

'Children come to believe they are valued for what they memorize or produce or achieve.' As a result, hot housed children might be at risk of developing achievement anxiety. He added that although authoritarian teaching environments could have negative effects on young children's development, 'this does not call for the antithesis, a libertarian, anti-authoritative posture.' Or, as a colleague paraphrased him, 'Hot housing ain't so hot, but you don't want to have an untended garden either.'

Tamara K. Harevan of Clark University said: 'Hot housing is a minority phenomenon of the urban middle class.' Instead of spending our energies discussing it, 'we should devote our attention to all the children in this country who do not have the most basic educational opportunities.' Another academic produced an essay from *The Nation* magazine of 100 years ago, deploring 'overpressure' on children. 'We seem to remain anxiety ridden about the same issues.' But he added, 'I wouldn't hold my breath waiting for the super-people that these super-babies are supposed to become.'

A clinical psychologist, Judith Coché, speaking of the stress that hot housing could supposedly create in Glenn Doman's idealized families, said: 'When I work with families with young, overprogrammed children, they usually fall into two categories. Either the parents are living vicariously through their child's accomplishment, or the overprogrammed activity is a substitution for day care or baby-sitting' because the parents may be in fast-paced careers. In neither case was hot housing in the best interests of child or parents; 'What happens when a hot housed child lives with hot housed siblings and hot housing parents? All this can lead to fire – and someone in the family is in danger of burning out or up.'

It was the same story at the 1986 Atlanta convention of the National Association of Independent Schools. Cleveland Educational psychologist Jane Healy argued, 'We're seeing children as a perfectible product into whom we can quickly and efficiently pour some learning'. Yale psychologist Edward Zigler said bluntly that early learning had 'no long term effect on middle class kids.' He caustically condemned hot housing as a yuppie obsession, and decried the phenomenon of 'the gourmet child', in which parents try to transfer their own hyperambitious goals to their children. And for Marion Blum, of the Wellesley Child Study Centre, hot housing could create 'very nervous, anxious children afraid of failure and risk-taking.' Special scorn was reserved at the symposium for Glenn Doman and his ilk, such as the Suzuki music teaching scheme, which teaches two- to three-year-olds to play the violin. This kind of upbringing, it was felt, would bring about robot virtuosity with little understanding and no lasting gain.

In Washington late in 1986, as the hot housing topic was hotting up, the National Association for the Education of

Young Children held a news conference on the subject to stress that undue parental pressure on young children was threatening children's zest for learning – the very opposite of what Glenn Doman teaches, if you take away the loading inherent in the words undue and pressure. Dr David Elkind (author of *The Hurried Child*), the association's president and the professor of child study at Tufts University, complained that too many parents were regarding education competitively. 'We have to re-educate parents,' he pleaded, 'that education is not a race. There is no finish line. Education is a lifelong process. Pressured to learn through inappropriate methods, children may get turned off learning at a very early age.'

'About fifty per cent of reading problems come from starting kids reading not too late but too early,' he said, adding that children are not developmentally ready to read until about the age of six and a half, when they get their permanent teeth – or as Glenn Doman would have it, when their brains enter the characteristically adult state of unreceptiveness. Another expert, Dr Samuel Sava, reminded colleagues that in fifteen years, enrollment of three- to four-year-olds in formal pre-school programmes had doubled. 'We risk losing the developmental potential of early childhood education in a misplaced effort to mass produce little Einsteins,' he asserted, and added the frequently quoted fact that Einstein did not learn to speak until he was four. (The full story, for anti-hot housers, is that he could not read until he was seven, and his maths teacher thought he was stupid at twelve. Also for the record, the teachers *and* parents of Thomas Alva Edison were convinced that he was retarded. Furthermore, Newton and Faraday were from very ordinay backgrounds and were badly schooled, while Shakespeare has by some bizarre method been calculated to have had an IQ of the utterly average 100.)

William Kristol, chief of staff to the US Education Secretary was also in Atlanta to declare: 'There is a certain distressing tendency to have super-babies. Parents think if their children are not multiplying by age four, they won't get into Harvard at age eighteen. Our sense is that the evidence does not support that. There's too much pressure on parents.' No comfort is forthcoming either from Dr Berry Brazelton, the famous Harvard paediatrician, who holds that hot housing methods are largely a hype designed for ambitious young parents.

So what about Professor Hans Eysenck, generally perceived as a hardliner and (with reservations) an IQ test and hot housing fan? He believes a society should look after its prodigies, certainly – a relatively contentious view, it has to be said, in modern Britain. 'I think it is very important if a society wants to prosper because after all, it is genius which creates new industries, new jobs and so on, and it is the very bright people who make for success. If one had a choice, would one rather have a bright or a dull judge, a bright or a dull leader of business affairs, doctor, or politician? I don't think one needs to put the question in order to know what the answer would be.' Professor Eysenck starts to doubt whether it is a good idea, however, systematically to accelerate the learning of youngsters. 'You can raise the IQ, of course, but not the intelligence if you see what I mean.'

As to the more pragmatic matter of whether hot housing works, and if so, on which kind of children (normal or already gifted), Eysenck cites the experience of the Russians and East Germans, who seem to make fewer moral judgements in concentrating on the job of providing their countries with the best and the brightest. 'They are selecting children of special mathematical ability and ability in the physical sciences and taking them out of their background, segregating them in special schools where they are taught by university professors,' says Eysenck. The results, particularly in maths, have been good, but he adds: 'It is possible that the Russians and East Germans are doing too much. I spoke to the director of the programme in East Germany, who was rather worried about segregating children and bringing them up rigorously and rigidly as future geniuses. He thought this might have a bad effect on their personalities, and in my view, it might well do so.'

If hot housing can be made to work on bright or gifted children, could it bring ordinary or even dull children up to speed? Here, opinion is also divided. 'It can probably work with mediocre children. I am actually rather doubtful about the bright,' says Eysenck. 'It depends really on what you want to achieve. If you want to achieve children who are very knowledgeable, then it probably works with bright children too. It you want to have children who are original and creative, then it may be counter-productive, because you may destroy the very motivation that would normally lead them on to working things out for themselves.'

Eysenck's question is repeated by many others; is information the same as intelligence, and is intelligence the same as creativity? All the answers seem to lead towards a total rejection of Glenn Doman's ideas and those of the other hot housing gurus. Yet are these academics saying that hot housing simply does not work? The answer is, not quite. Ask them directly, not if they approve, but if the systems have an effect or validity, and they are far less equivocal than in their public pronouncements; in fact they will normally answer 'Yes'. Whether you can sustain the advantage, they are not so sure. Whether hot housing is necessary or desirable, they are not at all sure. Perhaps it is just not fashionable or politically acceptable to say, 'Yes, I think kids should be put under pressure'.

It is, after all, exceedingly difficult to assert that Glenn Doman achieves nothing. Many of the children are frankly breathtaking in their abilities, and not just in rote learning. Psychologists may have no worthwhile method of measuring creativity or originality, but that is not to deny that it can, apparently, be stimulated. Perhaps the 'professional' world disapproves of Doman because they do not think his pedigree is up to much. The glossy Better Baby brochure is unusually reticent on his professional qualifications with the very good reason that the sixty seven-year-old Doman does not have many. Son of a Philadelphia private detective and later physical culturist, a much decorated war hero (Lieutenant Colonel, Company K, Battle of the Bulge) Doman's qualification, according to his own press office, is as a registered physical therapist at the University of Pennsylvania. 'Nothing wrong with that,' you say. But it gives scholars who look at his four-year-old Japanese-speaking athletes and say, albeit metaphorically, 'a horse could do that' a chance to say further 'Aha – *That's* all he is!'

The significant hole in the anti-hot housing argument tends to open up in the case of disadvantaged children, the handicapped, and, strangely, where musical and dramatically inclined children are concerned. Few people would deny that London's Royal Ballet School – a hot house 'on points' – is an effective star-producing enterprise. The success of clinics for spastics such as that run by Andras Petö in Budapest (of which more later) and Doman's own early work with brain-damaged children are less often called into question. And nearly everyone wants poor kids to be given an educational chance. People may question the end product of that education, whether, for example it teaches children no more than to be than good capitalists or communists, but few of us would reject the entire concept of study and self improvement; and there is strong, though not conclusive evidence that hot housing the young disadvantaged has a beneficial effect. Dr Bill Durden director of John Hopkins University Talent Search (an attempt to identify the best and brightest ten to fourteen year olds in the United States and bring them together on the Hopkins campus for an intensive Honours program) has been involved in a great deal of research on accelerated learning. He concludes that the intensive teaching (hot housing) which is appropriate to the very brightest students, has impressive results when applied to those at the bottom of the academic heap. Hot housing works, he maintains, and it works on everybody. 'Through intensive after-school work with disadvantaged minority youth – many Hispanic, many black, we can radically improve their achievement levels, and yes, they can qualify for our program. We know it will work – we have the evidence.'

What offends the academic world most is undoubtedly the spectre of middle class children being hot housed with a view to becoming even more privileged than they already are. Academics, particularly in Britain, are loath, it seems, to see a world divided between the haves and the have-even-mores. That just is not nice – except, perhaps, for the kids. Later we shall look at research that challenges the common view that you cannot be hot housed and happy, that an intellectual giant marrow will never make a tasty dish.

3

Case studies: The Hot House Flowers

With the number of theories, opinons and counter opinions on the subject of hot housing children, perhaps it will be valuable above all to look at the children themselves in these 'experiments'. Some were gifted from the start; others seem to have been born normal but hot housed. All are remarkable.

It was mathematics class, and six-year-old Michael De Battista was showing irritation with the teacher, who was asking questions he regarded as obvious. There is nothing to suggest that Michael was born notably brilliant. 'Michael,' the teacher asked, 'what's two times five?'. 'Ten,' said Michael with a yawn. 'Then what's five times two?' 'Ten,' he replied impatiently. 'OK, then, what's two to the fifth power?' 'Sixty four,' he answered quickly. 'You're not multiplying, you're using two as a factor.' What is more extraordinary than this interchange itself is that Michael is considered a perfectly 'average' child. There is no suggestion that he was born gifted, or with a specially high IQ – and neither were his fifteen classmates. Their brightness is not accidental, but coached. Michael is one of Glenn Doman's 'Renaissance' children, trained and hot housed on the Philadelphia campus.

The Caputo family, Janet and Frank and daughters Cara and Adriana, actually live the Doman theory as a family on the Philadelphia campus. Frank is a member of the institution's staff; the children provide an interesting test case of Doman's ideas. Cara started as a Doman-ite when she was five. Her younger sister has been brought up from babyhood according to Doman's precepts. And, insist the proud parents, it works! 'Adriana had all the benefits of doing everything earlier, and physically I put her on the floor more often so she would be able to crawl and creep around the house,' says Janet. 'I taught her many intellectual things, which just made her take in facts at a faster rate. If you put the children side to side, that would be the major difference – that Adriana can assimilate facts faster. Just look at how that would affect the entire world. Geniuses? If that's part of it, that's great!'

Three thousand miles away, in Oxford (perhaps the oldest hot house of all), fifteen-year-old Ruth Lawrence, possessor of one of the most distinguished first class honours degrees ever gained there, is at work. It is impossible to tell if Ruth is a product of nature or nurture, or of what balance between the two. She has never been to a normal school or mixed with her contemporaries. At her home in Huddersfield, she was hot housed from infancy by her father, computer consultant Harry Lawrence, who eventually gave up his job to chaperone Ruth in her undergraduate (i.e. eleven to thirteen) days at St Hugh's College. At the start of her course there, her tutor told the other maths students not to regard their time at Oxford as a competition, 'because you will lose'. The bulk and quality of Ruth's work turned out to be staggering, even though some tutors were unhappy at the ubiquitous presence of Harry Lawrence. But there was no question of her solo ability. 'It is not her age that interests us. It is her brain and the sheer range of what it can do,' said her tutor Dr Mary Lunn.

Over her ten finals papers, she answered eighty one questions ('State the monotone convergence theorem for the Lenesgue integration and indicate the main steps in its proof') against an average of thirty two. She gained enough marks to get two Firsts, though being only thirteen, had to toast her achievement in pineapple juice.

A conversation with Ruth, [noted the *Sunday Times* journalist Stephen Pile] is like an intellectual assault course . . . No question is answered unless it is rigorously worded and precise. I asked, for example if there had ever been a subject that she had found difficult. It provoked hours of discussion. 'What sort of question is that? I can't possibly answer it.' Her father, who wore sandals and had his trousers tucked into his socks chimed in: 'That is a subjective question. Introspection is not a subject she has studied. It seems to me you asking at least two questions there.' I said it was a perfectly simple question of the kind asked every day by non-geniuses. 'No question is ever simple,' came the triumphant, if rather pat, chorus from father and daughter . . . It was the most taxing conversation I have ever had, and also among the least interesting, like a football match that is constantly stopped by the referee for technical infringements.

Perhaps obnoxiousness is a necessary by-product of being precocious. A visitor to a New York hot house school found himself seated at lunch next to an eight-year-old. As it was just after Christmas, he asked the obvious question – what had been the boy's favourite Christmas toys. It was a terrible *faux pas*; 'I am an intellectually gifted child, and I don't use toys,' came the reply. Maybe the brusqueness is a cry for understanding. The mother of one hot housed/gifted child (the two can be inseparable) in the US tells of finding the eighteen-month-old sitting at the bottom of the stairs crying. She asked him what was wrong. 'I don't have the words to tell you yet,' he replied. Some are perceived as being deeply unhappy, perhaps half mad, anxious, neurotic, the children of pushy parents, withdrawn, angst-ridden; they are probably computer wizards, white or oriental, but *never* black.

Nobody ever complains, however, about David Huang, aged ten and a veteran university science student in Houston, Texas. David, America's youngest college student, studies chemistry, maths and computers, and achieved A grades in his first year at the University of St Thomas, when he was just nine. For all that, he remains charming, happy and sociable.

David is the only son of immigrants of twenty two years' standing from Thailand; his father, one of eleven children is a chemical engineer by training and runs a wholesale prawn business. David's mother, Rtie Huang, who is forty one, is probably the power behind the prodigy. She admits she taught David intensively while he was still in the womb. Hot house children are essentially the product of their parents, far more so than in the usual parent/child equation. A remarkable number of hot housing parents are upwardly-mobile recent immigrants to their country, determined that their passport to success should be through a bright child. 'Better to be smart than to be stupid,' she says with undeniable logic. She read books on raising a child's IQ and applied the lessons – all the familiar stimulation routines – enthusiastically. When he was last tested, he scored an IQ of 159. David read at two before he could talk, and at four managed to teach his father BASIC computer language. Rtie now devotes herself full time to David's education, although her rôle is almost entirely restricted to carrying his books – literally. A skinny ten-year-old, he is dwarfed by some of his textbooks. Each day, she drives him to the campus, walks him across the street, and then retreats to her car, where she waits, reading the Bible and writing letters. 'If he can be rich and famous, it is fine,' she says. 'If he cannot, it doesn't matter to me too much about the money. You can have money, and not be happy. I just want him to be happy.' She adds that David once got angry with her because she could not discuss logarithms with him; and he can be stubborn. 'I have to spank him when he's stubborn,' she says. David's needs can also prove expensive, such is the importance of things like high-powered telescopes and computer bits and pieces.

He wants to be a doctor, preferably a surgeon, but realizes that at present rates he will qualify when he is sixteen – five years before he would be legally allowed to practise. 'I'll just have to go and study something else, like, er, I like astronomy. Maybe I'll go and learn astronomy.' Money? 'It would be nice, but I actually want to help people though,' he says. When he left high school at eight and first was accepted by the university, they wisely kept his presence secret, until they could see if he would fit in socially. He is there on a full scholarship. The thoughtful university need not have worried about David fitting in; his co-students, the youngest ten years older than David, accept him totally and were upset when he missed straight 'A's in his second year (he had forgotten to do one term paper). They work with him, and by all accounts the relationship is on an equal basis. He does not date the girls, however.

Every hot house child gets bored with the inevitable question from visiting journalists; 'What's it like being with kids older than you?' Most, like David, will tell them they do not know, as they have never been with anyone else. David's relationship with his college friend Yolande, who is twenty one, is interesting. While she and other young women are extremely maternal towards him, they will all defer to his superior knowledge. Half child and half man, they pat him on the head, then ask him questions; he watches *Dr Who* and chatters about the properties of fibre optics. He also lisps appealingly, telling you breathlessly about dithtillation, and likes to play little jokes on strangers, like cooking up a horrid black hand-staining compound in his lab and handing it to them as a present. But the quite astonishing thing about David is that, unlike some of the 'accidentally' gifted children, he is not just a small old person. He has friends of his own age. 'I just like playing on my bicycle, playing basketball with my friends, and programming my computer. The ones I ride bikes with are five or six.' He watches TV happily; 'I like watching, *Nova, Dr Who* and cartoons like *Scooby-Doo, He-Man* and *She-Ra*', he explains, his concentration elsewhere, as he plays in the laboratory — today at making his own glass test tubes and condensers. Anne Pinkerton, one of his teachers, says:

> David is quite extraordinary for a ten-year-old. I have not been exposed to many students of his calibre, really, in my entire years of teaching. It's incredible. David is capable of just about anything. He grasps concepts very easily. There just doesn't seem to be too much that he doesn't get – and without much effort on his part. The University has been very careful about what David has been permitted to do. We did not put him in philosophy and theology or English, which we require. But this year, he is taking on philosophy and a first year English course, and as I understand it both from David and from his professors and others, he's doing just fine.
>
> David can make high A, low A, high B. It really doesn't bother him at all, and you know that he spent the time riding his bicycle, watching *Scooby-Doo*, in the library, playing with the computer terminal and getting all lost in time – and he's achieving, without pouring hour after hour into studying. He doesn't do that. He can be a child now, and walk him into a science lab and he's an adult.'

But she adds: 'David can't go back to spending his entire day with children his own age. He's too far beyond them.

So has hot housing in David Huang's case been a good idea, or was it just an essential method of bringing up a naturally bright child? 'I think it's inevitable. I had some questions at first about whether it was a good thing. But after you spend a year with David, I'm convinced we are not doing the wrong thing letting him come to school here and learn, letting his mind be challenged, letting him learn at whatever speed he can learn.' 'He's a joy to have in the class. When you walk into a large classroom of 104, what you see is the top of a head above a desk. And you notice two little feet that don't reach the floor. It's very hard not to teach "to" David, because his eyes don't leave you. In fact it's difficult not to direct everything towards him to the exclusion of all others!'.

But David is not a swot, and he does not make straight As. 'He doesn't write everything down,' says Anne Pinkerton. 'He sits, and his little feet are going and his eyes are dancing and if you ask a question, he's ready to volunteer or call out to give an answer. It is just great fun to have David. He still teaches me. I'm not really a computer literate person. David knows how to do an awful lot more. He comes in from time to time, and we log on to the computer and he'll say "Let me show you how to do this," or I'll say, "David, do you know . . . " and he'll say, "Oh, sure, that's easy". '

In the same city of Houston lives a five-year-old called Paul whose parents are both NASA astronauts, one of only three astronaut families in the world. As if having progenitors quite so resolutely of the right stuff were not enough, Paul, son of Dr Rhea (pronounced Ray) Seddon, who is also a medical doctor, qualified test pilot and space shuttle crew member, and Robert 'Hoot' Gibson, one of the most accomplished fliers in the world, is being brought up largely *à la* Glenn Doman. Rhea, forty, is an ardent supporter and frequent speaker at the Institutes for Human Potential in Philadelphia. So keen is she that Paul should live up to his potential, as she and her husband have done, that she has been photographed with the child in identical silvery-blue astronuaut's suits. At Glenn Doman's HQ, where it hangs, the staff call the picture 'Rhea and her Astro-tot.'

'I think a child is extremely receptive in the early years as their brains are still growing; they have sort of to learn the survival skills,' she says, echoing Doman almost word for word. 'The things that Paul was interested in early on, we sort of fostered. If he showed an interest in dogs, we had all kinds of books and pictures of dogs, and now that he is interested in cars and trucks, he's learning to read by reading the names on them. It's important just to foster those things they are interested in and enjoy doing. I want to make it easy for him to learn; we use every opportunity to teach him something. We talk to him a lot, we point out things as we are driving in the car or going through the supermarket, and he absorbs those things. I think certain children won't be ready for reading or counting or colours or art at a particular age, they won't show any interest in it or skill with it, but I think you should present it to them, that so when they are ready for it, it's there for them to learn.'

Paul is a delightful blond ball of energy, but it has to be said, has shown no exceptional abilities to date. He shows no undue interest in being taken around the mock-up of his mother's Space Lab, and performs no amazing feats as he looks at its thousands of gauges and buttons. His parents profess no interest in having a super-baby – they are more than happy with their late addition. Their pride and happiness simply that they are 'doing right' for their son may be seen as a different type of testament to Glenn Doman.

Rhea actually came into contact with the Doman system after her Space Lab mission as medical advisor and robot-arm operator on the Discovery shuttle, which followed Paul's birth. Work on frog spawn in space had indicated that the reproductive ability can be damaged by zero gravity. She was seriously concerned that a second baby (which has not yet come) might be damaged in some way as a result of her job, and wanted to check out Doman's work. She signed up for a course after the flight.

> You would like to think that if they get a good start, if they learn to read early and have an enjoyment for reading, if they are curious about things, if they ask questions about things, and you can show them where to find out that information, they will have an advantage. I don't think it's terribly important for us that he should be outstanding; it's more important to us that he should he happy. He may be happy being a professor in an ivory tower somewhere. We would like him to have as many options in life as possible, if he wants to be President or if he wants to be a truck driver or whatever.

(Paul has shown the interest you might expect in being an astronaut. He has a lot of fun coming in his childhood. Gibson

Snr., apart from his real flying, also pilots some of the meanest radio-controlled model aircraft in the world.)

'I think the ego build-up you get when people say you are doing a good job, you made straight 'A's, sort of teaches you as an encouragement that you can do anything you want to do. That perhaps tells people they can be astronauts, they can be physicians, that they are competitive. But you know, other children just accomplish that in their own time. They are not pushed or accelerated in any way. They are just smart. But I think that I for one would like to help Paul along that course.'

And Dr. Seddon's recipe for success? 'I think working hard is probably the most important thing and having a bit of luck; but I think the harder you work, the more luck you have.'

The Genius Factory: the formula which worked every time

Hard work is certainly the trademark of the Susedik family of suburban Chicago. Their idea of success was raising geniuses, and they seem to have a formula which works – every time. Joseph Susedik and his Japanese wife Jitsuko have four daughters – all with IQs of 150 plus. They claim they can develop the same abilities in any child, and indeed are thinking of starting a school to teach their methods. The Susediks met as penpals; he was working as a prospector in the Mojave desert and bought twenty Japanese names and addresses from an advertiser in the *Alaskan Sportsman* magazine. Jitsuko, who was teaching English at a Tokyo finishing school for ladies, was one of them, and had been advertising for an American man in the local *Japan Times*. 'I always wanted to improve myself,' she says. 'Japanese men are very fine, but they want the woman always to be on a lower level.'

According to their parents, none of the four Susedik babies

ever needed to cry when they were hungry or wet. All were born virtually talking, and were able to make a stab at (but never grizzle) the words 'Food' and 'Wet' when three months old. The oldest Susedik daughter, Susan, is now sixteen and a PhD. student in anatomy at the University of Illinois. She wants to be a doctor and has shown particular interest in spinal cord repairs to prevent or repair paralysis. The second daughter, Stacey, entered university in Chicago at twelve. The two youngest, Stephanie and Johanna are each five years ahead of their peers at school.

'They are really unique, the first case I've ever heard of of so many gifted children in one family,' said their local school psychologist after spending a day and a half administering intelligence and achievement tests to the girls. 'I was amazed. On some parts of the test, Susan went right off the scale.' (At ten, Susan in fact got the highest maths score ever achieved by a girl in the standard scholastic aptitude test. On the basis of that, she entered college.) Joseph Susedik told *Time* magazine then: 'If everybody raised their children like we raised ours, one eighth of the kids in this country could be smart'. Mr Susedik, now a brawny, retired maintenance mechanic with thirty three jobs behind him, from bartender to construction worker, dropped out of school. Academic researchers who have interviewed him have called him 'eccentric'. He claims to have been taken aboard a flying saucer at the age of nine and under hypnosis he can relate many of the details of the trip. He is a stong believer in ESP and reincarnation. Joe Susedik is also an amateur inventor, with a design up his sleeve for a magnetic motor that does not require fuel. He says he develops his inventions during periods of earthquakes or volcanic activity.

None of this interesting c.v. is instantly obvious when you encounter Joe Susedik – an unassuming, amiable 'ordinary Joe'. His exotic history and unexotic personality have to be seen against the facts of what he and his wife have produced in their daughters. The chances of four geniuses being born to one family have been estimated at a billion-to-one. Geniuses? Most alleged geniuses cannot be properly verified, but the Susedik girls are such a phenomenon and their parents so willing to talk about them that they have been tested and probed by almost every expert that the American education system could throw at them. Irving Sigal of the Education Testing Service at Princeton was specially detailed to visit the wilds of Ohio, where the family then lived, to make an objective assessment of the four girls. 'They are, indeed, geniuses,' he concluded. Whether they are geniuses born or made, he does not know – but he says that although Joe Susedik is not highly educated, he is extremely bright, as is Jitsuko. It is just possible, therefore, that the Susedik phenomenon could be an amazing genetic coincidence – a sort of biological grand slam.

The principles the Susediks worked out were to start lessons the day the babies came home; to watch their eyes, stop the second their attention began to wander – and always keep learning fun. 'We brought ourselves down to the infants' level and tried to think like they think. Infants are very curious, their minds are like sponges. The day Susan arrived home from hospital, Jitsuko showed her pictures of large block letters, and started sounding out words, clearly, never in baby talk.' Within weeks, the Susediks assert, Susan was saying 'Mama' and 'I love you'. The babies never cried because they were hungry or needed changing, their parents say. They used rudimentary words to indicate every need; when hungry, Susan would say 'Opei', Japanese for 'breast'.

The standard flashcards rapidly became flashier; 'When you get a cold, your body makes antibodies to fight the particular virus that comes into your system' read one, in big block letters on bright paper. Another solemnly spelt out the Pledge of Allegiance to the flag. Another still contained the Japanese alphabet, though the children were never taught Japanese in any detail because Jitsuko felt her own language was too inept at expressing emotion. Stories and music, though, were constant. At three months, Susan could carry on a conversation in full sentences. At two years she found *Sesame Street* too juvenile, and she played the organ at three. She was a high school freshman at five, having entered kindergarten and skipped through the rest of primary school in a matter of weeks.

'Generally, when not showing off at their parents' request, they act like any other group of happy, well adjusted little girls,' noted reporter Jay Branegan in 1981. 'They scamper about the barn as dad takes the animals out to their tethers. The little ones pick flowers and run to give them to mama. When it is time to pile into the family station wagon to go out for lunch as a treat, one of the older ones helps Johanna on with her shoes. 'Susan says, "Oh, neat!" Says the very likeable Joe Susedik: 'They're just ordinary kids with a little head start. I don't see the sperm bank coming over and knocking on my door; we know the girls' success is because of the teaching — they weren't born geniuses. America has to change its whole educational concept. We have to develop our scientists, our engineers so we'll stop being the suckers of the world, falling behind the Japanese and others.'

The three younger Susedik girls, despite their accomplishments, strike the visitor as relatively normal, pleasant, if unusually shy by American standards. Yet the girls are so accustomed to being with older people that they somehow cope. Stacey at thirteen goes away to college, where she gets on well with her nineteen-year-old room mate, though does not date boys — 'Because I can't find anyone to date, but if I could I probably would!' Stephanie, eleven and at junior high school with fifteen- and sixteen-year-olds, just wishes people wouldn't call her Stevie, her father's nickname, which has stuck to her irritation. Jojo, nine, says she has to study hard to keep up with her eleven- and twelve-year-old class mates — and they don't come over to her house after school.

Susan too, sixteen and a Ph.D. candidate studying with

twenty two-year-olds, shows a reassuring – perhaps a little too reassuring! – lack of messianic mission. She loves and thanks her parents very much, but has some doubts about the future as a doctor she thinks she might embark on. Asked 'Do you have great ambitions? Would you like to contribute something that's really important?' Susan told us: 'Not really. I guess it would be nice, but I don't really want to spend the rest of my life chasing after the hope that I can make a great contribution. It's more important for me to be happy in my personal and social life. I might have a career for a couple of years after I get out, but my main goal in life is just to get married and have children. I don't really think it's my duty because I have this ability to go out and try to save the world if it's not what I'd be happy doing.' And would Susan like to be rich and famous? 'I'd like to be both, but not really by doing cell biology. I'd love to be an actress or a singer, a glamorous person, you know?' Susan was as shy as her sisters while she was still at home, but has adjusted to college social life with huge enthusiasm. 'If my father knew some of the things that happen at school he'd hate it,' she giggles.

An interesting insight into the internal dynamics of the Susedik family came one day at breakfast in a restaurant near the Susediks' home during the filming of *Hot House People*. When a waitress asked Stevie Susedik how she would like her eggs she did not reply. The waitress referred the question to Jitsuko, who said, 'When the child wants to say how she would like her eggs, she will say.' An extremely long and embarrassing silence ensued; nothing from Stevie. Mrs Susedik insisted again that no pressure of any sort should be brought to bear on the child. Eventually one of the younger girls whispered, 'Fried.' 'I assume,' said the waitress, saving (in fact rather winning) the day, 'that your elder sister would like her eggs the same way.'

Wombs With A View

Even before her little genius, David, was conceived, Rtie Huang says she took care of herself, particularly her diet (no food that would 'retard the growth of the baby's brain'). While she was pregnant (no coffee, no tea) she used to read books and play Beethoven to David the foetus. 'You can teach your child when you're pregnant,' she asserts. David Huang could be said to be a startling example of the worth of pre-natal stimulation of what many insist is the oddest kind.

Like the Huangs in Houston, the Susediks in the north taught their brood and developed their talents not only from birth but before it, talking to the Susedik foetuses and (loudly) reading them *in utero* stories. 'We use ESP in our pre-natal work, because the baby doesn't have a solid skull, it's just got skin across the brain,' says Joe Susedik, 'So if we visualize very deeply before birth and after birth while we're teaching, we can impart more knowledge to the child. The child gets a three-dimensional picture of what we're trying to teach. I see us as pioneers.'

Fluffy caterpillars in children's stories were explained in terms of cocoons, butterflies, pollination and all. You could not vacuum the floor near the pregnant Mrs Susedik without her giving a detailed explanation of the internal workings of vacuum cleaners. All available children would gather round Mrs Susedik's tummy to talk to the next baby down the line. 'You know,' says Joe, 'a theology student called me and said, "You aren't the first" because God spoke to Job and Jeremiah in the womb and they were the smartest people of their time. It's environment. The scientists are finding out that chickens talk to their eggs, their eggs answer them back, the cow talks to the calf, the dog talks to the litter inside of her. It's simply instinctive pre-natal teaching.'

Pre-natal learning, eccentric as it may sound, has its adherents. Dr Edward Zigler of Yale University is not one of them, but he points out with characteristic wisdom: 'It's crack-pot in the sense that it has not been proven to make any difference. But I think in the sense that a mother learns, in that situation, "Hey, what I do makes a difference," it's very impor-tant. So if a mother has that attitude, I feel, just let her go ahead and do some crackpot things, as long as the attitude those things represent also means she's going to do something very wise, like making sure she doesn't smoke and drink during pregnancy, and that she gets pre-natal care that guarantees as sound a baby as she can produce.'

In recent years, developmentalists have turned their atten-tions to the unborn child. In the 1960s, researchers in South Africa treating toxaemia in pregnancy with decompression techniques suggested that you could create your own genius by decompressing the abdomen, thus increasing the efficiency of the placenta. Imogen Barker, the wife of a headmaster in Kent, England, was one of the guinea pigs, and wrapped herself in a huge plastic bag for half an hour every day in the last three months of her second pregnancy, inflating it at half-minute intervals. 'It certainly made the contractions less painful in the early stages of labour,' she recalls. 'Whether it made a dif-ference to my daughter's intelligence we will never know for sure.' Today, Rosalind, still at school, is an academic high-flyer – but so is her uncompressed elder brother, Jolyon. Was that genes, or was it decompression? No one can be totally sure, but a follow-up in South Africa did not note any difference between the babies who had the treatment and their peers.

In an Essex maternity hospital, psychologist Clifford Olds found that an embryo moves away from music it dislikes. 'Rock will make the embryo kick in protest, and what is generally known as classical music causes it to move slightly in the womb, as if to hear more clearly,' he said. 'And the foetus is already developing a personal taste – it does not always react favourably to a tune its mother enjoys.'

Today in the run-of-the-mill suburb of Hayward, outside

San Francisco, stands a smart obstetricians' practice, over the road from a maternity hospital. Here Dr René Van De Carr runs what is colloquially known as the Pre-Natal University. It is Dr Van De Carr's own tag, and though he does not go so far as to put it on his brass plaque he is quite serious about it. 'Graduates' of the 'University' – that is to say, newborn infants delivered under his care, are presented with a certificate and a cute red and white T shirt emblazoned with the legend 'PRE NATAL UNIVERSITY' and the institution's distinguished motto, 'Pat Pat, Rub Rub'.

Mothers-to-be sign up when they are pregnant. The 'teaching' of unborn babies takes the form of getting them to connect a particular sound with a corresponding activity. The doctors help the mother to discover where the baby is lying. She will then learn to say 'Pat Pat Pat' while patting her baby, 'Stroke Stroke Stroke' while stroking, 'Shake Shake Shake' and so on. Then a xylophone tuned to a certain note will signify some other action. If the mother does not speak loudly enough, Dr Van de Carr has paper megaphones just the right length to reach a pregnant woman's tummy. Fathers also speak to their unborn babies; 'Hello, baby, this is Daddy speaking. I love you, baby.' The Pre Natal University also does some work with bright lights – which the beleaguered embryo can see through the stomach walls. Babies tend to move away from them.

According to Dr Van de Carr and his associates, five hundred pre-natal university graduates have shown enhanced physical, and mental development; pre-natal stimulation is said to lead to early speech, physical agility and healthy parent-child bonding. 'They begin using sentences earlier,' the doctor says. 'They can recognize a hidden object, what we call object constancy. They know that if you drop a ball inside a cup, the ball still exists – hidden inside the cup. We think there may be some neuro-muscular acceleration phenomenon. We think it may trigger actual development of parts of the nervous system.' The babies born after pre-natal stimulation also seem puzzlingly to have a preponderance of hair, some baby teeth and surprisingly long finger nails – though Dr. Van de Carr does not want to commit himself to asserting that these phenomena are due to early neurological stimulation. Further anecdotal-type evidence is that Van de Carr's babies seem to talk earlier than most. (One Indian couple's new born girl seemed, when we were at their side twelve hours after the birth, to open and close her eyes on demand.) Van de Carr denies that there is no proof of his theories. Like Glenn Doman, he says that no known measurement can accurately quantify the gains his methods achieve.

He has resisted having the children he delivers IQ tested:

> We've tried to avoid the issue of super-babies. I think it's putting numbers on something that is so beneficial in a wide range of areas that we hesitate to do it. Because after all, we're working on communicating with the baby, making the baby more social. We humans are very social creatures, and we think the baby inside can actually learn to be social in this exchange.
>
> We recently presented a paper in Austria which indicated that the babies that were communicated with pre-natally are physically healthier at the moment of birth and when re-assessed five minutes later, they score significantly better than the group that has not been communicated with. So we are saying, yes, we think, feel, that we can make healthier and more socially adjusted children. Intelligence? Yes, I think they are more intelligent – intelligence in the broadest sense, in that it helps them deal with life in a more complete, more total way.

Why does Dr Van de Carr suppose that there is so much hostility to the idea of creating so-called super-babies? 'There is always a counter-reaction to anything new. Almost any movement or new idea will be met by a counter idea, something trying to hold the status quo. People tend to resist change even if it's beneficial. I would say we are working at improving our ability to get along with each other, and if that's social engineering, then that's what we want. It is more acceptable to most people than *genetic* engineering, so why not give it a try first?'

There is no doubt it is what hundreds of Dr Van de Carr's patients want; but all give the characteristic justification of wanting anything but a super-baby. They can be positively touchy on the subject. 'No super-baby is in our plans,' said one father. 'Just someone to be close to and be able to communicate with, talk to.' A mother insisted; 'that's not what we're looking for, but if the baby is born with a little bit higher intelligence, or manages to get along with children that are above his age level, that's fine. There's nothing wrong with that.'

One child, six-year-old Erin Abbadie, came along to see us with her mother, Cathy. Erin was Dr Van de Carr's first graduate. She is undoubtedly an attractive and self-possessed child. 'She seems a lot older and more independent, and she does a lot of things children of her age don't do,' said her mother proudly. 'She snow-skied when she was twenty two months, and now she's really fast, in the races and everything. She was always just more aware of everything, I think. And she picked up on reading very early.'

Dr Van de Carr enthused over a new delivery; 'This is a beautiful little baby. She's less than twenty four hours old and she's really alert. She's got good neuro-muscular activity and I think is fairly typical of many of our babies . . . Notice how docile she's being, passed between Daddy and myself, and she's not upset by the experience. She's pretty calm, relaxed and comfortable, and look at that head of hair! Isn't she cute?'

The Body Beautiful – at five months!

One of the stranger activities that Glenn Doman's super-children get up to is described by him as 'bracciation' and involves swinging hand-over-hand on a climbing frame between lessons, giving a good impression of small chimpanzees. They are encouraged to repeat this many times each day for better neurological development. Behind this practice lies a theory developed by Doman from his work with brain-damaged children. He believes that lost abilities can sometimes be found again by establishing new pathways in the brain – literally rewiring the brain – and bracciation and crawling can enhance the neurological development of the brain and encourage the 'cross-referencing abilities' which are thought to correlate with reading skills. Children who skip the crawling phase are believed by some experts to stand a statistically greater chance of developing reading difficulties including dyslexia.

In California, land of the body beautiful, many competitive mothers believe that kids in the fast lane need a headstart, physically as well as mentally, on the grounds that one thing leads to another. This has resulted in a proliferation of 'junior gyms' where toddlers can develop superior minds and bodies before they are fully toilet-trained. From twelve to eighteen months onwards, Jed Heller's Junior Gym in Los Angeles runs 'Mommy and Me' classes in a huge warehouse of a room with a padded floor and a padded obstacle course. With mother's help, the babies are encouraged to perform amazing feats of derring-do even as they take their first steps. The eighteen-month to three-year-olds, tiny arms akimbo, walk a padded balance-beam, and swing by the knees (fearlessly) from double wooden rings suspended from the ceiling. Mothers and babies sit around a huge circular silk parachute, put coloured balls in the centre and shake them so they look like popcorn. In another game, the kids run through a swarm of bubbles, trying to catch them in their mouths. 'It's not just play,' says Jed Heller, 'as much as the children may think it is. We design activities in a distracting manner so they are having a good time, but we know that there's a purpose for everything we do. You can't separate the mind from the body. Research indicates that improved coordination, early neurological development, may well lead to smarter children – more confident with their bodies. Furthermore, they excel socially because they don't have to spend much time worrying about the physical ability to perform or look good or feel good.'

The mothers at Jed's Junior Gym readily admit that they are looking for their children to gain a headstart at school; but is it not all a little too competitive at such a tender age? 'I don't really notice that kids are competing with other kids,' said one mother. 'I think they take pride when they do something right.' 'Super-babies?' says another mother with unusual frankness. 'Sure! I'll do anything I can to help develop them!' She tells us that she follows the teachings of Glenn Doman between work-outs.

A similar, though less earnest and frenetic version of the Junior Gym movement, swept through Britain in 1986. It is called Tumble Tots. The idea behind Tumble Tots is that there is an acrobat struggling to get out of each of us, and that the time to make the most of the acrobatic urge is at the moment a child can walk. The concept was developed by two British Olympic gymnastics coaches, Bill Cosgrove and Nik Stuart; they describe it as 'How to make your body do what you want it to do in increasingly challenging circumstances'.

4

Poor Kids can be Geniuses, Too

Nowhere is it decreed that hot housing must be an exclusively private enterprise activity. But even in the US, examples of educational hot housing in the publicly-supported sphere are not exactly legion. It should be said at the outset that although hot housing sounds to be the very essence of middle class social aspiration, it does not have to be so. If children – any children – are *expected* to become more intelligent, an important piece of research published in 1968 showed that their teachers will then perceive and treat them as such, aiding this kind of growth. (R. Rosenthal and B. Jacobson, *Pygmalion in the Classroom: Teacher Expectations and Pupils' Intellectual Development*).

For a long time, the public perception of the genius has been of a white, middle class child, or possibly an oriental computer whizz. Teachers believe that there are vast reservoirs of undiscovered talent in less predictable strata of society, but few public education systems have done anything about it. New York City, however, has been prepared to fund publicly a school for geniuses – on the strict understanding that the school should reflect the demography of the urban area as a whole. It was an optimistic gesture – a real act of faith – since it assumed that enough very bright children would be found from each racial, ethnic and social group in this incredibly diverse city to fulfill the brief. The result has been an object lesson for anyone tempted to believe that it is a waste of time looking for talent amongst low-income families, living in bed and breakfast accomodation. When we asked one Hispanic mother in a welfare hostel if it is truly impossible for the unemployed to raise geniuses, she answered, 'Crap'. She should should know; her six-year-old son Carlos has an IQ of 160, and attends a school known as Hunter.

In a huge, nearly windowless, red-brick building, a former armoury on the fringes of Spanish Harlem in New York City stands the Hunter College Campus Schools, a vast human laboratory attached to the city's Hunter College. The school's position is symbolic – with posh Park Avenue to the south, and Harlem to the north. Here highly able children, selected for their giftedness in a large range of attributes, are concentrated from all over the city. The Elementary School (kindergarten to sixth grade) comprises 400 children, with a staff/pupil ratio of a respectable (but not extraordinary) fifteen to one. The teaching programme is said to emphasize the development of thinking skills and creativity, along with a solid traditional academic foundation. The High School takes 1,250 students selected by its entrance examination. To get in, you have to demonstrate by a 'standardized achievement test' ability at least four years above your grade level in mathematics and reading. Selection of the youngest hopefuls – if that can be the right term – is at age two to three. The competition is intense and legendary in souped-up Manhattan. And no wonder – the alternative, if your child is Harvard-bound, is private schooling, where the fees might typically be $10,000 a year.

Hunter does not pretend to work with 'ordinary' children; it charges itself with winkling out and nurturing extraordinary talent no matter where it exists. Every student goes on to university. The city, with one of the highest welfare budgets in the US, cannot afford, says Hunter's Dean, Dr Rich, to waste anyone or anything. Hunter graduates of all ethnic backgrounds have gone on to become outstanding citizens; the school numbers among its graduates a Metropolitan Opera star, Martine Arroyo; Maria Muldaur, the jazz-rock singer; State Supreme Court judges, prominent politicians, mathematicians, scientists, union leaders; Pearl Primus, the dancer choreographer and Hortense Calisher, author.

'The curriculum is designed to foster a love of learning, as well as to provide a solid traditional liberal arts foundation. Independence and freedom of thought and spirit are both valued and encouraged,' reads the school brochure. Around one third of the students are black or Hispanic; many more are Oriental. A proportion of students have parents on welfare. What the children have in common are IQs of 135 and over. When you visit, you might happen, as we did, upon a group of seven year olds enjoying an art class talk on pointilism and having a chance to try out the technique. It is clear that for these children, recreation is study and study recreation; they sometimes have to be stopped, say teachers, from doing too much homework. In the 'recreation time' between classes, the High School students sprawl over the corridor floors surrounded by scratch designs for computer programmes and graphics. Every child is expected to have a 'mastery' of at least one foreign language. The school chess club meets at lunchtime, and happens to have two of America's junior chess champions in it – one black boy and one white girl.

A black eight-year-old girl works quietly on a piece of poetry, discussing syntax with two friends. A wise guy in a sweat shirt complains during filming; 'Come on, we're wasting time.' Three children, one black, one half black and one Jewish sit on the floor by the lockers discussing their projects. 'Mine's on lizards, what's yours?' 'Living in the Negev. What's yours?' 'Petroleum,' says the black boy. 'Otherwise known as oil,' says the girl mockingly. 'It's better than plutonium,' shrugs the boy.

Parental involvement at Hunter – the common factor of hot housing in *all* its manifestations – is heavy and considered vital to the progress of the children. Parents are encouraged to monitor classes and mix freely with the children in the corridors. The black Dean of the school, Dr Evelyn Rich, strolls the hallways, stopping for a brief chat with everyone. She is part educator, part social worker; on this particular day, she was worried about Carlos's parents. Mr and Mrs Alvarez had lost their home and been re-housed in bed and breakfast accommodation more suitable for New York City's population of cockroaches. Many of the parents, she says, are in the direst social circumstances, some living a half-life in welfare hotels. We talked to Mr and Mrs Alvarez after they had been rescued from their emergency housing. 'I am unemployed, and there is no way I could afford this kind of education for Carlito without Hunter College Elementary,' the father said. 'We were in the family shelter for three months when the school found out about our situation. They got the Hunter network in operation, and they actually helped us to get out of the shelter and into an apartment. It's been the saving grace, actually, for my family.' How did Carlito come to be like he is? 'We're definitely not wealthy, but we just stimulated him in the right way, and he just came out like that. I think anybody could do it as long as you put in the time and effort, and the love.'

'These days' a previous school director told the *New York Times* in 1977, 'after years of hearing educational élitism put down, it's socially acceptable to talk about gifted children again – although the nation still doesn't really care about them. We could fill half a dozen more schools like this with bright students eager to learn.'

Most Hunter kids describe the school as 'demanding' and 'challenging' often adding that they were bored at previous schools. A self-possessed girl from Queens told the *Times* that, 'If there were any boys around to impress, I'd be out there impressing them. Hunter makes you put your mind on learning, and if your grades start dwindling, you feel bad.' Some said they had previously felt isolated from their friends; a girl from Harlem said, 'I feel among my own people here. You can show your whole potential.'

'These youngsters are not an élite,' insists Dr Rich:

That's one of the myths about gifted youngsters. They have a right to be properly served as do youngsters who have other kinds of handicapping conditions, and we believe that in serving the gifted, in the long run we're serving all of the population. These are youngsters who may not be President or Secretaries of State or university people, but often they do provide the intellectual rationale behind the scenes that make the difference in a country or a corporation, in a school system, in some small business, and ultimately, everyone benefits.

We have kids here whose parents are mail people, probation officers, or who do very menial work like construction or perhaps domestic work – as well as parents who are teachers and social workers, surgeons and performers in the arts. We will not discriminate against a kid because of the economic circumstances into which he was born or currently lives. Many parents see our school as an alternative to a private school. That's not how we perceive ourselves; we see ourselves as providing a unique education for kids who are truly gifted, and at the same time we have a commitment to build gifted programmes in public, private and church-related schools.

Not all of these youngsters are going to achieve prominently in fields that we are going to know about. That's another commitment, and we recognize that some will live lives which appear to be quite ordinary, and there's nothing wrong with that. What's wrong is our failure to identify these kids and to give them the opportunity to develop these gifts and maybe live in some obscure city in the mid-west or out on the West Coast or perhaps abroad. At some time, there are others who will be Nobel prize winners. They will be statesmen, doctors, librarians, they'll run the gamut, but deep down inside, they will feel an inner sense of self recognition and self-worth. That's very important and the kind of thing you can't measure in money.

Dr Rich is particularly proud of the school's selection process. 'It's a fascinating process. We recognize of course that all of the techniques for identifying gifted children are in a very preliminary stage.' The school starts with IQ testing, but also has developed, with the help of outside consultants, a series of tests which enable them to identify 'divergent thinkers'. 'We give them tests which focus on similarities, differences, fluencies, flexibilities, imagination, and we look at the kids in a group setting to see what extent they exhibit leadership qualities, and ultimately, we make our choices based on these criteria. One is intelligence, second is what we call task commitment and the third, creativity. We're very lucky because we rely largely on parents to identify their kids and bring them in to us. The research shows that the most effective identifiers of gifted children are the parents. Now with minority parents, we work closely, because the indices of giftedness that you or I might traditionally search out and look for are not necessarily highly regarded in certain minority communities. For example, black parents often discourage youngsters from exhibiting verbal skills, and we find that they are a high predictor of giftedness, and we meet with those parents and talk with them about how to nurture and encourage their kids to exhibit these gifted skills.'

What exactly should parents be on the look-out for? 'We have found that self-motivation is a good predictor of gifted-ness, a youngster's inner desire to find out and discover new things. We have also found that persistence is another factor, the ability of a kid to tackle an assignment and follow through on it in new and creative ways. We have found other indices, such as the ability to think analytically. Now a parent in a ghetto might not know what that means, but in our minority recruitment nights, we sit down and we talk with them about the characteristics or the traits, and try to give them examples of what these things mean and how they express themselves, so that when they present their youngster to us, they can do it effectively.'

She concluded: 'This could significantly improve the public school systems throughout this country and thus make it possible for youngsters who are truly gifted but who have not been identified as such, to begin to blossom. Often people say that a Mozart or a Beethoven could be found in the rain forest of Zaire. We would argue that he could be found on 126th Street in East Harlem, and that it is the obligation of educators to find him, identify him and nurture him so that all of us can enjoy the symphonies which would result.'

The Hunter school in New York is not the only institution to hold a direct talent search, attracting super-able children through its doors. Johns Hopkins University in Baltimore conducts a nationwide talent search for young people who may be particularly promising in maths or language; pupils who live near Baltimore spend their Saturdays on the campus dipping their toes into undergraduate work. Other children go to high-powered summer courses. On the west coast, in middle class North Hollywood, California, is Walter Reed Junior High School. This is not a separate school for gifted children, but its Individual Honours Programme (IHP) is probably the most famous in the USA. This is the only junior high in America or anywhere in the world that functions at college level for the benefit of eleven- to-fourteen-year-olds.

In a typical Reed class, Paul Mertens, a Belgian with a masters degree in history from UCLA fires the questions. 'What does Herodotus say? Plutarch? Xenophon? Where do they agree and disagree? Why? How much of a democracy was Athens?'

By a happy twist of fate, three very gifted teachers happened to come together at the same place at the same time; Paul Mertens, Judy Selsor and William FitzGibbon. They are the secret of success at Walter Reed; if you want to teach gifted children, it is almost essential to start with gifted teachers. In a nearby room of the vaguely Spanish style schoolhouse, William FitzGibbon, an MIT science graduate, sketches a physics problem concerning the path of a falling projectile on an overhead projector. The twenty students punch numbers into their calculators, shouting out the object's coordinates. One student does so looking up occasionally from an Agatha Christie mystery, another from a biography of Eugene Debs. The atmosphere is loud and chaotic, but nobody leaves when the 3 pm bell goes. A young girl points out that the teacher has been applying a shortcut formula to the problem, and that his answers will not work in every case. 'People think I'm crazy teaching junior high with an MIT degree,' FitzGibbon says, 'but these kids are so sharp. I need to keep up with them. I hate to put it this way, but it doesn't work if you have 180 IQ kids being taught by 120 IQ teachers. These aren't the kind of students that are considered ideal by most teachers. They don't hesitate to correct a teacher, and if they don't respect him, they'll challenge him. That causes some of them problems when they leave here and don't get the same calibre of work and instruction.'

Walter Reed has 150 academic superstars (*Time* magazine's expression) on its register for the Individualized Honours Program, and is probably the most successful junior high in America. Nearly half its pupils go on to the very top US universities, such as Stanford, Yale, Harvard and MIT, and they are pre-eminent in such strange brain jousts as the US International Chemistry Olympiad and the National Language Arts Olympiad.

The Walter Reed students' achievements in advanced maths and science are only the school's more demonstrable successes. The IHP course also emphasizes English and social studies – areas in which attainment is far more difficult to quantify. The course aims to produce well-rounded students who can read and write and speak in public, as well as calculate; who can exercise criticism of conflicting historical analyses as well as plot the path of that projectile. In an English class eleven-year-olds discuss the subject of scapegoats – was Lee Harvey Oswald or Jack Ruby the bigger scapegoat? A young girl broadens the debate – surely Dreyfus was a bigger scapegoat than either?

The formula at Walter Reed again is simple – obvious, in fact – and familiar; excellent teachers, parental backing, a strong respect for some traditional educational methods (but without traditional behaviour – these children are not repressed, and have no fear of the teachers, whom they call by their nicknames. Mr. FitzGibbon is addressed simply as 'Fitz'. They are not disrespectful, however), the creaming off of eager children with IQs of at least 145 from the entire Los Angeles school system, all combined with a determined colour blindness. 'We don't even know the race or nationality of the students when they apply,' says Mertens.

All Walter Reed IHP students take Latin. The maths course combines straight computation with sophisticated problems in symbolic logic. ('A student's aptitude for abstract maths is not necessarily reflected by his previous record with ordinary computation,' says FitzGibbon. 'The great poets didn't necessarily start off as good spellers.') Standard textbooks have been all but abandoned. Pupils study from original sources. 'We don't read about Marx, we read *The Communist Manifesto*,' says one teacher. In the English class, each student must keep a running journal filled with stories, poems and personal observations.

What do IHP kids go on to do? The oldest are only twenty six now, but they are already making their mark. The school cites Ron Unz, a twenty three-year-old National Science Foundation Fellow and doctoral candidate at Stanford; then there is twenty five-year-old Kelly Goode, black, BA in Government at Harvard and now working for CBS TV, as manager of comedy development. Lisa Greer, twenty six, Princeton, Yale, now practising civil law in the Los Angeles District Attorney's office. Children there now speak of being archaeologists, electronic engineers (making medical equipment to help people – but *not* Star Wars developing technology, a boy insists), biologists, lawyers, doers of great things.

One of the problems about the IHP course is that once pupils go on to ordinary, even expensive private schools, they have little to do but tread water until they go to university. Another difficulty is that local egalitarians are often hostile to the carefully maximized advantage – charges of élitism are occasionally heard. But says Mertens: 'To put these highly gifted children in a regular classroom would be to punish them and hold them back. Some people think democracy means being absolutely equal and having the same curriculum for each student. But in a real democracy, we owe to each individual the opportunity to develop his talents to the utmost.'

Adds FitzGibbon 'Most of the talented people that are born that way do *not* develop it. There are many mute inglorious Miltons around. They need encouragement or else they will not flourish, and that's what I'm trying to do here, and trying to see other schools do – that is, to develop potential to its full limit.' Does hot housing work on these bright children, making the bright even brighter? 'Of course,' says Judy Selsor, teacher of English on the IHP. 'We all need to be pushed, even the brightest. People rise to the occasion – they always do!'

Kelly Goode says she was not a child prodigy – just a normal kid, daughter of a schoolteacher. What was the most important thing the Reed course (which she says was her best educational experience until Harvard) taught her? 'I think to have confidence in myself, to know that I am a smart person who is capable of doing good things and of achieving success, but more importantly, becoming a knowledgeable person. I think that was the single most important thing to me. I think that sense of self confidence was able to help me take risks along the way, to go out a little bit on a limb.'

She knows that working for CBS TV is not exactly saving the world, and is also involved in Amnesty International and other volunteer work. 'I don't think you can necessarily save the world through your work,' she says. 'I think that if I worked eight hours a day in social service, or I were able to earn money and give them $50,000, they might want to have the $50,000 rather than my time, every day for eight hours. I think that there are many ways to save the world, and you don't necessarily have to be a crusader to do that.'

Up by the Bootstraps

Elitist? Of course it is. But the same cannot be said of the federally funded experiments in 'municipal' hot housing in the US, the best known of which is Project Head Start, started in the '60s and still continuing today.

Head Start was a practical outcome of many things including the national psychological trauma caused by the launch of the Soviet Sputnik in 1957. Overnight, people used to thinking their school system was pre-eminent had to re-examine that belief. The nation had fallen behind in the Space Race; it had to try harder. Americans looked with new eyes at perhaps their most vital resource – smart children – and realized the nation's future was in their hands.

In the relatively liberal years of the 1960s, this idea was translated into a notion very much in tune with the civil rights movement, that the potential of all children must be developed, and that increased stimulation of disadvantaged children in early childhood would prevent social discrepancies appearing in the first place. Project Head Start was the first ever federal attempt to give disadvantaged children of four upwards the first class educational experience they lacked, thus pulling them up to speed – or at least ensuring that they did not fall irretrievably behind early on. Head Start did not address itself so much to IQ as to the general notion of competence. It was that which was seen as the key to social mobility, to people making the most of themselves in life.

Though the project was politically popular at the time, many educators now consider it a practical failure. Participating children at first seemed to show improvement but gains were not sustained when they left the programme and entered school. Why did Head Start fail?

The generally recognized answer is twofold. First, the intensified teaching began too late – many children who entered the programme at age three were already behind their peers in language and measurable intelligence. Second, the parents were not involved. At the end of each day, Head Start children returned to the same disadvantaged home environment. Many of the problems of Head Start have been ironed out in a more recent experiment taking place in the highly conservative state of Missouri, which had one of the worst standards of public education in the United States. The State gathered together a panel of experts to create a local equivalent of the national Head Start programme. There was a strong belief among them in the 'three is too late' theory of raising children – they knew that they needed to 'get at' children long before they reached school age. The population of Missouri is particularly diverse. The same programme had to work on Ozark hillbillies living in rough shacks and black families in St Louis's inner city. After thrashing out the requirements, they launched, in 1981, the 'Parents as Teachers' Project. At present it is being viewed as a breakthrough.

Four widely different school districts in the state have just concluded a three-year assessment of the value of teaching 380 sample sets of parents how to rear their babies – what to say to them, even before they can speak, how to present information, what toys and books to choose. The families came from a wide range of backgrounds, from 'disadvantaged' to affluent, black and white, from urban St Louis to rural farming communities. An army of 'trainers' visited all the participating homes to teach parents to observe, stimulate and oversee their babies' development. The results, independently and rigorously evaluated, were strong stuff. Toddlers of all backgrounds, by age three, were said to show mental and linguistic growth far exceeding that of their peers. Language ability scores for the hot housed group were on average twenty points higher than for non-participating children. Some child development experts take the view that children who fall behind early on are never able to close the gap. One of the most exciting findings of the study was that children from 'at risk' families, (meaning the educational level of the parents was low, or they lived in poverty, or single-parent families) showed achievement equal to those from affluent families with better educated parents. The crucial factor, it appears, in creating these quite breathtaking results, was the degree of involvement of the parent.

The State was interested in creating not *gifted* but *competent* children. Educators wanted to prevent early failure, and to even out opportunities for all income groups. 'Our goal was never to create super-children,' says Mildred Winter, State Director of the programme. 'Our goal was to develop well-rounded competent, lovable, happy, healthy three-year-olds, who in turn would go on to find success in school.' So impressive are the results of the Parents as Teachers Project considered, that a new Missouri state law, the Early Childhood Development Act was passed by the legislature in Jefferson City in 1986. It is now mandatory for all districts to make the parent-trainee programme available. 'Human resource in the state of Missouri happens to be developable and expandable,' says a delighted State Governor John Ashcroft. 'If I were to tell you that I could develop and expand the amount of oil beneath the surface of my State, you'd laugh at me. But this resource is more important than oil.'

In the Missouri project, the parents were mobilized from the start, soon after pregnancy began. In other words, the home environment was effectively transformed. Success, just as in Glenn Doman's system, seemed to depend on hot housing parents alongside their children. Now one of the Missouri Project's most outspoken supporters is the effective founding father of Head Start, Dr Edward Zigler. He has taken its lessons on board. The education guru says now: 'My own reading of "Head Start" experiments is that we must change an entire family system so that it is a better background for the development of the child.' But Zigler has certain reservations. He does not agree that 'three is too late.' 'I think the attitude that it's too late means that we give up on vast numbers of children, and that it is a social error. You never give up on a child. Some very interesting programmes in Israel are directed at adolescents.'

Another child development expert, Dr Burton White, one of the architects of the Missouri Project, couldn't agree less. 'You know, it's such a sad, un-American, un-Anglo-Saxon thing to say, but the reality is that a child who is three years old and has the developmental status of a child who is two or two and three months doesn't have wonderful prospects,' he says. 'We like to think it's never too late, but the reality is that it very often is. We still have to try, and we always will be trying, but if you look coldly at the realities, children who are weak developmentally at three by and large stay weak for the rest of their lives.' Einstein? Dr White believes 'couldn't talk at four' stories to be myths: 'How many people took a close look at Einstein's developmental status? And talking isn't really what's critical in a three- or four-year-old, anyway. It's what they understand of language.'

Dr Zigler, a great believer in the effectiveness of educational 'intervention' programmes, nevertheless bristles at the term hot housing: 'An idiotic concept, this notion of the gourmet child, that there is some way to spend vast amounts of money and guarantee that this child is going to grow up to be some kind of paragon,' he says. 'All of these efforts to force-feed children intellectually or socially get in the way of the really supportive ways of encouraging growth and development, which are less dramatic and much more sound.'

Perhaps it all depends on your definition of hot housing. 'The Missouri Project,' Zigler says, 'is at the cutting edge, I think, of what's best in our intervention programmes. You get the child very young. In fact, if anything we would like to pick up mothers the day after they become pregnant and guarantee very good pre-natal care. And then you get the mother to interract with the child in an instructive way that optimizes the intellectual and social potential of that child. At every single age, including those nine months in which the child is developing in the womb, there is a way to provide environmental nutrients to the child.'

The Missouri Project caught the public imagination and gained support because it is not a ghetto programme, but one that can produce gains right across the social spectrum. But the true test is whether such programmes produce an effect where it counts, with disadvantaged children well on their way to becoming society's write-offs. Cathy Harris, a twenty three-year-old black single mother, lives in one of St Louis's worst slums. The smell or urine in the apartment block's lifts is so strong that visitors prefer to use the glass-strewn stairs to reach her seventh floor home. Cathy lives there with her two-year-old son Geovonden '(Von' for short). 'I think this programme has made him much smarter and much brighter,' she explains. 'He's more motivated and it's helped him a whole lot, as well as me, because it gives me the help that I need to motivate him and keep him interested. I love motherhood, because I feel I'm helping my son – and I'm very proud of my baby because I feel he's a little bit above the kids his age – and some older.'

Another local mother explained, 'I don't think it makes them smarter, but I think it gives them the tools to live up to their potential.' And a professional journalist, the father of a two year-old son put it like this: 'It's taught me a lot about his limits, both the upper and the lower limits. I thought my wife and I were pretty well-read on family upbringing and child rearing, but the kind of things we're taught by personal visits and personal contact, where they can show what he is learning, the ways he is using language, wouldn't have been appreciated without this kind of programme.'

'OK,' conceeds Wilma Wills, a roving Parent Educator on the Missouri project, 'we're pragmatists. One of the things that we are doing is trying to inculcate, I guess, more middle class values, especially as relates to school. We're trying to help children, when they go to school, to be more successful there, and we know that for many of our children, this is the way to improve in life. Poor parents don't talk to their children any less than middle class parents, I think they talk to them in a different way, in more direct terms. They say "Yes", "No", "Go over here, go over there," and don't elaborate so much. We try to encourage the parents to use expressive language.'

She continues to describe a more exalted and energetic version of the 'Health Visitor' system long familiar to new parents in Britain. 'We tell a parent of a new-born baby that the baby will be asleep most of the time and when it is not, it will be crying usually. Some parents who don't know a lot about child development think that babies cry to irritate them purposely. I tell them that some babies are just difficult, so the parent doesn't have to think she's doing a lousy job. With older children, they are expected to go through a period when they are just really obnoxious, they say "No" to everything. No matter what you say, they want to do the opposite. We try to tell the parents that that's expected – children who *don't* do that need to be looked at very carefully. I think babies are remarkable – they tell us exactly what we should be doing in terms of their feelings. If your child is interested in jumping and climbing, well, provide safe opportunities for him to do so. Then you cut down on a lot of friction. If your child is contrary, determined to exercise his independence, (the terrible twos,) you can give him choices. Say at breakfast time, for example, if there's always a big fight over whats going to be eaten, "We can have eggs or we can have Cheerios",'

The lumber and mining town of Cranbrook, British Columbia in Canada has none of the problems of downtown

St Louis, but its teachers have decided that the town's children need an academic kick-start. So the Superintendent of Schools went to Vancouver and Professor Geraldine Schwartz, who runs the Vancouver Learning Centre there – a school devoted to teaching the art of thinking. 'We chose the town for a study because of their enthusiasm,' says Professor Schwartz. 'They just came to our door asking us to do something.' The result is that from September 1987, Cranbrook – population around 15,000 – will become another large scale human laboratory, dedicated to improving the intelligence of its next generation.

You could describe it all as 'the acceptable face of hot housing', and it happens in many places other than North America, motivated by a different (though not enormously so) ethic from that operating in the openly aspirational bastions of the American working and middle class.

Following a 1969 experiment in Israel by Dr Avima Lombard of the Research Institute for Innovation in Education at the Hebrew University, Jerusalem, thousands of families in Israel, Turkey, Peru, Bolivia and South East Asia are attempting to 'improve' their young children using a system known as HIPPY – Home Instruction Programme for Pre-School Youngsters. Former Education correspondent of the London *Daily Telegraph* John Izbicki described it as 'one of the most successful early childhood experiments since Friedrich Froebel opened the first kindergarten in the first half of the nineteenth century.'

HIPPY was designed for the nearly 200,000 refugees who came to Israel from Africa and Asia in the 1960s. The Afro-Asian Jews (like those who came as late as the 1980s from Ethiopia) were very religious, exceedingly poor, and entirely unsophisticated. Their children were often physically and emotionally neglected while their parents were struggling to establish themselves in their new home. Exactly as was happening simultaneously in the US, Dr Lombard sought to give disadvantaged schoolchildren a better start in life by improving their performance at school. At the same time, she wanted mothers to feel more adequate as women. Dr Lombard sent field workers in to the immigrants' homes armed with folders of 'educational' material.

First, the children were alloted easy copying tasks, tracing round straight, squiggly, rounded or squared lines. The mothers were asked to promise to spend fifteen minutes a day supervising this activity with their four- to six-year-olds. Once the easier tasks were mastered, there would be harder work, such as pictures. The mother would say, 'When a person rides a bike, he has to put out his arm to show which way he's turning. Show me a picture of Joey putting out his arm.' Or she might turn on the radio and say, 'This is a loud sound/this is a soft sound' and repeat the exercise until the child could easily distinguish the two. Eventually, the child would start school at six, well prepared. Youngsters who have gone through a full HIPPY course are reported to be finding themselves at a noticeable advantage over those who have not; their ability to read, write and do arithmetic is measurably superior to that of a control group. And, as in Dr Zigler's view, at least of the US programmes, the real success is perceived as being not so much in the children's performance, but in increasing the time the average mother spends with her children. Career mothers are often heard to console themselves with the thought that the limited time they spend with their children is, at least, *quality* time; but there does seem to be a certain minimum *quantity* necessary, too.

In 1979, under the last Venezuelan government (and continuing under the present one), started possibly the most ambitious experiment in human engineering ever undertaken – a hot housing spectacular with the country's entire population of fourteen million as guinea pigs, an unprecedented attempt to raise the intelligence of a nation.

The architect of this Brave New (Third) World was Luis Alberto Machado, poet, philosopher and the world's first

Minister of State for the Development of Intelligence. Machado was in charge of teaching millions of schoolchildren, illiterate peasants, civil servants, old people, factory workers and soldiers in a nation already beset with Third World problems, how to think. With the help of special Harvard-educated consultants, he soon constructed a programme – an amalgamation of America's Head Start, the teachings of Dr Burton White ('Three is Too Late'), the tenets of the controversial Cambridge 'lateral thinking' guru Edward de Bono, and a pinch or two of Glenn Doman. Machado, a charismatic, prophet-like figure in his own country, believes mental capacity can be augmented at any age. The political demand was that results should be demonstrable and, above all, fast. Having accepted the proposition that education is the only long-term solution to the country's problems, its leaders could not afford to wait for evolution – they wanted visible improvements within a generation.

A group of Venezuelan teachers were first hot housed in de Bono-ism and the teaching of Glenn Doman. Then they were sent into slums and rural communities to teach parents, many of them illiterate, to teach their children. It soon appeared to them that what worked in the suburbs of Philadelphia indeed had direct application in the shanty towns of Caracas. The core teachers went out to teach other teachers the new methods. Formal thinking classes were introduced into the curriculum, and appeared to be successful even with average to slow children – resulting in greater speed of response, improved reading skills, general enthusiasm and an immense gain in self-confidence. Finally, teachers went into maternity hospitals to teach new mothers how to stimulate babies. Methods were demonstrated in special nationwide TV programmes and distributed on video tape.

A tribe of nomadic Indians had by 1983, under Machado's aegis, been taught in two months to play the violin sufficiently well to take part in a televised orchestral performance.

(Whether they particularly wanted to is not recorded – but, as we said in the first chapter, nobody, including nomadic Venezuelan Indians, will stand up and have their *intelligence*, of all things, challenged). Peasants in a remote mountain village had formed a symphony orchestra and the Venezuelan equivalent of the Vienna Boys Choir.

By 1983 also, two thirds of the babies born in major cities were undergoing stimulation exercises in the hope of improving their intelligence. Poor mothers from Caracas slums watched bemused as volunteers subjected their new babies to routines designed to accelerate mental skills – lights were shone, rattles rattled, legs and arms exercised, unusual tastes tasted and smells wafted. A ragged child could be found standing on a litter strewn hill playing a shining new violin, part of an 'Integral Creativity Project' which aims to give every child *and adult* the chance of artistic genius. By 1984 it was reported that 42,000 teachers had been trained to teach in the new ways. When the government changed, Machado's Human Intelligence Ministry was incorporated into the Department of Education. The work continues; stand by for the Venezuelan Space Project?

Another, far more modest, version of the Philadelphia programme is now operating in Rio de Janeiro, Brazil, where again, parents from different backgrounds are trained to teach their children by disciples of Glenn Doman. Doman himself visits Brazil every year to apply his ideas in the hardest test of all; he goes into the jungles to try out his methods on Amazon Indian children. 'Primitive' children can be geniuses too, Doman believes; what proof does he have of this? None, perhaps, that many developmentalists would support. What is it that he from Philadelphia wants these children to be doing that they do not now already do? Speak Japanese? There may be a very weighty question mark poised over the whole enterprise, but Doman has been knighted by the President of Brazil for the 'benefits to children' of the Institutes' work.

The kind of work that set Glenn Doman off, with brain-damaged children, is still advancing, largely due to the lifelong efforts of a Hungarian doctor, Andras Petö. Petö is the inventor of 'conductive education' an intense, hot house method of expanding the physical potential of children with severe forms of spasticity, spina bifida, atoxia, cerebral palsy and athetosis (a particularly acute form of spasticity where the sufferer cannot stop moving about). Adult sufferers of strokes, Parkinson's disease and multiple sclerosis can also be helped.

Petö developed his methods from the psychology of Russians such as Vygotsky, Luria and Pavlov. Conductive education is an attempt to educate subjects to overcome their handicaps, rather than just learning to cope with them through the help of wheelchairs and gadgets. At his Budapest institute, children and adults are taught to move normally by rigorous, near-militaristic drilling in the small movements that build up to complex skills. Patients shout out a description of their movements as they perform them – Petö believes that language is a vital factor in re-establishing motor control of the brain. Remember that internationally, a major component of hot housing programmes for normal, undamaged children is this notion of the link between the physical and the mental.

Children are wheeled or carried into the Institute, but work begins as soon as they are there. Walking will usually involve gripping the baton held out by a 'conductor', who walks backwards, encouraging and reassuring as she goes. Their efforts may start as the wildest lurching, agonizing to watch, but grasping the baton, walking, holding cutlery, learning to speak or get dressed all seem to develop eventually.

The hot housing causes consciously developed movements gradually to turn into automatic routines; two thirds of the institute's registered child pupils have gone on to attend ordinary Hungarian schools. Most of the handicapped adults who go through with the often quite harrowing course (as with Doman's techniques, its very intensity has the potential to ruin family life, exhaust parents and create harrowing emotional crises) re-enter mainstream society, even the most severely affected victims of their diseases. The Petö method is rapidly gaining adherents outside Hungary; the first (privately financed, it has to be said) British conductive education clinic is scheduled to open in a redundant school in Birmingham in 1987. The Hungarian work gives hot housing enthusiasts another chance to ask, if it can produce such results in damaged children, just imagine what we could do with normal kids. What the rest of us have to ask is, is this kind of programming ethical? Even if it works, is it imperative to do it?

Meanwhile, In Space . . .

Nothing, it might be thought, could be less similar than the Petö institute and NASA's Ames space research laboratory in California; yet both in their different spheres are pushing forward the frontiers of the potential of the human brain. And because both exist as state enterprises, and are thus free of commercial pressure, they cannot in any case stand accused of being profit inspired organizations.

Dr Ralph Pelligra, NASA's chief medical officer, and therefore well accustomed to future-think, believes that since most of the problems confronting the human race – such as war and pollution – are generated by the human mind, the answers must also reside in the brain. For many years, NASA has been assessing the effects of zero gravity – 'zero G's' – on astronauts, and extrapolating the results to consider how young children might function in space colonies. As one might expect of a consultant to the Glenn Doman institutes, Dr. Pelligra strongly believes early education is one answer to developing people who will deal most effectively with these problems. He is happy to speak of a 'smarter generation', 'smarter not necessarily in terms of having more knowledge, but being able to deal with problems, which I find is the real definition of what smart is – flexibility.'

But where Dr. Pelligra steps a little outside the sphere of Doman is that he believes children raised in outer space colonies might be the answer to our need for Better Babies. For what will be missing in space stations is gravity – and gravity, Dr. Pelligra argues intriguingly, is what has limited human potential, and held 'Super-babies' back. 'If you observe a new-born infant, what he is doing is struggling with gravity,' he says.

> He's trying to programme his nervous system so that he can overcome the effects of gravity, which are tending to keep him pinned to the Earth. The way he first does that is by making random movements with his arms and legs, and before long, he begins to recognize that some of these movements lead to a forward motion and others don't, so he begins to programme his system to include some and exclude others. Before long, he is up on his hands and knees, again trying to defy gravity. This takes a period of a year or so. Now in a zero G environment, this whole process could be expedited, because he wouldn't have this over-bearing force acting for such a long period of time.

> In doing so, by allowing him more access to his environment earlier, he would improve his mental growth. But you would have to expose him to higher gravitational forces so that he could develop his bones and muscle mass as well – and in a circulating space settlement, that would be quite easy to do. [The reason for this is that a revolving space station would set up several *different* gravitational forces; in the centre, astronauts could experience weightlessness, at the periphery, could work out under double Earth-gravity conditions.]

> You could just move the infant out to, for instance, a two G gym, where he would be able to exercise at a very early age in a way that's not quite possible on Earth. He could do tumbling in a half G environment, and develop his vestibular sense, but do strength exercises in the two G environment for a very brief period of time.

Zero G, according to Dr. Pelligra, could also be a way of increasing the life span of space pensioners. 'The characteristic features of old age,' he goes on, 'are pretty much the effects of gravity winning the battle against the human and attempting to grab him back into the Earth. And so you will see the body hunching over because it can no longer resist this force; you will see the skin and the organs sagging, the heart, for instance, losing its struggle to keep the blood pumping to the head. (This could be a solution to the problem of senile dementia, for elderly astronauts, at least) Then there are the brittle bones, and the problems of arthritis. In fact, not even necessarily in old age, many of our medical problems are related to the effects of gravity – the backaches, some of the heart problems. In space it is conceivable that many of these visible effects of the ageing process could be delayed, in that an older person could be much more active, witless of many of the consequences of age. In the circulating space station, as a person got older, she or he could move closer to the centre of rotation. You might imagine a discotheque at 0.25 G where you could dance all night and not feel the aches and pains the next day.'

How Tokyo Rose

You do not of course have to journey into space and ahead in time to see a type of Brave New World. You can just look at Japan. With the exception of Venezuela, no other country has seriously set out to improve itself on such a grand scale. The statistics proving Japan's pre-eminence in industry are dizzying, tripping over themselves in their profusion; no one can fail to get the message. In IQ terms, the Japanese have left the world standing. Japan's average IQ is ten to fifteen points higher than that of Britain or the USA, a repeated finding that has enlivened a sense of racial superiority largely dormant in the country since the end of the war. Crown Prince Akihito and

Princess Michiko of Japan are pictured deep in discussion with Glenn Doman in his Better Baby sales brochure. The intelligence question is *hot* in Japan. According to studies by psychologist Dr Richard Lynn of the New University of Ulster, average IQ in Japan has risen measurably in the past thirty years. This has been accompanied by increased weight, longevity and height, though the latter is attributed (by Japanese advertising for McDonalds hamburgers) to nothing more than the relatively new habit of meat-eating! But Big Mac consumption alone can hardly explain Japan's IQ increase.

The education system underpinning this economic miracle can only be described as a fierce form of hot housing, the lesson, that such force feeding, by what ever mysterious mechanism, works. Under the right-wing prime minister Yasuhiro Nakasone, the always-rigorous Japanese education has become more authoritatian. Nakasone believes Japanese children have become too soft and pampered by the high technology society, even though to the visitor, seeing the lack of shiftless, menacing youth on the streets, they seem a well behaved, self-disciplined, graceful bunch. Displays of youthful non-conformity are highly restrained and, well, conformist.

Japanese education is in most ways fiendish. The competition is so great that some of the booming cramming colleges (*juku*) now offer courses in how to get into others! Babies take tests at 'pre-nursery' schools to get into the best nurseries. Kindergarten children are enrolled in crammers to secure places in the best primary schools. Children work twelve- and fourteen-hour days in the hope of one day securing one of a dwindling number of the legendary 'jobs for life'. Hot housing summer camps are a common feature of life.

Computers are rarely found in Japanese classrooms; the Western fascination for the devices has yet to reach the Japanese with force. The learning is instead primarily rote memorization, the examinations a parroting of the facts. The cost to the children in stress and suicides is great, though most child suicides are prompted by the vicious bullying endemic in schools – presumably another symptom of pressure.

Exam time is known as *shiken jigoku* – examination hell – and groups of schoolchildren can be found at the crucial periods in March praying at *Shinto* shrines for success. The exams have been described as a modern initiation ceremony to determine whether the young Japanese is fit to become a *sararyman* – a life-long salaried employee of a large corporation. The foreigner is stunned by the range of subjects in which the seventeen-year-old Japanese has to demonstrate mastery; languages, literature, mathematics, physics and chemistry. Children who show talents in a particular area are actively discouraged by their teachers and advised to broaden their interests to meet examination needs. Success is as important to families' social standing as to the student himself. As in pressurized, middle class New York and North London, the strategies involved in getting children into this or that school become obsessional. Parents in Japan tell friends and neighbours the name of a school or university their child is aiming for, but this will often *really* be their second choice; this white lie avoids loss of face when the child actually only makes his second choice.

At the end of this first, almost unendurable part of their education, however, ninety per cent of high school students graduate, and over a third go on to university, some of whom, in Tokyo, will have done their final cramming in manic mass-learning sessions in the city's largest Sumo wrestling stadiums.

Ignoring the more peculiar aspects of the system, an American investigation of Japanese education published in 1987 pointed out areas that the USA, embarrassed by Japanese success, could do well to follow. The emphasis on early training was said to be worth noting, as was the intense parental involvement. (Japanese mothers supervise homework and often carry on running communications with teachers through notebooks sent back and forth from home to school.) If

commercially-run *juku* were set up simply for remedial purposes, individualized and in small groups, they might be helpful. The order and discipline that generally prevails in the
Japanese classroom also means that students spend a third
more time learning than American youngsters. And finally,
teaching in Japan, the investigators noted, was a highly prestigious profession. The pay compares well with industry, and
there are five applicants for each teaching job.

Japanese technological progress is a moot point. It is impossible to spend a day in the country without being impressed by
the extent of automation and technical novelty. Nothing, it
seems, can be left alone, no simple function performed, without a tinny electronic voice from a loudpseaker assisting in
some unasked way. Lifts talk to you, immaculate trains give
their own (pre-recorded) running commentary on passing
stations, the distance to the next stop and so on, restaurants
revolve furiously, taxi doors open automatically for you: no
other nation on Earth seems to have been capable of installing
heated shaving mirrors that cannot steam up in hotel bath-
rooms.

It goes without saying that Japan can *make* things like no
other industrialized society, in quantity, design, quality and
packaging. How innovative on the historic scale heated bathroom mirrors and talking cameras are is another question.
Their education system produces an astonishingly – enviably
to an industrialist – positive-minded and co-operative workforce, willing to work all hours. Many *sararymen* have gone
years without taking their holiday entitlement – there is a very
real risk of coming back from a week in Honolulu to find your
prized job being done by somebody else. But there are indica-
tions that the system equally stymies individual creativity.

A recent survey of 48,000 high school students demonstrated that while they are good at solving problems by set
formulae, their logic and original thinking is very poor. They
were good at multiple choice questions, but an astonishing

thirty three per cent were unable to construct a coherent, logical sentence in Japanese. In social studies, most students could not answer questions that spanned two areas of study.

It is deeply troubling to the Japanese that while their country is the second, and will shortly be the premier manufacturing nation in the world, the country has won just six Nobel prizes, all awarded to people educated before the war. Sleepy old Britain, decaying and de-industrializing, with a smaller population, where hot housing is still something you do with cucumbers, has won eighty. But perhaps the lesson the British should draw from this is to try to resist laughing or sneering at Japan, and just imagine how systematic hot housing might improve their performance too.

5

Is Everybody Happy?

Why do the Japanese hot house their children to such an extraordinary extent? The easy answer is that they do it for the glory of their country, that national gain is a worthy cause in itself. But it is not very easy to imagine people putting themselves or their children under such pressure for quite such an intangible reason as national pride. They must surely, in some very major part, do it for reasons of personal satisfaction.

Just as nobody anywhere in the world wants their intelligence impugned, it is a truism that everyone, everywhere wants to be happy. But can hot housed or gifted people (there is always a blurring of the two categories: the hot housed are often gifted early on and vice versa) ever be happy? And if they are unhappy, is that an inevitable consequence of their somehow knowing too much – i.e. comprehending this world a little more vividly than most of us? Is their misery because the rest of us, with our Neanderthal sensitivity and intelligence, just cannot tolerate swots? Or is the pressure placed on the gifted/ hot housed simply intolerable?

It was long a generally held view that children who are hot housed grow up to be anxious and self-critical, and make very peculiar adults. That notion was revised by what is now described as the Terman Study (of which more in chapter 6). Professor Lewis Terman was the Stanford University psychologist who set up a long-term study of high IQ subjects in California in 1916. Over the years, the 'Termites', as his subjects came to be known, turned out to be anything but inadequate. Research, done at regular intervals throughout their lives revealed that they were happier, more satisfied, in better mental health and even richer than average. Because of the Terman study, the commonplace that the very bright, for whatever reason, tend to end up as lonely, unhappy brains on stalks, brilliant idiots, stage-managed by eccentric parents working out their own feelings of inferiority through their progeny, has come to be seriously challenged. It seemed to be with some pleasure, however, that the London *Sunday Times* writer Stephen Pile seized on the strange misfit nature of Harry Lawrence, father of genius Ruth, with his sandals and trouser legs tucked into his socks. Few people would regard Ruth as destined for great happiness, on her own or anyone else's terms, in the future. And, in a strange way, many will be gratified if Ruth digresses from the pattern of Terman geniuses and does not even become rich.

The archetypal failed child genius was the prodigy William James Sidis, born in 1897 of American immigrant parents. He could speak at six months, read the *New York Times* at eighteen months and Homer in the original Greek at three. At six he spoke seven languages, entered Harvard at eleven and graduated in maths at sixteen. His parents, themselves extremely gifted, had concentrated on making him even more of a prodigy. In his teens and as an adult, Sidis dressed strangely and behaved oddly. He showed little social sense, confiding in reporters, among other peculiarities, his desire for a monastic existence and a lack of interest in females. Girls at Harvard made unmerciful fun of him. Eventually, he gave up his academic ambitions and started to take lowly-paid routine jobs and drop out – a scheme ruined by reporters irresistibly attracted to the story.

Brilliant academic performers' frequent failures in 'real life', particularly in school and later in the employment market, continue to be a favourite topic of press interest. When psychologist Michael Bradley was made chairman of Mensa, he was earning a pittance running a backstreet community centre in a rough area of London. 'Clever people see life in a wider perspective than simply making money and gaining material possessions,' he was quoted as saying. Bill Wright, then producer of the BBC's popular *Mastermind* contest, said, 'Winners require photographic memories, the ability to take decisions and make quick changes of mind – all the qualities needed in the competitive commercial world. Yet few of our winners are what people would recognize as successes in the outside world.'

Organizations for the parents of gifted children regularly warn the public of the ease with which the very clever child can become maladjusted, and the danger of this happening is well reported. Children who do not 'go off the rails' have been known to cope with their giftedness by 'adapting down' to fit in with other children below their intelligence level. Very bright children have a marked tendency to be perfectionists, who refuse to try things when they believe there is a risk of failure. They rarely say, 'I don't know'. Teachers face problems dealing with ultra-bright children capable of outwitting them, complained Lord Boyle, a former Conservative Education Minister at a 1972 conference in London organized by the National Association for Gifted Children. He also pointed out that Britain had no schools exclusively for gifted children other than in the specific fields of music and ballet – a situation that still applies today.

One American authority on gifted children has asserted that, 'in the inner city, where the gifted youth isn't challenged, he's likely to become a gang leader.' And today the belief persists that many of the cells in our prisons are filled not with the intellectually primitive but with the gifted who were never identified and given the appropriate educational challenges.

The *Daily Mirror* in 1974 examined British children, 'in a class of their own'. Anna from Manchester, then a dainty blue-eyed eight-year-old with an IQ of 168, was described by her mother as 'a pain in the neck, a horrible child. She must know everything, win every argument and every game.' Martin, from Birmingham was dreamy and 'very unhappy at school. At nine,' said his mother, 'he was a living question mark. We have to explain to him how democracy works, how communism operates in Russia and China.' Colin, the ten-year-old son of a car worker had an IQ of 150 and an 'I know best' attitude which infuriated his teachers. At junior school in Birkenhead, teachers ignored him when he put up his hand. Said his mother; 'he was furious. Night after night, he would march home like a soldier, get behind the curtain and cry. "They think I'm invisible," he would say. At one stage he refused to go to school. I didn't have to smack him. I just explained the law and the Education Act and he gave in. You can always reason with him.' Eric, five-year-old son of a West Indian single mother picked up reading and writing at two from *Sesame Street*, and now, said the mother, 'needs constant attention. He asks questions such as who is God?", "Why am I black?", and "Is God black?" '

Dr Anne Mathieson, an Essex doctor, told parents and teachers at a conference in 1981 that there were five types of hidden genius in classrooms – and often more than one to a class. There were the clowns, bored by school who turn their intellect to confusing the teacher – and entertaining the class. There were the daydreamers, who escape from boredom into a fantasy world and become inattentive and socially isolated; some children would hate getting high marks because it made them unpopular; some bright children would lose confidence because they had brighter brothers or sisters. Others would sail through primary school, and become disheartened in a secondary because the competition was fiercer.

Some of the unhappiness sketched in these examples could, it might be argued, be mitigated by hot housing, by educating these children, who might be bright for any reason from

genetic accident to deliberate early stimulation, alongside their
intellectual peers. Carl Heye, an eighteen-year-old from the
roughest part of Brooklyn NY explained in a 1980 ABC TV
20/20 documentary that he remembers a downhill slide before
his giftedness was officially recognized. He missed classes,
toyed with drugs and considered dropping out until his talents
were noticed. Then he was on the point of going to Harvard
and set his sights on a law career – but many of his former
street friends had turned against him.

The fifty four-year-old pianist Ruth Slenczynska told how
being pushed as a child made her flee both the piano and her
father at the age of sixteen. Today she is teaching and performing, but believes she never fulfilled her promise because her
talent was not allowed to develop at a natural pace. The same
fate could have befallen violinist Pinchas Zuckerman, who as a
child had a busy concert schedule in his native Israel. It was
only because Isaac Stern discovered him, cancelled all his
concerts, and brought him to America to direct his energies to
study, that he can now enjoy international acclaim – without
having to look back on an intolerable childhood, he believes.

A symposium at Columbia University in 1980 gave gifted
children at Hunter College Elementary, the New York public
'hot house', a chance to express their feelings about being
intellectually or creatively talented. First, Lorin Hollander, a
thirty six-year-old pianist who now works with bright children
to help them 'discuss their dreams, thoughts and inner states'
spoke of his talented youth. He had been aware even before he
could articulate it, that he had a special affinity for music. His
father, who was Toscanini's associate concertmaster, encouraged his musical development. At five, he gave his first
public performance. 'It was on a day in kindergarten called
"Circus", Hollander recalled. 'I played Bach, and got beaten
up in the schoolyard.' He survived to make a Carnegie Hall
debut at eleven. He now says the gifted feel with extraordinary
depth a variety of emotions. 'They must learn to grip hold of

the emotions and fold them into new shapes. The creative child often feels he's damaged because early in childhood, he saw something his peers didn't, and those things torment him until he learns to use them. Many of them are frightened by their own feelings. We must show them we understand.'

None of the eight Hunter children, however, attested to these internal turmoils – even though it has yet to be seen whether they will match his artistic accomplishments. Margaret Laster, twelve, said: 'I know we're not Einsteins, but people treat us either as if we're the pits or as geniuses. We're just a little bit above average.' Jenny Schwartz, twelve said: 'Being gifted does put a label on us. I made friends with someone from a regular public school and spent a week with her. One day, I corrected her grammar. She got mad at me and said, "My mother told me not to be friends with you because you're too smart".' The children's feeling of being unusual, said the school's principal, was minimized by being amongst their own community at Hunter. 'Kids understand that if they're doing badly at Hunter, they shouldn't feel inferior because they got into the school and others didn't,' said Leslie Kane, eleven, and one of triplets, all at Hunter.

In England, Tom Holt, son of writer Hazel Holt, started writing poetry early, scribbling down verses at eight. With a book of poems in print at age twelve (Philip Larkin saw them and said they were exceptional but that he would 'like to see what he writes when he has been over the cattle-grid of experience') and being proclaimed in the press as a genius, things might have gone awry. 'Tom was a withdrawn child with everyone except me. He hated and despised other children,' says Mrs Holt. 'He was perfectly satisfied with his own company and totally absorbed in the passion of the moment. When he was four, it was dinosaurs, and I had to read out scientific manuals with Latin names. Then it was model soldiers, which he used to re-fight all the battles in the Iliad . . . He had no childhood at all, really. I did try to take him out to tea and so on, but he hated it, and I sympathized, because I was the same kind of child myself. At parties, I was always under the table with a book . . . He has always been the perfect son to me, and I think we are closer than we have ever been, intellectually, of course.' Tom is now a postgraduate student of ancient Greek history at Oxford and is writing two novels simultaneously. 'It's obviously dodgy to be regarded as the most important thing in the world,' he says, 'but that is how my mother regards me.'

Over on the West coast of America, at Walter Reed Junior High, fourteen-year-old Sayuri Sayuridesai, one of the students on the Individual Honours Programme spoke of the ubiquitous 'other kids': 'They think we're nerds with calculators on our belts and thick glasses,' he complained to *Time* magazine. But the pupils report almost universally that their school work is so varied and interesting that they never get bored — and barely watch TV. At Reed, the day we were filming there, some of the children had set up a study group in the corridor. Four little boys organized the group to review the latest books on astronomy. One wanted to know why a particular book did not discuss black holes — his favourite subject; 'Black holes are not the premise of this book,' another twelve-year-old told him sharply. This was fun time.

According to Professor Hans Eysenck, writing in the London *Mail on Sunday* on William James Sidis, exceptionally bright children have shown that on the whole they are not weak, puny, emotionally unstable and socially maladroit, but rather *above* average in physique, stability and social presence. 'On the whole, they become first-rate practitioners of whatever discipline they choose,' he writes. 'Most of all, a prodigy needs sensible parents.'

How Clever?

'First rate practitioners'? Yes, but . . . Selma Wassermann, a professor of education at Simon Fraser University in British Columbia, Canada, was fascinated to fly down to South California to see for herself a group of gifted children aged ten to twelve give a demonstration of higher order cognitive skills. Her attempts to establish rapport, she wrote, were not very successful; she asked them how they supposed birds fly. ' "What do you mean?" asks Chris. "I don't understand what you want us to do," says Mark, his body shifting uncomfortably. "We didn't study birds yet," ' says Ann, explaining the lack of response. 'The children are clearly troubled. I make several attempts, using a variety of open-ended tasks that have no clear, definitive answers, to tap the creative thinking abilities of these children, and I am dead-ended every time. Again and again, I encounter responses in which the pupils try to manipulate me into helping them "get the right answer". The more I avoid doing this, the more tense they seem. Their dependency, their rigidity, their intolerance for ambiguity, their inability to take cognitive risks and their anxiety are astonishing.'

Later, Wassermann was shown the 'low achievers', and asked them how they might weigh a giraffe. They rose to the challenge. ' "You put 'em on a bathroom scale," says Marla. "Dummy, he ain't gonna fit," says Benedetto, smiling at his wisdom. "You gotta use two scales. Put his back feet on one and his front feet on the other." More and more responses of equally refreshing ideas keep coming. Then Sam offers: "I'd get a big truck and fill it with food that giraffes like to eat. Then I'd weigh the truck. Then I'd hide inside of it and call 'Here, giraffe, here giraffe'. When he got inside I'd slam the doors and weigh the truck again.' I am astonished at the difference in responses of both groups and even more concerned about the "Single right answer" orientation of the pupils identified as gifted. I am flabbergasted at their limited personal autonomy and their difficulty with questions that do not call for single, correct answers.'

Later, the gifted children confessed to her their constant and pervasive anxiety, their worries about school performance and grades, the pressure from parents and teachers. 'The children are always on guard. They use their considerable talents to try to figure out what their significant adults demand of them, and their lives are tilted in the direction of performance – up – to expectations. They are crippled by fears of making mistakes, and their anxieties are manifest in a variety of stress-related physical symptoms. Because school tasks are largely of the "single correct answer" type, these children have become gifted lesson-learners – excelling in the lower order cognitive tasks found in traditional textbook and workbook classes.'

All this, she speculated, could make it difficult for them, handicapping them, even, if they are to take on higher order tasks of problem-solving. And the low achievers? 'Most of them are out on the streets involved in many activities that require high levels of problem-solving abilities. They have become "street-wise" – experienced and talented problem-solvers, while the gifted and talented attend music lessons and French lessons and do prodigious amounts of homework.

A British educational psychologist Sue Roberts is perhaps more generous to gifted children. Some, she said, 'are very bright children who feel life's problems are too much. One wrote an essay saying, "man is like a cancer spreading disease on the face of the earth". I tell teachers these children need special projects, but they are afraid of making them feel different.' Some, she says, threaten suicide. And some do it.

When a brilliant seventeen-year-old student from Dayton Ohio, James Dallas Egbert III, shot himself in 1980, his parents, a doctor and his wife, received calls from the parents of another boy, who had been so troubled by his inability to communicate even with his own family, that he too had killed himself — just four days previously. The mother who called said her six-year-old son felt 'as if he were in an iron cage, because his mind had developed so much faster than his body. Another mentioned a son so alienated from his peers that 'he could understand just how Dallas Egbert felt'. Egbert had known his alphabet at two, could read at three, finished high school at fourteen and entered Michigan State University at fifteen. He was described by schoolfriends and teachers as a loner, isolated by his brilliance coupled with his immaturity. He had an IQ of 145, but computer science teachers whom he out-witted said the score did not accurately reflect his intelligence.

The dead boy's parents, hearing about the troubles of other children like their son, set up a memorial fund intended to create a clinic to help other gifted but troubled young people. It will come about far too late to have helped one of the most notorious genius suicides, Lenny Ross.

Son of a Los Angeles showbusiness accountant, Ross was always uncomfortable with his contemporaries. When his mother, Pauline, took him to trendy restaurants as a child, other people would stare in amazement as he discoursed eloquently on national affairs. At seven, he attracted national attention by passing the exams for his Federal Communications Commission ham radio operator's licence. Pauline seemed to relish being a 'stage' mother, and entered him on many of the TV quiz shows that reached their peak in the 1950s. At ten, with a performance of precocious answers about the stock market, Lenny won $100,000 on *The Big Surprise* and at eleven, a grand prize on *The $64,000 Challenge*. Lenny 'had too much publicity during his lifetime,' Mrs Ross was to complain after he went for a suicidal swim in a motel pool in 1985, and was found face down at the bottom, his arms crossed. He was then thirty nine. But a lot had happened in his life.

At Yale Law School in 1963, he appeared a manic, puckish,

witty character. (At eighteen, he was four years younger than his first-year colleagues, but he looked younger than that.) He had come billed as a prodigy, but his co-students were sceptical. However during his first month at Yale, the lucid excellence of his answers to questions on torts and contracts sent 'a chill down the collective spine of the class,' a contemporary recalled. He completed the first term's reading in a month, and then marked time by helping and coaxing his friends through the course, with the generosity of spirit that he always displayed. 'He was like a cross between Portnoy and Woody Allen,' recalled a Yale roommate. 'He was immensely ambitious, neurotic, energetic, full of ideas and always hustling.'

Benno Schmidt, the dean of Columbia Law School said, 'I've never seen anybody grasp problems so quickly and see the implications on so many different levels.' He had a dazzling, original sense of humour, that could make sudden, unexpected connections between James Joyce and a McDonalds advertisement. 'He never wanted to say anthing in an ordinary way because he was afraid of being banal, and he was always jumping ahead,' another associate said. He was always thinking up schemes and setting himself targets; it might be memorizing thirty words a day from a Spanish dictionary, or a plan to make money elegantly by buying unfashionable art and inflating its value by loaning it to museums.

He went on to teach at Harvard and at Columbia, and worked in high-level posts in the administrations of former California governor Jerry Brown Jnr. and President Jimmy Carter. But it was in this political work that the constraints of reality began to depress him. 'He became aware in a very direct way that this wasn't a world in which you just got to the right place and then got to the levers and really changed things,' said a friend. His manner became stranger, his sentences would stop halfway. 'He started to feel his inadequacies vis-a-vis well-rounded people. He never felt quite on top of things,' says Professor Samuel Popkin of San Diego University, a close triend. His eccentricities began to get worrying. He would spend enormous sums on good furniture and plants, then leave the furniture askew and piled with papers, the plants dead. He often ate frozen bagels and frozen peas because he could not bear to waste the time defrosting them. He would only write with collaborators who would finish what he had started, everything from books about economics to a popular guide to everything from police stations to pizzas called *The Best*.

After politics, he tried to slit his throat with a broken bottle. He went back to California to lecture. One day he stood mute in front of a class of expectant students for half an hour before they straggled out, embarrassed; another time he was found lying under a car in the carpark rehearsing a lecture. He volunteered to have a brain operation, to sever a circuit in the brain concerned with emotion and motivation; it failed. In the end, suicide was a rational act for Lenny, one of his friends thought. A fellow law professor at Columbia, his friend Bruce Ackerman, said at his memorial service: 'What could account for Lenny's remarkable decline and despair? What is it about the world that made a genius like Lenny find it so intolerable? I do not know. I do not even want to know.'

The Japanese Experience

No culture, of course is as associated with suicide as that of Japan, which to the West appears educationally to be one enormous hot house. In fact, although there are nearly 1,000 suicide cases amongst under twenties every year (typically four times the British rate) only about a quarter are what might be called hot housing suicides – children for whom the 'examination hell' system proves too much in life. It may be that, adjusted for various factors, the proportions of young people killing themselves because of educational pressure in Japan and in the West are not dissimilar.

What the other effects of Japan's education system might be are another matter. Widespread nervous disorders and ulcers are the physical manifestations. And, despite the personal and industrial discipline which has led to the country becoming, in just three decades, the world's second industrial power, Japan is also suffering a record level of juvenile delinquency. Between 1977 and 1982, crime committed by high school students rose by fifty five per cent. Classroom violence is rife, teachers being beaten up and put in hospital by frustrated youths a common event. Police at the Komatsu high school in Tokyo have to protect staff at graduation ceremonies. On the day a thirty-year-old Tokyo teacher was taken to hospital seriously injured after being kicked and punched for reprimanding a fourteen-year-old boy for tampering with fire equipment in a corridor, police took sixteen youths into custody for attacking ten teachers in a provincial city. In one case, police had to close an entire school when it was taken over by youths with steel pipes and chains. In another, a mother strangled her delinquent son and then killed herself. 'The previous generation were obedient and polite when they were at school,' social scientist Ms Yoko Watanabe told the London *Times*. 'This could be evidence that Japanese society is on the brink of drastic change.'

The Japanese authorities are quick to explain that the violence in schools is caused by 'delinquents' and it would be hard to dispute that on the surface. However, could it be that a large proportion of those rioting in Japanese schools are, by our standards, brighter than their docile colleagues? To many Westerners the principal characteristic of schooling in Japan (apart from its success in some pretty crucial respects!) is its extraordinary slavishness. It often takes a bright slave to rebel, even though in Japan there is little or no provision for drop-outs. The late developer, the brilliant, lateral thinking misfit is given far less latitude in society. Not all the delinquents in Japan's schools can be super-bright; but what *does* happen to the country's wayward geniuses?

The Down Side

Hot housing is often blamed for stress and pressure on children and perhaps with some justice. Dr Irving Sigal of the Education Testing Service, Princeton, New Jersey, certainly thinks so and has little regard for the phenomenon.

> The argument is that the world is getting more complicated and full of all kinds of competitive requirements [he says]. You know, dollars, money, cars and all that. I want my kid to have all that. How's he going to get it? He's going to get it if you toughen him up. You make him tough so he can be a competitor – to hell with his psyche. It's like programming a computer.
>
> But I don't accept that. There is a heart and there is a soul in this stuff. The thing that I get concerned about is that we are making these people highly focused on accumulation of knowledge, highly competitive, without enjoying the process. Parents seem to want stars, but we can't all be stars. Most of us are also-rans and also-rans have a lot to contribute.

The Up Side

So is it all bad news?' Is Irving Sigal's conception that hot housed tomatoes are de-natured, pallid tomatoes actually true? We may speculate on how decent a life, by our standards, Ruth Lawrence leads and will lead. But to assert baldly that she must be unhappy would surely be a mistake, and rather an arrogant one. Obviously the archetypal suicidal geniuses must be rare exceptions; understandably, the good news hinted at by Professor Eysenck does not get so readily reported. A few examples of children who are hot housed and unfashionably happy do slip through the media net, however, and parents are still prepared to go to enormous lengths to make their children into stars.

Two researchers looking into 'enriching the background' of

poor black children in Minnesota in 1975 – which meant seeking out children who had been adopted by white middle class families – concluded that their IQ scores could be enhanced by the process. Controversial stuff; but the descriptions of the 'good' homes where the black children did best are interesting. Far from discovering dour, pressurized home backgrounds, Dr Sandra Scarr-Salapatek and Dr Richard Weinberg wrote of parents who were, 'generally warm, comfortable, free of anxiety and relaxed with their children'. Such parents, 'run democratic households in which adults and children participate in many activities together'. And they suggested there were many other signs of a 'rich' home – the numbers of books used, the amount of talking and listening to children, the choice of toys, the opportunities of play and peaceful study.'

Think of the four brilliant Susedik children – are they unhappy? The eldest, Susan, now sixteen, has taken to university social life (she has been there since she was ten, and is now a postgraduate Ph.D. candidate) with gusto, a little more gusto she candidly admits, than her parents might approve of. As she chatters away about college, grades, the complicated details of the American school system, her boyfriend, how she 'relates to' various people, she sounds like any other American teenager, until she gets on to a subject such as cell biology, when things get a little serious. Susan is now specializing in the behaviour of bone marrow cells. She is by no means without a sense of humour, though. 'I don't know, you see these girls who are having all the fun and they're always the dumb blonde type, so I figure I can always pretend to be dumb, and I'm working on the blonde part.'

Ask Stephen Baccus, (a Miami prodigy who enrolled with an IQ of 190 at New York University five months before his bar mitzvah) if he is happy, and he will have little doubt that things are going well. At twelve, he had already had parts in eight films and TV shows, thirteen plays and several commercials.

The youngest of the six children of an attorney and a school counsellor, Stephen first showed his abilities at six months, by differentiating between a honeybee and a bumblebee in a child's picture book. With the help of *Sesame Street*, he could read at two. His theatrical talent came to light at six when he got bored with toys and started taking acting lessons in the vacations. 'I wouldn't say I'm smart,' Stephen told *People Weekly* in 1981, 'I just learn fast.'

Eugene Volokh, a pint-sized computer whizz from Los Angeles wasn't as sure as Stephen about not being so smart. He told the *Wall Street Journal* in the same year and at the same age (thirteen) 'there's a natural tension amongst children of certain ages, and it was worse when they weren't as well educated as I was.' Eugene, the son of immigrants from Kiev, had an IQ of 206 and had just landed a job in his vacations from UCLA as a consultant with Hewlett-Packard computers, where his father, Vladimir, is a programmer.

The company were fascinated not only with his computer ability, but with his commercial instinct. 'It would be truly naive for companies to buy from me and treat me special (sic) just because I'm thirteen,' he told the *Journal*. 'We work together for a profit, and that means a no-nonsense relationship. It's all symbiotic – when I gain, my customer gains too.' Being in the adult world seemed to suit Eugene perfectly, as he had never been able to communicate with his peers. He fitted into Hewlett-Packard, said the company, 'just like he's another engineer.' He declined an invitation to appear on the popular TV show *That's Incredible*, saying he didn't want to be on a programme where the next guest might be, 'a man who eats dirty laundry.' But he readily accepted a dinner invitation from the physicist Edward Teller, the co-inventor of the H-bomb and, at seventy nine, still one of the most fertile scientific minds in the West. Dr Teller is a special advisor to President Reagan on the Star Wars project. 'They discussed maths,' reported the *Journal*, 'and Eugene presented him a problem based on probability theory, which Dr Teller solved. The physicist then beat Eugene in two games of chess.'

Eugene Volokh may appear precocious – but unhappy? On the contrary. Eugene was clearly in a heaven of his own impeccable design – with one slight problem, that dogged him until he was old enough to be able to drive himself to business meetings; he had to be chaperoned by his long-suffering grandmother.

Billed as 'the cleverest woman in the world,' Marilyn Mach vos Savant, forty-year-old wife of the artificial heart pioneer Dr Robert Jarvik, writes political and satirical books because, she says, 'I've learned that it's more important for me to spend my time writing and talking to interesting people than trying to change the world.'

Born in modest circumstances in St Louis Missouri, Ms Mach vos Savant's IQ of 230 was discovered when she was ten; she still confesses to having found maths (her best subject) hard to understand at school. Now she says she finds it more exciting to sit in Paris cafés than in research laboratories. 'I have always been popular and I've got no sympathy with so-called boffins who make themselves physically and socially unattractive to fit a stereotype,' she told the *Daily Mail*. 'Nor have I ever had problems with men. I have never intimidated them.' Born long before the infant-hot housing Missouri project revolutionized education in St Louis, she says she was put into a gifted class at school against her will. She remains unsure of how to treat gifted children; 'Some parents want to believe that their children are very bright when in fact they're just hard workers,' she says. 'The children end up unable to communicate with other people and they become socially screwed-up.'

Perhaps happiness should not be discussed purely in terms of the feelings of clever *children*. Behind every child prodigy, it seems, stands at least one *parent* with a vision. And hot housing according to many of its protagonists, requires above all a nurturing, supportive, adoring *mother*. It is a problem which understandably disturbs thinking women, particularly if the product they happen to be hot housing is itself a small girl. Even Professor Lewis Terman, when asked to define the rôle of bright women, replied 'to raise bright sons'. What, women might well ask, is the point of hot housing a super-girl if her ultimate role in life is going to be not running the world, but hot housing the *next* generation in the hope that it might run things. One of the side issues discovered by the long distance Terman study of bright children was that many exceptionally gifted women who marry and have children say in their later years that if they could choose again, they would have chosen to have a career. They will have drawn some reassurance from the findings of a 1986 study done for the American Psychological Association, which asserted that children of working mothers do better at school than those of women who stay at home to look after them, have higher IQs, are absent less, have better communication skills and are more self-reliant.

Glenn Doman on the other hand encourages a 'Born Again' form of motherhood. 'I think a great many women have been made to feel guilty because they are not the first lady Pope, or because they are not the president of the galaxy,' he says with some justice. 'I think a great many women have been made to feel guilty because they are *only* mothers. *Only* mothers?' Fathers have an important rôle as well, he concedes, but Doman mothers are made very proud indeed to be 'only mothers'. Janet Caputo, one of Doman's on-campus mothers is a typical product in that she would not consider taking a job while her children are young: 'I think kids really need a Mom around, and even now that they're older, I'm always home with them when they're home. I think that's very important.'

Jitsuko Susedik, mother of the four Susedik prodigies, never took a job. Joe, her husband, she said, 'says it makes women feel too independent. A marriage has to be a team effort.' The

Susediks' view of Jitsuko's rôle as a woman seems to be curiously out of step with their cosmic goals for the children. Susan Susedik's stated ambition after becoming a doctor – to marry and have children – seems to confuse matters even more. Perhaps it is only to be expected, however, that she should want to imitate her mother in some respects.

Child expert Dr Burton White is the guru of the 'three is too late' school of thought. He wrote the best-selling childcare book *The First Years Of Life*, which encouraged a generation of parents to believe that there is a critical period in which to enhance the abilities of small children, which ends at the age of three.

Dr White is in effect the godfather of hot housing. He does not insist that the significant parent must be mother, only that one central grown-up should remain on duty full-time: 'It can be dad, it can be grandma A, grandma B, or grandfather A or B. The only thing that mother can do better is to breast-feed. It turns out that breast-feeding is a very good thing to do, especially if the baby is a boy, and the breast-feeding can last six months or longer. After seven months of age, our position is very straightforward; one of those six should be with the child for the majority of his or her waking hours, and that leaves plenty of time for shared work by adults, it leaves plenty of time for substitute care up to three, four, five hours a day. But for the majority of the time, when a child is learning the basics about the world, he should have a guide who is crazy about him. And you cannot hire that irrational caring about the baby – you can only get it from those six people most of the time.'

Dr Edward Zigler is even more amenable to working mothers; 'Stay-at-home mothers do not have smarter children,' he says. 'There's no question that children require great effort and there is probably some loss to children by mothers working in the out-of-home workforce, but so many do so because of economic necessity. To denigrate those mothers and say they're doing something wrong is really a mistake, because they are there to provide the wherewithal whereby children can grow and develop. As for the ones who work because they *want* to, it is not a bad thing because one of the phenomena we encounter is that it's not very healthy for a child to be cooped up all day with a mother who would rather be somewhere else. If I had my pick between a mother who was at home and didn't want to be there versus a mother who had a child in good care and was out doing what she wanted to do, if that family system is a happy system, that child benefits.'

Another prominent child expert, Professor Jerome Kagan of the Harvard Department of Psychology, supports the view that a mother who stays at home naturally produces a cleverer child; 'But there is a point of diminishing return,' he warns. 'Some mothers put so much pressure on their child that the child becomes anxious, the anxiety turns to hostility, and now we have a child who is worse off than when his mother went to work.'

None of which cuts much ice with Glenn Doman; who mistrusts most 'expert' opinion: 'Two hundred years ago there wasn't a professional anybody. There was no paediatrician, no child psychologist or child psychiatrist; a teacher was somebody who could read, at least in the United States, and without any professional help at all, mothers managed to take us from the caves to the Age of Reason.

Then the professionals came along and in a mere 200 years, we have moved from the Age of Reason to the atomic age; that is a very questionable piece of progress.'

6

The Hot House Child Grows Up

When Professor Lewis Terman invented his IQ test at Stanford University during the First World War, it was the tool he needed to prove a theory – that inborn intellectual ability might exist in people of all social backgrounds.

In 1921, Terman began a study of gifted children in California to test the fruity local metaphor 'early ripe, early rot' – the popular perception that a spectacular intellectual start in life would eventually be marred by physical or mental burnout, eccentricity or social inadequacy. 'If you were very bright as a kid, you were supposed to become crazy,' explains Professor Robert Sears, now seventy-eight, who took over the Terman study after the originator's death in 1956. Sears has managed to combine the rôles of researcher and subject. A professor of psychology at Stanford, he was also one of the original study group of 857 boys and 671 girls who became known as the 'Termites', joining the cohort at the age of five. Sear's father had been a colleague of Terman.

The Terman study is unique in its duration and comprehensiveness – though it shares the fascination of other research into how children 'turn out' (such as the British TV documentary series *7 Up* which tracked the lives of a group of children at seven-year intervals, from the age of seven). The idea was to identify a group of gifted children early, and to examine them at regular intervals in order to assess the quality of their adult lives.

Critics have pointed to some flaws in the study's structure; perhaps it was biased in that it documented the experiences and attitudes of a homogeneous group – namely white, middle class urban Californians; perhaps Terman should have established a control group of children whose IQs according to his tests did not fall into the 135 upward bracket.

Nevertheless, the results of the Terman study, which is now drawing to a close as the respondents die off, are absorbing. They help lay to rest the notion of the agonized genius, and lend support to the idea that an early lead in life *lasts*. This has been backed up, in Britain, on a smaller scale, in a study on the Isle of Wight, in which IQ was found to be an extremely reliable predictor of how children of all backgrounds fared in adult life. The Terman results can be interpreted simply as proof that smart children are 'born lucky'. Equally, they can be viewed as support for the wisdom of hot housing – a rationale for coaxing children into the fast track early in life. The advantages of growing up gifted are summarized by Robert Sears: 'The Termites turned out very well indeed. Statistically, they live longer than most other people, their health is a little better, they work longer and harder and seldom retire at "normal" retirement age. They are far more successful in the kind of things they do, they have much higher level occupations and, happily for them, are considerably better off than most of the population. Their incomes, when last assessed in 1975, were (on average) *four times* the national average.'

Geniuses, says Sears, enjoy relatively happier and more fulfilling lives than 'ordinary' folk – although he concedes, as a psychologist, that most measurements of happiness are necessarily crude. 'Well,' he says, 'they don't commit suicide any oftener than anybody else does. That's one thing. They *say* they're happier; when we ask them "how happy are you compared with most of your friends?" they always say very much happier. You take that with a grain of salt, of course, because a lot of people will say that. I think it's fair to say that their mental health is very much better than that of the general population, and that that is a sign of happiness. There are relatively few alcoholics compared to the general population. There are only three hospitalized psychotic cases, and that compared to a general population where it is something like a hundred out of a thousand. So the behavioural signs that you use to say that somebody is happy or getting along well are pretty good.' There is also noticeably less senile dementia amongst Terman subjects than amongst the population at large.

The names of the Terman subjects (apart from that of Sears) are not well publicised. But Sears says the group turned out to include a 'highly successful motion picture director of the 1950s', three child movie stars who were well-known in the 1920s, two scientists doing high level medical research, eight appellate court judges, a nationally-known science fiction writer, a female metallurgical scientist and a father of the H-bomb. (Only two members of the group had at sometime received welfare payments.)

But to apply the question some would argue is the true test of genius – did any of the Termites change the world? There were certainly no Nobel prize winners amongst them. 'Everybody changes the world a little bit, and they were pretty influential', says Sears. 'On the other hand, Leonardo da Vinci changed the world a good deal more than any of our group did. So did Einstein, and so did Shakespeare. We had no one comparable to Einstein or Leonardo at all. There were several very high-level, active people among the scientists. One, I'm afraid changed the world; he was very active at Los Alamos. He was director of one of the major parts of the atomic bomb development team back in the 1940s. But others have been just very skilful, very excellent doctors, lawyers, businessmen, scientific researchers . . . top second division people. They are by-and-large good and successful people by common standards of what it means to be successful in the middle class. There is something,' he concludes, 'about real genius which is more than a matter of high IQ. It's the creativity, the imagination. Psychologists haven't found out what it is yet. We don't know, but there is something extra that marks off the real geniuses from those who are just awfully, awfully good. Wouldn't we all like to know what it is?' ('So, was Einstein a happy man,' we wondered. 'Oh, very happy,' replied Professor Sears 'I knew him.')

Sears concedes also that intelligence as measured by IQ may not be responsible for all the very impressive life histories of his fellow Termites: 'I think it's partly that they grew up in better family circumstances, better environments, better health care, probably better schools. And growing up in an environment that is advantageous is very likely to produce happy people.' Does he consider that his own life has been typical of those taking part in the Terman Study? 'I'm certainly happy. I've certainly had a very successful occupational life. And, yes, I'm richer than most people in the country, not richer than most rich people, but I've done very well. I think I'm a perfectly good example of the group. My health has been good until just this last year, and I'm 78 . . . So it's a good life.'

Psychologists consider the Terman study to be among the most influential in forming modern theories of how to educate the gifted child. 'It started the gifted child movement,' according to Julian Cecil Stanley Jnr., director of the Study of Mathematically Precocious Youth at Johns Hopkins University. 'It dispelled a great number of sterotypes about gifted children, and it's been the fountainhead of all gifted children work since then.' Most importantly, perhaps, the experts say that Terman has dispelled the belief that acceleration of bright children in school is harmful. 'There is a new climate in the country,' said Stanley in 1984, 'which enables highly able youngsters to enter college several years younger than was typical.' (Stanley received a Ph.D. in pure mathematics from Princeton when he was 20.)

Another fascinating finding of the study, which challenged the idea that people get more conservative as they get older, was that over a period of forty years, the Termites' attitude towards marriage had changed. The women particularly, when interviewed in their seventies, tended to favour more egalitarianism in marriage, supporting the same standards of sexual morality for both husband and wife and placing less importance on the dominant role of the husband. 'The data show that the perception that people get more conservative with age is not always accurate,' concurred a researcher into the Terman study from the National Institute on Ageing.

Towards The Perfect Person

There was little that was conservative about Aaron Stern when thirty-five years ago, he gathered the media at a Brooklyn hospital for a remarkable event. Stern, who was a doctor of philosophy and had been a prisoner in a Nazi concentration camp, was about to launch perhaps the most flamboyant and brazen hothousing extravaganza of all time. 'Gentlemen of the Press,' he announced as he was photographed by the cot of his infant daughter, 'I'd like you to meet my daughter, Edith. I am going to make her a genius – and a perfect person.'

Edith was to be a human experiment. Her father, who now lives in Miami, had developed a theory that the world's evil, which he had witnessed in the raw in the German camps, was the result of nothing more than barbaric stupidity. If men and women could be made more intelligent, he reasoned, they would henceforward be less likely to mindlessly follow another Hitler. Edith was to be the incarnation of his ideas, and in our cynical world, of course, something of a hostage to fortune.

Aaron Stern could not work, as he was disabled by his time in the camps, so, like Ruth Lawrence's father twenty years later, he begun to devote his time to teaching and developing his child. He spoke to her constantly, holding forth on philosophy and explaining the theories of Darwin and Freud as he fed her from a bottle. His wife Bella was not permitted to nurse the baby. That, said Stern, was valuable learning time; Edith could read by the time she was two. He purchased second-hand volumes of the Encyclopaedia Britannica and placed them in her cot. By the time she was four she'd read them. Aaron Stern took Edith to museums and operas. In fact, he took her everywhere he might want to go, reading, training, explaining, even when he could not tell if she understood.

She was able to speak in full sentences by the time she was a year old. From that moment onwards, while living in conditions of some deprivation (one room in Coney Island, without a window) he conducted a running dialogue with her; she could read at two, play music at three, chess at four. At the same age, she started her mornings with Rice Krispies and the *New York Times*. One day she telephoned the newspaper to demand that they write an editorial deploring the West's crocodile tears, but lack of action, in helping the people of Hungary in the face of the Soviet invasion. One day, on the New York subway, her father asked if she knew how the subway trains worked; when they stopped at the station, she went to a public telephone, called up the Transit Authority and asked them how the trains moved. They asked why she was so interested, but Edith did not rest until she learned that there was a third rail.

During Edith's early childhood, Aaron was twice in hospital with cancer of the jaw, probably brought about by a beating at the hands of a Nazi guard after his wartime escape from a German cattle truck. Aaron even turned this traumatic time in hospital into a chance to teach Edith about biology. She learned to read her father's electro-cardiogram, and was encouraged to question the doctors' diagnosis; and, not unnaturally, she announced that she would like to grow up to be a doctor, so she could make Daddy better. (The statement was to rebound on her years later when she went into computing; 'She did it because it was the only place she could go where she knew I could not follow,' Aaron was to say.)

School was not a happy time for Edith. One teacher called her arrogant; another said she knew a lot of stuff, but had a mediocre mind. Her father withdrew Edith from state school at the age of nine to educate her full-time at home. She had made no long-term friends, and entered college at twelve. At fifteen, Edity became an assistant professor of mathematics – the youngest in American history – at Michigan State University, while she studied for a doctorate.

Edith was not, Stern now stresses, a natural Einstein, but today she has an IQ of 203 (or, on other occasions, 150; 'It depends on the day of the week and the phase of the moon,' she says) and works for IBM in secret computer software research and development in Boca Raton, Florida – one of the fronts, it might be said, in the international War of Intelligence. 'We're trying to identify where it would be helpful to have machines do the work instead of people,' she told the *New York Times* ten years ago. 'I don't think that my childhood cramped my emotions or anything like that. I am pleased with the results of my father's experiments on my mind. When I have children, I plan to raise them in exactly the same fashion.' And she went on to do just that.

Edith was never conventionally pretty. Her father thought her overweight as a child and a teenager, and she admits to having disliked her body. 'When I go to work in the morning,' she said, 'I wish I could leave it behind.' She was not a perfect person in her father's sense. She was, however, always good for quotes to inquisitive reporters. 'How can imperfection create perfection?' she asked rhetorically as a teenager.

In most respects other than the physical, it would seem that as an adult, Edith Stern comes near her father's ideal, though he sometimes complains now that she does not really love him.

'She doesn't have the love she should have for a father with a pacemaker', he says. ('Do you love him?' we asked. 'Sometimes, yes,' Edith replied.)

Now thirty five, with shoulder-length brown hair and glasses that constantly slip down her nose, Edith is softly spoken but blunt and impatient, and does not suffer fools – or journalists – gladly. Conversation can be something of an obstacle course. She has the strict, often defensive preciseness of Ruth Lawrence, but Edith's conversational obstacles and questions in reply to questions have the patina of experience, maturity and, often, great wisdom. Her defensiveness may be understood when someone has spent a lifetime being referred to in the newspapers as 'The Edith Experiment' or 'The Edith Project.'

'If you want a definitive answer on the nature versus nurture controversy,' she insisted in reply to the question, 'Was she born the way she is or made?' 'I'm afraid you'll have to go speak to some of the geneticists and behaviouralists and so forth. I see no reason to try and discover which facets of life are attributable to one or the other. I believe that my father's training of me, his working with me, had a great deal to do with it, but again, it seems rather difficult to separate out what would have happened otherwise. I think he'd need a properly controlled scientific study to do that.'

Edith and her husband, a computer programmer, live in a house full of books, with one entire room full of science fiction. Her father thinks her preoccupation with science fiction is a waste of time; she regards it as a wonderful mental exercise and both she and her husband are active in the local sci-fi society. For our interview, she wore a T-shirt bearing the legend 'Feed Me', based on the strange man-eating plant Audrey that was the focal point in the musical *The Little Shop of Horrors*.

Edith is the mother of a six-year-old son, whom she teaches and hot houses much as her father taught her. Her son, Daniel, was doing 300-piece jigsaw puzzles at three, and is in gifted classes in the local public school system; he has been IQ tested, but the tests have produced a wide range of scores, as they have with Edith herself. She will not disclose what his scores have been; 'I don't have a real good feel for their validity,' she says.

Why did Edith specialize, in common, it would seem, with a high proportion of hot housed children, in computer mathematics? Did she have a natural inclination towards the subject? 'I had some inclinations *away* from things; I have no talent whatsoever for art, but I enjoyed doing most of the things I did. I did them all as well as I could. I enjoyed maths, and it seemed I could do more with it than I could with some of the liberal arts, and so I followed that discipline.'

So what was the point of being so precocious? Has it made Edith successful, rich, happy? She remembers that strange childhood as 'pretty much' happy: 'It is one of the things that makes me happy, not so much having been in the news or having gone to college at an early age, but having the wit to read something that was written by a great mind and appreciate it, that makes me happy. Whether it makes me successful – I think it's no doubt a factor.'

Does she believe that you get out of children what you put in? She tries to 'make every moment a learning experince,' and admits that she would be very disappointed if young Daniel did not turn out to be intellectually superior, but says, 'I don't think you really look for a return on investment. I don't raise my son to get something out of him.' But does she believe that parental input produces results? 'Again, you're asking for a nature versus nurture decision. You do the best you can, you optimize all the factors, and then you cross your fingers and hope for the best. If you're asking whether my father got a proper return on his investment, well, that's his problem, not mine.'

Edith denies that her father stands out in her memory as a larger figure than her mother. She is resolutely against the idea of mothers staying at home: 'Trying to say that a dedicated mother should stay at home implies that all mothers are good at nurturing children and teaching them, enjoy it and are magically fulfilled by it. If I stayed at home all the time, I would become a screaming lunatic, and do terrible damage to my son. He is far, far better off with teachers that enjoy teaching small children and are trained for it and are good at it.' And she believes resolutely in accelerating intelligent children. But she adds 'If you are talking about some global rat race, where you are trying to give your child an edge, then I consider that to be a somewhat impure motivation. It is certainly worth encouraging them to be as bright as they can be. I am not sure that driving them beyond that gets you anywhere. If a child is not able to accept the teaching, then it will do no good at all. I believe that a lot of children are not being taught as much or as well as they should be or could be. I don't think you can push a rope.'

So how important is high intelligence? 'Compared to what?' challenged Edith. Compared to being *average*? 'I thought you were going to say compared to being healthy, or compared to being musically talented or artistic,' she snapped. 'Compared to being average? Average could be that you have a great lack in one area but a great bump of talent in another, so that technically you would be average. I don't think that's a question with meaning.' Do we need geniuses? 'It would be lovely if we had people able to make the kind of technological and philosophical breakthroughs that would help the species as a whole advance; I prefer penicillin to not having penicillin,' she said. But personal breakthroughs, she strongly feels, are not for her: 'I don't feel driven to make great breakthroughs. I don't really have any ambitions in that area. I suspect a lot of my ambitions have already been satisfied.'

Aaron Stern is, frankly, a little disappointed with his Pygmalion project. 'I hoped she would dedicate her life to the pursuit of the improvement of human life by being either a physician or being engaged in a project that would lead to a cure or therapy for cancer or heart-disease, because she has the ability to do so,' he said, his voice filled with emotion. 'Obviously, she has chosen the green pastures and become interested in IBM work, which is not directed to such objectives, I believe. To me material values are of lesser consequence than attainment of noble objectives.'

He still says he was entirely serious when he promised the world to make Edith a perfect person. 'At the time, I realized that mediocrity reigned supreme, and that every effort, intensive effort, on my part, would enable the child to go so far beyond what is expected that she would become nearly perfect, within the scope and framework of educational limits imposed by society.'

When asked if Edith is, indeed, a genius, he seems to hedge his bets. 'I would say Edith is a genius in juxtaposition with her peers, because mediocrity is looked upon as something very desirable, so our youngsters do not fulfil their potential. As far as I am concerned, she could do much better, but then there is no limit to one's growth; intellectual growth is practically limitless. Without my coaching, I think she would have been ordinary, because I don't believe she has any genetic advantages over other kids. I have seen brighter youngsters than Edith who have perished in a valley of tears because society doesn't expect them to go beyond that. I have been very aggressive in my desire to advance Edith, and she has succeeded.

'I love her very much,' he concludes. 'Had she been a street cleaner, I would love her also, but I am pleased my labour has not been wasted, was not in vain, in that I have proven beyond a shadow of a doubt that intellectual growth begins at birth and ceases at death only. We can do so much better than the reality of life suggests. We have any number of people who have reached the highest plateau and they are dumb and they are idiotic in their behaviour, and they are cruel. Cruelty goes

hand in hand with stupidity in my judgement, you know.'
Were Hitler and Stalin not, at the very least, intelligent? 'No',
says Aaron Stern 'they possessed no intellect.'

Whatever Happened to the Quiz Kids?

While Aaron Stern was still a prisoner of the Nazis, a new craze
was sweeping the United States, a radio programme started by
a Chicago producer and called *The Quiz Kids*. For ten years
from June 1940, first on radio, later on TV, a group of five cute
children each week would answer questions on anything from
the Venerable Bede to aeroplanes. Hot housed in the full glare
of national publicity, these children are living examples of the
final results of life in the hot house. The programme's
audiences were enormous. The Quiz Kids toured the country
and raised $118 million for the war effort; They posed for
pictures, looking quite ridiculous with mortar boards on their
little heads. They made films, records and headlines, were
turned into cartoon characters and paper doll cutouts. They
received fan mail by the sackload; babies were named after the
cutest kids. Adorability and kid-next-door appeal were a pre-
requisite for getting on the show, along with 'Encyclopaedic
Knowledge.'

One of the most popular and cleverest of the stars from the
start of the series was Ruth Duskin, just seven in 1940 and
already the possessor of an IQ score of over 200. The producers were fascinated by the idea of a little girl with long
blond pigtails who was interested in chemistry (her father
taught the subject). But it was literature that was attracting her
attention most of all. Her mother read the Bible to Ruth and
her sister every lunchtime. Then, starting with Lamb's Tales
from Shakespeare, she graduated rapidly to Shakespeare himself.

Everyone knew Ruthie. She was adored from coast to coast.

Competitive and cute, she was a godsend. She appeared with
Chico Marx, Bob Hope, Jack Benny, The Lone Ranger and
Silver. America's greatest stars made guest appearances on the
show and inevitably went down to graceful defeat at the hands
of Ruthie and the Quiz Kids. All the attention did *not*, it seems,
turn the superkids into monsters. Ruth maintains that many
were not fully aware that they were broadcasting on the radio,
imagining that they were performing before a live audience
only, in order to assist the war effort. Growing up on the show,
and reaching the ripe old age of nine, Ruthie was asked which
character from Shakespeare she would like to marry; she chose
Hamlet, then changed her mind because he was indecisive, and
she would prefer 'a man of action'. At about the same time she
was invited to represent the schoolchildren of America at a
prestigious luncheon in New York. Ruth and her mother
approached a room that had a sign over it saying 'Celebrity
Room'. She backed off from the door and said the room was
only for celebrities; her surprised mother said, 'But you are a
celebrity – don't you know that?' Not long after, she sang a
duet on TV with Bing Crosby and burst into giggles in the
middle of it; Jack Benny gave her a gold ring.

Ruth went to university at sixteen, and at nineteen, torn
between a career and her mother's idea that the highest good in
life was to have children, married a student lawyer, Gilbert
Feldman, partly to escape the unreality of her short life so far.
After graduating, she had three children, worked as a teacher
and journalist and wrote a book *Whatever Happened to the
Quiz Kids: Perils and Profits of Growing Up Gifted*, based on
her research into the adult lives of eighty-five of the 600
children that appeared on the show. A large proportion of the
Quiz Kids, like Ruth, were from working class and lower
middle class non-entrepreneurial Jewish homes, where parents
(according to Ruth) saw the show as 'an opportunity for
families who had not yet made it in America,' both in terms of
the recognition and fame, and the $100 war bond (which was

used to offset college fees) and which the children earned for each performance. (The producers were explicitly against what was then known as the 'Hollywood Parent' syndrome, and were keen to find wholesome children from wholesome families.)

When Ruth wrote the book, she found that generally the Quiz Kids were happy as adults, but did not achieve greatness, or, as some might say, fulfil their early promise; this was often their personal disappointment.

Their stories echo the Terman study in most respects, though one 1942 Quiz Kid, James D. Watson, did manage to change the world. He won a Nobel prize in 1962 for co-discovering DNA – the reproductive basis of life. Harve Bennett Fischman, class of 1945, dropped the 'Fischman', and became a big time TV producer (*Rich Man, Poor Man,* the 1982 Emmy winner *A Woman Called Golda* and the movie *Star Trek II*). His teammate Bob Easton became a dialect coach, helping Jaclyn Smith with her dialogue as Jackie Kennedy in a 1981 TV movie. Dick Williams was the first senior US diplomat in China; Jack Loukel was a Jesuit priest, the Vatican's representative to the International Labour Organization and very active in ecumenical efforts; Clive Brenner was an engineer involved in space missions.

As in the Terman group, there were a few sad cases, but not many; at nine, Gerard Darrow, an orphan, was pictured on the front cover of *Life* magazine, captioned as a Quiz Kid. He had a short but undistinguished career as a music announcer but in 1980, embittered by years of unemployment and alcoholism, he died aged forty seven. Ruth maintains that his problems were not precipitated by his stint on Quiz Kids. Raised by a maiden aunt, he showed emotional difficulties before the show existed. The ambitious aunt had called in the press when he was three, because he could recite all the names of common birds. Before he died, he claimed that his failure was caused not by his early years in the hot house, but because he was emotionally damaged anyway.

What surprised Ruth Duskin Feldman primarily was, 'that more of them aren't in top executive positions. They aren't earthshaking achievers. They tended to choose more individual enterprises, like entertainment, teaching and writing. Another surprise was how idealistic we turned out. Answering my question about life goals, most of them spoke of wanting to make a contribution to society. Hardly any mentioned financial gain. This was reflected in their incomes, which, while good, were not spectacularly high. Above a certain level,' Mrs Duskin Feldman has concluded, 'IQ isn't relevant to success. Hard work, drive, motivation, self-confidence, perseverence, enthusiasm and luck are at least as important as sheer intelligence . . . Some have a sense of letdown. Childhood acclaim can give you a false view of the world. Adult society doesn't automatically reward the quick or the bright or the artistic.'

She wrote of the way people expected Quiz Kids to be high-achieving, cute and modest, how their self-esteem would suffer if they did not achieve objectives. 'Often there's a fear of failure. Some gifted children become compulsive perfectionists. They're afraid to take risks because they might not live up to expectations. A child might just withdraw from competition and underachieve if the pressures are too great – or he may hide his abilities because he wants to appear average.' Many of the Quiz Kids, who tended to come from immigrant families anxious to 'make it' in America through the success of their children, *had* to do well on the show. Failure was not an option. You only stayed on week after week if you consistently produced correct answers. Families welcomed the appearance money; some of the pressure on the children was financial.

The Nobel winning James Watson was not in fact a great success on the show, appearing only three times. Ruth says: 'On his last time, I beat him on a Bible question, which still rankles with Professor Watson, I believe. He wrote a note on the questionnaire I sent out to him about why he left the show;

it said, "Failed the Bible", which says something about bright or brilliant people – that they do tend to focus on their failings.'

Another quirk typical of bright people that Ruth Duskin Feldman became aware of as she researched her book was what has since been written of as 'The Imposter Syndrome'. 'What it really means is that a lot of bright people, not only kids but also adults, have this feeling deep down inside that they're really not as good as they're cracked up to be, and that "somebody is going to find me out". A lot of people who are successful feel that they don't really merit their success, and I think one of the reasons for that is that bright people tend to measure themselves by a standard which is much higher than what the outside world will apply. "I know how much more I could be, I know what my lacks are, maybe somebody else looking at me doesn't see that"; it's kind of like the doughnut or the hole.' She confesses to disappointing herself all the time. 'I think in recent years in my case part of the problem was being a woman, and it was part of the problem of many gifted girls, but more so in those days, when bright girls were not expected. Even Professor Terman said that the greatest contribution of bright girls was to raise bright sons, which was, in retrospect, a horrible thing to say.'

Like all youthful prodigies, she is angry that more is not done for gifted children. 'Our egalitarian society pays lip service to "developing tomorrow's leaders", but resents favouritism for those who are already advantaged. Remedial programmes are taken for granted, but half our nation's two million bright and talented youngsters are not given the educational opportunities suited to their special needs.' Mrs Duskin Feldman differs from many of today's educators in her prescription for gifted children; 'Since the 1960s, the idea has been that what is taught must have practical, vocational value.'

Instead, she favours a liberal arts-type education, and believes that the more classics the child reads, the better. 'The liberally educated person is going to be the most adaptable in our civilization,' she asserts. For example, emphasizing the classics again, schools would better serve all youngsters. She also treats IQ scores with a certain scepticism; 'There are a lot of bright children today who are overlooked because they're not necessarily the best test-takers, but they may in fact be the more creative kids who are actually going to make the greater contributions in the long run if they are found and sought out and encouraged. I think it's a nice idea to be smart, but I don't think that pushing is ever a good idea. I think children should be encouraged. My mother had a very good motto; "Let the child lead". What parents should do is to have their antennae out there and try to pick up the vibes from the child. What is the child interested in? Give them the tools, give them the encouragement, be interested yourself, set an example.' She admits to having pushed her own son; 'You would think I would have known better,' she laughs.

One of the great benefits of the show, she strongly believes, was to demythicize the public conception of brainy kids, as the Terman study was already doing. The producer had had great trouble selling the idea to a sponsor. 'The image of bright children in those days was that they were little geniuses who had to be freaks or brats, and that if there were enough of them around to make up a panel of five, that nobody would want to listen to them because they would be so impossible. People were always pointing to those rare examples of child prodigies who committed suicide or went insane. What the show did was to really bring to the public's consciousness what Professor Terman was doing on an academic level. *The Quiz Kids* show put this on the public airwaves and later the screens, so that everybody in America could see that bright children were not all wan, bespectacled brats, but that they were in fact like the boy or girl next door. It was towards the tail end days of the show, in the early 1950s and after the Soviet Sputnik and so on, that suddenly public interest in bringing out the potential of bright children was aroused. The Quiz Kids paved the way for that.

7

Future Think:
Babies in Bottles?

If it is a fascinating exercise to examine and question children who have been played with as foetuses, then systematically hot housed as babies, then imagine how intriguing it will be one day to see how young Doron William Blake turns out.

Doron (meaning 'gift' in Greek, and an anagram of Donor) is the much celebrated Nobel sperm bank baby from California, the child of one woman of the future, psychologist Afton Blake, and an anonymous biological father known only as '28 Red'.

Fiddling around with nature is becoming perfectly acceptable in many areas of western life. The designer vegetable is already a reality in the USA, such has been the progress in using tissue-culture techniques and gene mapping to grow plants with desireable traits. And these are not triffids; ultra-crisp celery and sweeter carrots are being test-marketed in US cities. Meatier tomatoes are being sought by Campbells and Heinz. Potato/tomato crosses are promised. In Japan, tobacco that does not need to grow in a field is on the way; in Italy, they are developing super-hardy strawberries. In Sri Lanka, experiments are being done on improving coconut, rubber and tea. At Nottingham University in England, biologists are working on breeding rice plants from single cells. And in many developed contries there have been great strides in the area of human genetics – offering tantalizing glimpses of a brave new world.

137

A recent survey by the renowned New York polling firm, Yankelovich, Skelly and White revealed an astonishing trend. Researchers discovered that the mothers of the future will stop at almost nothing to produce children of higher quality than those of their own generation. It seems that members of the high-achieving baby-boom generation, having children now, fear for them. They fear spiralling unemployment figures and dwindling educational standards. They fear cruel competition and the enormous changes that will be wrought by the information technology revolution. They are anxious to breed babies who will come out on top in a fast-changing and increasingly incomprehensible world. It has made modern women somewhat desperate in their quest for the Better Baby, anxious that the traditional model is not well enough equipped for life in the twenty-first century.

Three quarters of them, the survey indicated, would opt for an abortion even for such 'defects' in the unborn child as a risk of heart disease. An estimated four per cent of women in the USA, would opt for a termination if there were a risk of a moderate defect, such as a propensity to asthma. More astounding, twenty-five million women were reported to be willing to use genetic engineering to make their children more intelligent – a figure that includes fifteen per cent of older childless women and those in professional and managerial jobs. Nine per cent would be happy to pre-order their baby's personality and emotions by some form of genetic intervention; three per cent would not object to altering the physical characteristics of an unborn child. Over ninety per cent, when the question is put another way, approve of the general concept of improving health by genetic engineering. Nearly forty per cent also approved of using artificial insemination if their partner were infertile.

This forty per cent stipulated, however, that the male donor would have to be of a high quality, intelligent and emotionally stable, and preferably athletic. Practical considerations seemed to predominate. More than twice as many American women said they would like a successful businessman as a donor than would select a lawyer, a scientist or a scholar. Only twelve per cent would go for Albert Einstein as a hypothetical donor. Choices such as Neil Armstrong, Henry Kissinger and Mahatma Gandhi proved even less desirable. Standards were high. When asked to customize a baby, nearly a third of the women surveyed could find no suitable blueprints on a list which included John F. Kennedy, Robert Redford, Lee Iacocca and Leonard Bernstein.

'It is clear,' commented the *London Standard* writer Jeremy Campbell, reporting from America on the findings, 'that American women are much more choosy when picking a sperm donor than they are when looking for a husband.' Ten thousand American women a year use sperm banks, yet have little idea what they are drawing from them. The banks are not regulated. Only half the states have passed legislation making the husband of the natural mother the legal father of the artificially inseminated child. A third of doctors providing the service do not keep records of the donors' details. That is clearly one reason why the Nobel sperm bank – more grandly known as the Repository for Germinal Choice – set up at the rear of the Pacific Coast Savings Bank on South Escondido Boulevard, Escondido, South California – has been such a big hit. Mothers terrified of defect, and in this age of contamination also of disease, get a detailed prospectus, outlining every fibre of a potential donor's being, including such defects as, say, a tendency to walk pigeon-toed. You know what you are getting, on paper at least.

'What chance is there that I could meet a guy like *this*?' asks Serita Stevens, a divorced thirty six-year-old Los Angeles romantic author, a typical Nobel sperm recipient, leafing through the Repository's catalogue: 'Ancestry, Ashkenazic. Eyes, hazel, brown hair, five-foot eleven. Born in the 1950s, weighed 150 at twenty four. Normal face [sales talk!] with strong, slightly dimpled chin. Extroverted, personable, very stable; enjoys swimming, skiing and photography, hiking, backpacking, bicycling and animals. Significant film director with law degree, produced scholarly published work in law. IQ 155, father a successful executive; mother, teacher. Music: evidence of good ability but untrained. Very competent swimmer; manual dexterity excellent. General health, excellent. Grandfather lived to eighty two. Defects: dental malocclusion, minus four diopters myopia. Proved non-carrier of Tay-Sachs.'

Dr Afton Blake, an attractive psychologist with an IQ of 130, was one of thousands of fiercely feminist American women, who, though they were aware of the Cinderella-like ticking of the biological time clock, did not happen to have found a stable relationship with an extraordinary man, and was damned if she would simply mate with the first suitable one. She would go for the best, and why not?

Doron, her baby, born in 1982, was the second child to be born through the efforts of the Repository, which went into operation in 1980. The bank was founded by the elderly plastic-spectacle-lens-king and social theory whizz, Robert Graham, with the expressed purpose of 'improving the human stock'. It would collect and freeze the sperm of Nobel-prize-winning scientists and give it, no charge, to bright, reasonably well-off women with infertile husbands. He did not actually mean the service to be available to single mothers like Afton Blake. The hit-or-miss old ways of improving your child's chances, moving to better neighbourhoods, enrolling in Glenn Doman courses and so on, were over. What was needed to pull society up by its bootie-straps was better genes.

The idea did not go down well universally. America, if you think about it, was an odd country to take a high profile in favour of *breeding*. That kind of nonsense was supposed to have been abandoned in the old world by the Pilgrim Fathers, who founded a 'meritocracy' in the new. The reason why the nurture side in the nature v. nurture debate has been so heavily supported in the US, legitimized by federally-funded schemes such as Head Start, is largely because the idea of achievement is so democratic and American. In fact the great attraction of Glenn Doman's ideas to many Americans is simply that they holds out the same promise for everyone.

The Nobel Sperm Bank had a bad start in terms of publicity and in all other respects. Recipient Number One, Joyce Kowalski from Arizona, applied to the Repository, saying her husband had too low a sperm count to father a child. In 1982, she gave birth to the scheme's first child, Victoria. Then it was discovered that her husband was her second, and that she had lost custody of her two children by a first marriage, after their father accused the Kowalskis of abusing them by expecting them to attain unreasonably high standards of behaviour and scholarship. The hyper-hot housing Kowalskis expressed similarly grand hopes for Victoria in a *National Inquirer* interview. ('It may have been a social blunder, but it wasn't a genetic one,' says Graham. 'Mrs Kowalski's got an IQ of 130 or 140.')

The Nobel sperm bank was criticized from its inception by philosophical types who said that brighter did not mean better, and that neither winning the Nobel prize nor possessing a high IQ was much of an index of social value or human worth. Scientists pointed out that genes do not have a lot to do with intelligence, and that even if they did, they could not necessarily pass it on reliably. Other unquiet souls were uncomfortably reminded of the Nazis' eugenics programmes of the 1930s and 1940s, in which they glorified certain traits and tried to reproduce them – whilst killing those who did not have them.

The Repository however had its supporters. A prominent one was William Shockley (IQ 129), Nobel prize-winning co-inventor of the transistor in 1956. Shockley is the only identified one of the three pukka Nobelists who leave their deposits, so to speak, in the Nobel sperm bank. The other depositors are best described as Nobel-ish, high-achieving, high-IQ (there is no official minimum, but the donors are said to range in scores from 140 to 182) scientists so far un-honoured by the prize committee. Amongst the virtues of scientists, claims Graham, is that, 'there's less conjecture about their standing than there is about men in other fields – anyway, we had to start recruiting somewhere.' Unfortunately for the Repository, even with young donors, half the sperm fail to survive freezing and thawing. Few recipients, as it turned out, were asking for Nobel sperm anyway, and none were impregnated by it; the women were not keen on the donors' ages, most being aware that older men's sperm is more likely to harbour defects. With the lack of younger Nobelists coming forward, Graham tried to recruit from a supply of precocious adolescents found in a study on the subject. The head of the study refused to hand over the names, however. The search became wider than a mere quest for IQ points.

'High IQ is far from enough for us,' explained Graham, 'although it's a fairly good predictor of what we're after. What we really want, there's no precise name for, although I suppose creativity might do. We expect a person to have demonstrated achievement and an interest in contributing something to the world. The Repository won't settle for just smart.'

That widening of what everybody thought were the criteria has led to some unexpected signings, like the Olympic gold medalist and the student signed up recently. The student (Light Green 40, IQ 150) had heard about the Repository and 'put himself in the place of couples who are trying to have children but can't'. He felt, and his wife agreed, that it would be 'personally gratifying' to help these folks out. 'Parents concerned enough to go to the Repository are likely to be people who also will provide the right environment for the child's intellectual growth,' the student reasoned. Now it has got around that anybody can try for what to many is the ultimate ego trip. While one reporter was researching an article on the Repository, Julianna McKillop, one of Graham's assistants at the time, was 'eyeing a visitor like a rancher surveying a slightly mis-shapen bull'. She lost interest in him when it turned out that he was short-sighted.

'Just then,' wrote Glenn Garelik, 'the proceedings are interrupted as another aide bursts breathlessly into the inner office. "Did you hear *that*?" she says. "Man came in, was crazy – wanted to donate". "What'd you say? Was he really? What'd he want? Was he crazy?" "Man was crazy. *Said* he was crazy – not in his genes, but the result of an accident. Genes're still good, he says. He wants to donate while they still are." "What was his IQ?" asks McKillop.'

Nearly forty babies have so far been produced by the Repository, and its slightly more down-market offshoot, Heredity Choice of New Hampshire. So what are they like? Afton Blake, who proudly claims genetic links with the Norwegian Royal Family on one side and the visionary poet William Blake on the other, happens to specialize in child development. She says Doron did not use baby talk except for demanding the breast, for which he would use the somewhat repulsive command, 'I want yummy'. At two, Doron displayed the qualities of a four-year-old, though she admits, 'emotionally, he's his age.' He is co-operative and considerate, if rather more uninhibited than some people like children to be. Ms Blake was very annoyed when Doron's school toilet-trained him. 'There's no containing him, and I don't try to,' she said, when the boy was three. A reporter found her, 'tense, nearly overwhelmed, but unyielding in her indulgence of her son . . . He has mostly lost the interest in the piano he evinced at two, but he plays his mother like a violin,' he wrote. Subsequent interviewers have always shown some satisfaction in pointing out how lively, if not downright normal, Doron is.

Doron's father is identified only as donor 28 Red. The one-page catalogue description which 'sold' his sperm said he was a blond, handsome athletic science professor who has won prizes for his classical music performance. The only drawback was a thirty per cent chance that he could pass on haemorrhoids to his children. The BBC TV producer Desmond Wilcox had little trouble finding 28 Red for a 1985 documentary. 'When I spoke to him I said, "Hello, we're from the BBC". "What's that?" he asked. I explained, and then I said, "You're Donor 28 Red. I'm pleased to be speaking to you because I've met one of your children," and a great wail came down the phone.' Fortunately, 28 Red had a sense of humour, and agreed to be interviewed, albeit anonymously. His mother he felt, would not be pleased to have 'My son the sperm donor' splashed over the small screen. It is quite surprising that more sperm donors are not worried about peopling the earth with their progeny. Do they never wonder what would happen if a man and woman they fathered met and innocently formed a relationship? Half-brothers and -sisters having children together when they do not even know they are related are hardly a recipe for genetic triumph.

Adrienne and David Ramm, from New York, know everything important about the father of their nearly three-year-old daughter Leandra, except who he is. He has an IQ of over 200, and 'has won athletic competitions'. He has blond hair and blue eyes. Consequently (or so they would have it) Leandra is everything they hoped for when the liquid nitrogen tank containing the sperm that produced her turned up by Federal Express parcel service from Escondido. Leandra is an extraordinarily pretty fair-headed, giggly moppet with a blue bow in her hair. Mother Adrienne is a former dancer whose postnatal euphoria has lasted for three years – understandable in one who longed for a child and weathered personal crises in order to have her. Adrienne probably interracts with Leandra more than most of the parents do with their kids playing on the swings in the local park. Back at home, in turn Leandra interracts enthusiastically with her computer – Dad's a computer operator. As ever, hot housing does not stop with the production of a super-baby; even a finely tuned car needs to be driven skilfully. 'Higher, higher!' yells Leandra on the swing, and little does she know it but mother is trying; the kitchen *chez* Ramm has some unusual appliances in the corner – a new set of liquid nitrogen cannisters marked romantically, if inexplicably, APOLLO SX-18. It is the twenty-first century stork. David and Adrienne are trying for another super-baby-in-a-bottle.

A jolly noise issues from the TV to which Leandra's computer is linked. 'What's that?' asks father, David. 'Telephone,' says Leandra. 'That's right, a xylophone,' coos the proud dad. 'The stronger the background, the higher, the better the genes, the better the all-round baby is going to be, so you might as well go for the best,' says David, who insists that the couple's use of the Nobel sperm bank was not prompted by the desire for a super-baby. 'No, we wanted a baby. It seemed a good choice because they screen them and so we know that it is not just going to come from anybody, but that it comes from a healthy parent.' In this AIDS-conscious age, such things are of deadly importance.

Leandra's biological father was denoted by the colour 'clear'. Adrienne found him by leafing through the brochure, though he was her second choice. Number One's sperm was ordered, but was 'not available'. Did David try to select from the Nobel catalogue a father for his child that was as much like him as possible, a good mathematician? 'No'. What was he looking for? 'Just height, [He is five foot eleven] I didn't want somebody that was five foot eight, OK? Just general characteristics, but that could have been almost any of them. Musical ability was fine, I don't have that but I can appreciate it. It could have been an athlete. I wasn't bad, but I was no big deal. It could have been a doctor. It doesn't make any difference as long as the person showed a range of qualities, you know, a rounded person who not only excelled in his field, but was good at other things, too, "clear" had good hobbies, other interests, so that he wasn't a one-dimensional person.' Brightness, David says, is fine with him, too.

The Repository did not go into a lot of detail about David and Adrienne's background, the couple say. The bank asked for no proof of IQ, but just checked that they were graduates, professional people and so on. Was Adrienne impressed by her sperm's pedigree? 'Absolutely, yes. We were, because the potential donors were very humanitarian men who had achieved something in their field. They were in so many ways wonderful people, I mean not just because they had high IQs, but what they had done with their work, with their brains, and that they were servicing other people. That they even wanted to help other couples who wanted a child. To me, this symbolized a very great person. Leandra's biological father was a happy person, a professor of science in a major university. He was goodlooking with a pleasant face, it said. And he liked gardening, reading, skiing. Slightly outgoing. He had two children of his own.' Leandra's brother or sister, however, will not be fathered by the same man. 'We can't get the same one; but we have another picked out. "Fuchsia" is an Olympic athelete; this seems very, very incredible to me, so we'll see!'

Fringe Sperm Banking

George Bernard Shaw (or it might have been Einstein – there are at least two versions of the same story) recognized the indistinct and unreliable nature of genetic inheritance. He was once approached by a beautiful woman, who suggested that with his brains and her body, they could produce superior offspring. Shaw wrote back: 'But alas, what if the child inherits *my* body and *your* brains?' The odds are indeed miniscule of even theoretically OK genes turning up trumps every pregnancy. But this does not trouble Graham, who admits, 'If we ever see a Nobelist out of this I'll be astonished. We're just happy to produce competent, creative, interesting people who might otherwise not be born.' He argues that the comforts of modern civilization had messed up natural selection by allowing the less fit to survive. His slips back into vague alignment with fellow hot housing theorists by saying that the process of increasing the high-quality human stock might bring about the birth of secular saviours, capable of extricating humanity from its various stalemates.

Robert Graham's split with his associate Paul Smith in 1983 was the artificial insemination customer's gain. Smith, a border collie dog breeder as well as a baby producer, is fractionally less fussy than Graham about the social standing of his recipient women – he accepts unmarried women happily. Nevertheless he is as idealistic as Graham about the value of selective breeding. 'I never reject a woman because she's too humble,' he says, in largely English accent (Smith lived in Britain for 15 years after being arrested in a 1965 anti-Vietnam War demonstration in Los Angeles). 'There's a lot of sperm to go around, and if a woman wants to get pregnant, she will. If she doesn't get it from me, she'll get it from a less illustrious source. So my only concern becomes, will she make a good mother? Other than that, and unless she's mad as a hatter, I don't try to screen recipients at all.' Of his single women, some hear the loud ticking of the biological clock and fear they're running out of time, others are lesbians in their twenties harbouring no illusion about meeting Mr Right.

Smith holds with the oft-voiced professional theory that a child's IQ will stand between 100, the general mean, and the average of the parents. Thus a 100/200 pairing – an average father, say, and an ultra-bright mother will produce a child scoring 125. Thus, he claims, he aims to improve the population average – not manufacturing genius, but shifting the average upwards. Smith's HQ, when visited by the *New York Times*, was a ramshackle farmhouse in a swampy New Hampshire wood. There, sperm from his talented donors – including

Doron Blake's father Red 28 – rubbed uni-cellular shoulders (well, nearly) with those of his prized collie stud, Kep.

Smith gets annoyed when you link selective breeding with totalitarianism: 'The Nazis didn't invent breeding,' he says. 'It happens every time someone chooses a mate or has one chosen by his parents. If a woman's not very attractive, she'll have to settle for a man who's not so great phenotypically. With artifical insemination, there become available to her some very, very desirable men.' Personally, he considers that good looks are little more than window dressing, but finds that, 'recipients wouldn't be happy otherwise. I'd be delighted to have a Stravinsky, but he'd not be popular with the ladies.'

Another Frontier

The Ramms, Afton Blake, and Irene Adkins all wanted a baby with a known pedigree. But coming very shortly, there may be a time when we will be able not only to identify genetic likelihoods, but also to *programme* babies, to grow them just as we wish, with the physical characteristics we choose – and, if we order it, with greater intelligence. Developments in the field of bio-genetics are moving forward at speed, as scientists learn more about the nature of cells, and the DNA in which genetic characteristics are coded. Some predict that we are five to ten years from the 'customized' baby.

In a series of modest, temporary-looking grey buildings in Torrance, a suburb of Los Angeles, stands one of the front lines in these advances. The signs say Ovum Transfer Centre; there are separate donors' and patients' entrances. The centre is run by a Chicago firm, Fertility and Genetics Research Inc. In principle, the technique they practise is simply a variation on the general theme of artificial insemination – but it has wide implications. In this case a woman incapable of producing ova, or concerned about a dominant genetic characteristic she carries and does not want to pass on to her children, 'borrows' an egg from another woman – it can be her sister, or a complete stranger. The 'donor's' egg is fertilized by sperm from a chosen male partner, and implanted into the recipient's womb. She then bears the baby to term, acting, in effect, as a 'host mother.' The Ovum Transfer Centre has effected eight births in this way in the past few years.

In one sense, this is simply the female equivalent of using a sperm donor, as the Ramm family did. For some infertile women, it is a welcome alternative to using a surrogate mother to carry and deliver a child, bearing in mind in particular recent cases where the biological mother has refused to give up the new born child having formed emotional attachments. But, as a medical breakthrough, the new technique of ovum transfer opens a Pandora's box of other possibilties as well. For the first time, it is technically possible for a woman to give birth to a baby who has no genetic connection to her at all. The development of 'host' motherhood moves one stage beyond all other forms of artificial insemination, by allowing the 'birthing' mother a virtually unrestricted range of genetic choices. No longer bound by the limitations of her own heredity, she can (in theory anyway) pick two perfect progenitors for her child, but give birth to it herself.

It must be stressed that the technique was developed to help one category of infertile women – yet potentially it is a new frontier in hot housing. And the process appears to be totally natural. Eligible couples can now entertain the idea of adopting an egg instead of a child – no fuss, no legal work (and the neighbours will think it is an ordinary preganancy). The adoptive parents also enjoy the whole natal experience, surely an advantage from their and the 'adopted' baby's point of view.

Five days after an egg and sperm succeed in coupling in the egg donor's body, something else different, and even more revolutionary happens at Torrance. The fertilized unit, fastidiously termed by Fertility and Genetics Research Inc. a 'conceptus' rather than an embryo, (the former term is considered less emotive) is then washed out of the donor's womb – a process called 'the lavage' – and examined in a glass dish for defects. If a recognised genetic defect is found in the conceptus (knowledge of how to spot these is still at an early stage) the doctors can oblige the patient by throwing it into the nearest waste bin. Technically this operation is not an abortion.

As present techniques of gene-mapping become more sophisticated, complex moral and ethical issues may arise. What is an 'acceptable' defect? A propensity toward pigeon toes? Bowed legs? Near-sightedness? Crooked teeth? What would happen if the doctors missed a defect in the 'conceptus', and a baby were born defective; the prospect is enough to wet a Californian lawyer's lips.

Dr John Marshall, who runs the Ovum Transfer Centre, balks at the idea of customized babies; 'That's not something we're involved with or that we plan on doing, but I guess theoretically it's a possibility. It's certainly something that's done in the animal husbandry business. I think we will be able to prevent, certainly in the near term, women from having children that bear significant and recognizable genetic abnormalities, and so, I guess, looking at the average, that there will be better babies resulting from that. But it's not tailoring a specific baby to a better floor plan, so to speak, it's simply eliminating some that have very bad defects that shouldn't be born at all.'

'I'm concerned that we do the right thing' says Dr Marshall addressing the moral issues looming just over the horizon. 'I am always very, very concerned that the donors, that the patient and her husband, fully understand what the risks are, what the benefits are, what the issues are. I have a responsibility to help them reach a decision with which they are comfortable. We have not seen anybody who has asked us to do anything that makes *us* uncomfortable . . . at this stage, we are simply helping couples who wouldn't otherwise be able to have children.'

Janice, a recipient mother at the centre who had to have her ovaries removed when she was young, is certainly comfortable about the procedure. 'This to us was an absolute miracle. I have had no opportunity since I was eighteen to even think that I could bear a child of my own, and this is a wonderful chance for me to be a complete mother from the start.'

The cost, says her husband, Mark, is $4,000 for the first try, then a further $2,000 every cycle in which an attempt is made at implantation. The donor is paid nothing more than expenses. A successful procedure can cost recipients up to $12,000. 'But how can you put a price on a chance to bear your own child, genetically half mine – and Janice gets to carry a baby to term?' Janice and Mark have not met their donor, but they have met others, and found them to be, 'just totally fascinating and wonderful, normal people. We have no concerns at all. Physically speaking, we know that the donor is a healthy, normal woman of child-bearing age. They're selected through a very tight screening process, and psychologically they are very heavily screened.' Few of the recipients are much concerned about the relative intelligence of donors. All must be high school graduates, they say, but then in America just about everybody is.

The motives of the recipient couple cannot be doubted; any chance of a baby is understandably welcome to people in such a position. The ovum donor's motivation is a curiosity, however, and appears to be a blend of altruism and some emotion. They are certainly not in it for the money.

'The thought struck me,' says Joanne, an ovum donor, 'that it was such a simple thing to do, to be so helpful to someone who could not have children, because having children is just one of the joys in my life.'

As far as the parents of 'her' baby are concerned, she says: 'I don't have any preferences as to IQ or intelligence or anything, as long as they have a great deal of love to give – that's my determining factor. I did have an opportunity to meet a recipient couple. They weren't matched with me in any way, but they were a very nice couple and from the moment I met them, I was in love with them. They were everything I had dreamed about the patient couple being . . . they're like my heroes, because they're pioneers and they're very wonderful people.' And does Joanne feel attached to this little bundle of cells she gives away? 'No, I don't feel attached. I care for the future of any human being, but I'm not attached because my body goes through the same cycle every month, and the egg is lost every month. It's something that can very easily be given to someone who cannot have children and I would gladly do that as often as possible.'

In April 1987, the London *Mail on Sunday* newspaper revealed to the world another extraordinary leap in the field of surrogacy. This time, the advance had been made in South Africa, at the Park Lane Clinic in Johannesburg. Forty eight is a late age to be pregnant, as Mrs Pat Anthony of Tzaneen, 300 miles from Johannesburg, would be the first to admit. To be bearing triplets at that age is still more remarkable; but in Mrs Anthony's case, the triplets, due to be born in October 1987, were not strictly 'hers'. The ova came from her twenty-five-year-old daughter, Karen Ferreira-Jorge, whose uterus had been removed in an emergency operation three years previously when she nearly died giving birth to her son, Alcino. Karen's ova had been fertilized by her own husband, Alcino Snr., a refrigeration engineer.

Mrs Anthony, who had herself had a traumatic time giving birth to her son Colin, twenty three years earlier, bravely went to the Park Lane Clinic when Karen received the devastating news that she would never be able to carry another child. There, a medical team headed by Drs Cecil Michelow, Joel Bernstein and Merwyn Jacobson told her that, yes, she could become the world's first skip-a-generation surrogate mother, and bear her own grandchildren. Four eggs fertilized by Alcino Snr. were later transplanted into Mrs Anthony. The news that three had successfully 'taken' was an amazing bonus – Karen had always wanted to have three or four children!

The South African triumph was not only a double first – first time a couple's egg had been transplanted into a surrogate mother, first time a mother had acted as a surrogate on behalf of her daughter and the first surrogate triplets – but also opened up the possibility of what might be regarded by many women as the perfect career-girl's method of having a baby – enjoy conceiving and then hand baby over to Mum to process!

Sorting the Geep from the Shoats

Most of the groundbreaking work in human genetics derives from early experiments with animals. Some forms of artificial insemination and manipulation of genes have been pioneered at the Ministry of Agriculture's animal research station in Cambridgeshire where scientists routinely clone embryos to produce uniformly excellent sheep. Selective breeding to improve a line of farm animals is of course a well known procedure, but cloning them short-circuits the process. 'You can produce some in months rather than in years,' says Dr Barry Cross, the unit's director. 'Breeding is a long process, you have to wait for them to mature, you have to wait for the offspring. Over the years you have had all sorts of techniques developed to accelerate the rate of genetic improvement of stock, one of which is artificial insemination. This is just the latest method that has been offered. With cloning, you know what you're getting. It's not quite so much a pig-in-the-poke as mating two animals and hoping that they will combine their genes in the most desirable way. Because you have your embryo, you know its constitution, and you simply split it up into other embryos and get four, five or six identical animals. They tend to have similar behaviour and look very similar, sometimes almost identical – although there are slight differences in the patterning and colouring of coat.' Perhaps it is the power of suggestion, but when they are together in the field, the cloned creatures seem to move and bleat in perfect unison.

Another technique perfected at the laboratory is the *fusing* of embryos of different species – sheep and goats for example – to form 'chimeras', creatures known jokingly as shoats or geep. The genetic mixtures (they are not cross-breeds, as every cell is half sheep and half goat) are of little agricultural value, but it is not difficult to work out applications for various combinations of animal.

But does this work have direct human application? Is the ultimate purpose of such research really just to improve agriculture, or is it an acceptable substitute for human experimentation? 'Anything you ever do in animals that concerns breeding is of potential value to human medicine,' says Dr Cross. 'Artificial insemination was used to breed cattle for at least twenty years before medicine used it for helping infertile women to produce offspring. Eventually most of these techniques like embryo transfer can be used in human medicine.' Dr Cross can see the benefits, if the law allowed, of transferring his type of work to humans. 'The prevention of children being born with particular genetic defects, the production of babies with longer life span, or better health prospects – all these things are theoretically possible.' He hazards a guess that we are ten to fifteen years from viable methods of gene therapy, the repair or replacement of defective genes.

'Theologically,' says Dr Cross in reply to the 'playing God' question, 'I suppose you could say that all scientists were created by God, and they're expressing, you might say, His will in exploring the secrets of the universe. All the objectives of scientific research are to acquire the sort of knowledge that will enable human society to improve, and that is certainly an objective of this institute and all others that I know of.'

Dr Michael Leyburn, a veterinary geneticist running a British company called 'International Embryo,' is frequently asked about the ethics of his profession, too. 'An eleven-year-old said to me the other day, "Aren't you afraid that you are doing what Hitler did?" I asked him who Hitler was and he didn't know. He's obviously heard his parents talking about it. It's a nonsense, just scaremongering. There's no doubt that this sort of work has human application somewhere along the line. Scientists are now exploring the possibility of repairing really serious defects and dramatically improving the quality of life for a certain number of individuals. I think the lobbies who are trying to argue that we should not do this ought to place themselves in the position of those individuals who have serious genetic defects, and try to decide whether they would have supported the manipulation of their genes at the embryo stage.'

One of the very, very few scientists willing to rehearse for us dispassionately the implications of such experimentation is Dr Leyburn, an honest and outspoken proponent of genetic manipulation in animals. 'We have switched growth genes from other species into mice and obtained mice which are three times the size of their litter mates. In other words, those which had the growth gene switched into them grew at nearly three times the rate of their full brothers and sisters in the same litter which didn't have the gene switch. We've also done that in pigs, and we're waiting to see the results. Essentially, the point is to make them grow faster rather than bigger. It's purely an economic situation, producing food faster and more economically.'

The point of producing a chimera, he explains is to show that it is possible to take *specific parts* of an embryo and fuse them to another embryo to produce better characteristics. 'For instance, to take a high-yielding dairy cow from Britain, which doesn't have heat tolerance or tolerance to certain tropical diseases, and take from a tropical animal which is a poor producer, that part of the embryo which codes for resistance to tropical diseases and heat tolerance, and put that bit into the embryo of the animal from Britain, producing a chimera which is a high-producing animal with high heat tolerance etc. That's what we're really looking for.

'The human is a mammal,' he continues, 'and although there are slight differences between the embryos of different species within the mammalian group, there's no reason to believe that you can't do with humans what you can with other mammals. We don't ourselves work on humans because we're veterinary people. But we see no reason why those procedures should not be applied to humans. Again, leaving out any sort of moral or ethical arguments altogether, there is no theoretical reason why one should not be able to manipulate and alter human embryos and therefore the resultant offspring. Once we know the gene map, where all the genes are on the chromosomes, then it should be possible to take out and replace every one of those genes. If one presupposes that any part of intelligence is hereditary (and we don't know how heritable it is) one should be able to increase intelligence by micro-manipulation of embryos and replacing certain genes.'

'Is it technically possible,' we asked Dr Leyburn, to fuse human embryos, or split them? 'Yes,' he says matter-of-factly, 'since the human is only another mammal.' 'Could you produce human clones?' 'Yes, it's technically possible now.' 'Could you choose a baby's hair or eye colour?' He feels this will be realistic within the next five years. The research, he hastens to add, has not gone further anywhere in the world than freezing human embryos for storage – in which the Australians are pre-eminent. 'I don't know of any case in which micro-manipulation of human embryos has taken place,' he says. But he adds that the techniques could be applied to humans 'within a couple of years'.

Gene manipulation, customized babies, programmed people: worrying stuff to Dr Leyburn? 'These things don't really worry me,' he insists. 'It seems to me to be a natural process. Whatever the human does is a natural and normal process by definition. I have no problem about the ethics of it all. These are emotive issues. One thinks about *1984* and *Brave New World* and so on, but I think that in common with other things which are being done for the good of the human race, these things will be handled in a way that in general terms the scientific community, certainly in countries like this and the United States and Australia have always handled them – they've been handled extremely well. Many people were concerned when artificial insemination first began on a large scale, and they said exactly the same things then – that we're going to produce monsters and that sort of thing. It's because people are afraid of the unknown – but it's not unknown to the people who are working on it.'

All the same, these glimpses of the next stage of biogenetic research bring into sharp focus the words of Dr René Van de Carr at his 'Pre-Natal University' in California. He maintains that his method of communicating with unborn babies to sharpen them up a little for the outside world will seem perfectly acceptable in comparison with the genetic engineering that will become common-place in the future. And it is hard not to muse on the possibility of a future where hot housing by gene therapy is the norm. In the same way as people now invest in plastic surgery or orthodonture, might we one day save up for an extra gene? Will we soon receive junk mail that instead of inviting us to buy a holiday timeshare apartment starts, 'Dear Sir, You have been selected by our computer as a potential donor to our sperm bank . . .'? And if by any chance intelligence were related to some yet-to-be-discovered, reproduceable genetic factor, what wonders (or horrors) might be wrought by the new tribe of super-smart people? The average mind boggles.

8

The Best of British

Professor Brian Cox of Manchester University, the president of the National Council for Education Standards, wrote in the London *Sunday Times* recently an impassioned plea for more government spending on education. 'By reducing spending on school books, the government is ensuring that more money must be spent on law and order. It's a crazy sequence,' he reasoned. This is a familiar *crie de coeur* in a Great Britain where education (the perceived dearth of it and its apparent social consequences) is arguably the most sensitive and emotive political issue next to unemployment. British school leavers are often judged the poorest equipped in Europe. Cox, a professor of English, and co-author of several of the controversial Black Papers on Education, gave some stark examples of what he means by under-achievement in education before coming to his conclusion.

A friend of Cox who teaches in a junior school in a depressed area had found a seven-year-old boy hanging about in the toilets. The boy said he was hungry. 'My friend was mystified until further questions revealed that the boy wanted to drink from the water fountain. He didn't know the difference between "hungry" and "thirsty" '. Another teacher nearby, Cox went on, had taken his class of eleven-year-olds for a walk and at one stage said, 'We'll pause here'. The children, not one of whom turned out to know what 'pause' meant, went on walking. These children were British and there was no second language problem. According to Cox many teachers of this age group assume that words such as 'return' or 'consider' will not be understood, and he reports the cases of some children who cannot distinguish between 'over' and 'under'. A child reportedly said, 'She's my brother'. Another wanted an explanation of the difference between 'Mr' and 'Mrs'. 'When they leave school,' the professor concluded 'they are almost unemployable except for the most menial tasks.'

It is not only in language ability that poor British youngsters seem to be in such bad shape. A reporter for the London *Evening Standard* set children outside a school gate a few basic problems, such as how much ten cans of catfood at thirty four pence a can would cost; none could get the answer. When a sixteen-year-old was asked what was ten per cent of £3.40, he looked blank; did he know what a percentage was? 'Yeah, it's when you take money off.' 'I don't think you were unlucky with the kids you talked to,' a maths inspector for the Inner London Education Authority told the newspaper. 'I agree that a lot of them can't do mental maths, and the situation has got to change. One problem is getting them to apply anything they learn in school to the outside world. They keep all their lessons in tight little compartments. Nonetheless it should be remembered that learning mental arithmetic the old way, out loud in school, was as humiliating for some children as corporal punishment. What we're working on at the moment,' the inspector continued, 'is deciding what children in the year 2000 ought to be able to do. There's no point teaching logarithms to children who have calculators, but it becomes very important that they learn to estimate answers quickly, so they know roughly what the calculator should say.'

It has to be said that self-flagellation over 'how bad things are getting' is a peculiarly British pastime, but the weight of public opinion, bolstered by such common examples and people's own experience with their children, can hardly be ignored or lightly dismissed. There is a universal demand from the public for education that gives children the chance to read, write and calculate. The non-competitive, relaxed style of education favoured in the past fifteen years, is now falling out of fashion in many areas, said to have destroyed the opportunities of the very people to whom it was addressed – low-achieving and low-income. At the same time, educational hot housing of a sort seems to be flourishing in Britain, in a booming private sector, where traditional academic values, modified to take account of the sciences, appear more nearly to produce the kind of rounding, mind-expanding experience educational idealists dream of.

It was once said that the battle of Waterloo was won on the playing fields of Eton. The twenty-first century 'war of intelligence' will, in all likelihood, be won or lost in the same place – since that is where the most able tend to congregate. The well-off, of course, have always been educated privately. But because there is no state provision in Britain for gifted children, the only solution for many youngsters of high ability and limited means is to apply for a grant from the local authority to pay for private education. If you are bright, in essence, the state education system is something you get rescued from, with the help of the state Assisted Places Scheme.

It is interesting that in Israel, where the better parts of Britain's comprehensive schooling philosophy have been adopted, the translation for that wet and woolly phrase 'underprivileged' is 'those in need of being cherished'. Most of the best cherishing in Britain is available only to children whose parents can afford it.

A Microchip Off The Old Block

With such a roaring enthusiasm in this private sector, one could expect there to be something to show for it, nationally. Certainly, Britain makes a living in the world, but according to some, is weak on innovation. Oil (which, it is predicted, will run out soon), insurance, banking, financial dealing all do well enough, but in an atmosphere often labelled 'risk averse' – anti-innovation, anti-technological, anti-enterprise and anti-intellectual. Deliberate, systematic, high-profile hot housing, in the pioneering sense of the USA, is regarded with some scepticism in Britain. The idea of a genius – a boffin – is encapsulated in the figure of Sir Clive Sinclair, inventor of the electric tricycle, the C5, launched as a great advance in technology and rejected as completely impractical by the entire public. It was said at the time of the launch that any five-year-old could see the C5 was going to be a disaster.

This is not to deny that Sir Clive is a brilliant individual and an innovator but the C5 fiasco exemplifies a fundamental British problem – an inability to hit the mark with well-produced, well-timed, innovative and marketable goods which satisfy or even create demand. It is said that the black-on-grey cold crystal digital display unit used on watches was invented at a British university, but never patented. The quintessentially French Perrier bottle, which carries French fizzy water around the world was in fact a British design, albeit based on an Indian club. A minute fraction of the manufactured items in a 1980 guide to 'cult objects' come from Britain. Among those that do, typically, are the green Wellington boot, the Barbour coat, the Burberry raincoat, the Mini, the E-Type Jaguar and the Morris Minor – all clever inventions, but twenty five (or more) years old.

Prince Charles, who is perceived by Royal standards as being open-minded and outspoken (he confesses to talking to plants) summed up the British problem succinctly in a late 1985 speech. 'Going to the US convinced me, and I listened to what people said there, that we do need a sense of urgency in our outlook on regeneration of industry, enterprise and so on in this country. Because otherwise, what really worries me, is that we going to end up as a fourth rate country.' In the wake of his speech, Sir John Harvey-Jones (the chairman of ICI until he retired in March 1987) put it another way; 'If we imagine the UK can get by with a bunch of people in smocks showing tourists around medieval castles, we are, quite frankly, out of our minds.' Brian Nicholson, chairman of the Manpower Services Commission put it more harshly still: 'When you compare Britain's adult workforce with our main competitor countries, we emerge as a bunch of thickies.' And the former Labour MP and respected political commentator Brian Walden wrote of 'the foolish view – very common in Britain in all walks of life – that we have a choice in the matter. We can, if we like, be unenterprising, slapdash, uncompetitive, uninterested in money and nothing very much will happen.'

It is something of a leap to link this acknowledged lacklustre performance in the world with the public education system. There are other possible explanations; a startlingly real, rigid class/caste system is one. But poor education, which parallels and consolidates the class structure, is recurrently the public's choice of culprit. And it is the uncompetitiveness of the education system which often angers the people most. They look back enviously at the industrial buoyancy of Victorian Britain and feel instinctively that however bad things were then, no one was afraid of competition. They look towards the competitive eastern bloc and see that talent there is painstakingly fostered. In East Germany, talented children can even be separated from their parents, to be accelerated in State-run hot house schools.

(There is an alternative explanation though it is not popular with the British left or right. The view was expounded by an eminent American journalist finishing his long tour of duty in Britain. He felt that the country was, though crumbling, heading for an admirable new post-industrial consensus, the basis of which was that the British had once scaled the heights of industrial development and had no need or desire to do so again. The future should lie in service industries and even those people in smocks showing tourists round castles; the far east and America could pollute their atmosphere and enslave their people making things that Britain would buy if it liked them.)

Britain has raw talent aplenty. The nation did not stop producing prodigies with nineteenth-century geniuses like John Stuart Mill (who learned Greek and Latin before he was five). But the country has few units which strive either to create or develop genius. Precociousness is widely perceived as a liability and there is little sympathy for the idea of 'special provision' for the gifted, either within or outside the comprehensive education system. Demand for such provision is often dismissed as 'élitist', and seen as a form of educational revisionism. British parents of highly able children are inhibited about lobbying outspokenly for a better deal and complain about being made to feel like stage mothers.

Indeed the notion of giftedness has never won full acceptance in Britain. Teachers and psychologists mistrust the ambiguity of the definitions and indicators, and great scepticism surrounds the methods employed to test high intelligence early in childhood. (An eleven year old boy genius once accurately perhaps encapsulated national attitudes when asked by an interviewer on BBC Radio 4 'Just *how* intelligent are you?' 'Not intelligent enough,' piped the lad, 'to answer that question.') Other educators fear that concentration on a talented élite, if that is what the gifted are, breeds jealousy in others, plus dissatisfaction; that it is no more than a prescription for a lonely life. To concentrate on a fortunate few is proportionately to deprive those who are 'exceptional' in a less happy way – i.e. who are handicapped. Anyway, this view runs, 'geniuses' all turn out to be middle class and white. An official of the National Association for Gifted Children spoke in 1975 of 'pronounced apathy and even downright hostility in staff rooms, changing steadily to a realization that a teacher's service kit must include attention to the potentially brilliant, just as to the slow learners'. The NAGC's view is that it ill-befits those who care for children to let their hackles rise when the term 'gifted' is used – it may be emotive, but it is a perfectly correct description of a natural endowment.

'My IQ was 147 at the last count, though it has previously been estimated at 150 and 153,' said an anonymous writer to the London *Daily Mail* in 1978. 'At grammar school, I was almost always near the bottom of the class. Since I started work as a hospital doctor, I have always been conscious of having something to feel guilty about. For the last year, I have been on the dole ... Psychiatrists warned me that my "unusual ability" would always be a handicap in this country and that I should either give up the work for which I am trained or emigrate. One added, "In no other country would your ability be such a disadvantage."' Mrs Frieda Painter, author of the book *Living With a Gifted Child* (1984), wrote of young children frustrated at school, having tantrums, using scrawly handwriting and daydreaming. The dropout syndrome would continue later in life, where she knew of first class physicists becoming lavatory attendants and philosophers on pizza production lines. 'I'm not interested in the wishful thinkers, I'm interested in those who, with more sensitive schooling, will develop into leading contributors to society and fulfil themselves better on the way,' she said. David Lewis, a research psychologist and author of *How To Be A Gifted Parent* is struck by how uneasy such parents feel about their children. 'There are exceptions, of course,' he says, 'but they're not like pushy show-biz mums. They're often really troubled by their kid's apparent difference from others – sometimes with reason.'

Often in Britain, more than anywhere else, a contradiction is seen between intelligence and children's happiness, despite the evidence of the Terman study indicating that smart children have a *better* chance of happiness (whatever method of measuring happiness you care to apply) than most. At best, only sketchy, *ad hoc* arrangements are made for enriching the curriculum for gifted children. Britain is virtually the only western European nation with such scant provision.

As for 'disadvantaged' children – no nationwide attempt on the scale of 'Project Head Start' has ever been made (or even contemplated) in order to pull them up to speed. Less still has there been any organized effort to 'hot house' or accelerate the performance of 'average' children. The proportion of British women who, at the extreme end of the hot housing scale, would be prepared to consider genetic engineering to enhance their child's potential, is believed to be about a quarter of that in America.

The experiences of British children apparently born with unusual talents can often read almost like hard-luck stories. Emily Holt, a twelve-year-old pupil at the fashionable (though state-aided) Camden School for Girls, is a strange case in point. Emily is a highly talented designer, and spends her time making curious puppets out of latex, and furniture models, chairs, tables and so on, from cardboard. The models are remarkable. She spent much of last summer making twelve-foot high puppets for a musical to be put on early in 1988 at London's Shaw Theatre. Emily knows pretty well what she wants to do in life – to be a film set designer; she was particularly intrigued when the Muppet creator Jim Henson invited her to his workshop when he was making the models for the film *Dark Crystal*. For the moment, all she wants is to study design and technology, but her voluntary-aided school, chronically short of funds, does not have a course, never mind a workshop. Unfortunately, Emily too is short of funds. Her father, who was a talented industrial designer, died recently of cancer. Emily's mother, Anne, is a graphic designer herself, but private education is financially out of the question.

Emily's response to all this is perhaps the characteristically British make-do-or-mend. She has decided to raise money for her school, in the hope that it might be able to fund a course. At the age of ten she began a letter campaign, writing to almost every captain of industry in Britain. 'I state my case,' she explains. 'I say that I am at Camden wanting to do design and technology and it is a voluntary-aided school, and that I'm trying to raise money for a course. People I've written to so far [such as Lord Sieff of Marks and Spencer] generally write back saying that's great and we will put in so much.' Some of the recipients of Emily's letters, like ICI, responded by writing back offering to 'show her round the plant', invitations which she has taken up willingly, travelling up and down the country in her quest for information and inspiration. What Emily has done might be described as self-hot housing, constructing her own course. It is the only avenue open to her in Britain.

'A talent in music is well encouraged in state schools,' says Mrs Holt, 'but Emily's field is a fairly new subject, particularly for girls, so she is posing something of a problem. I think that if the country is to make its way forward rapidly in technology and industry, it must support the children who are good at that. Emily works long hours, so we all stay up quite late. She has to make do and mend for materials particularly. She has learned to loot builders skips, which is quite good; it gets the materials in when she needs them.'

Camden School, Mrs Holt says, is good academically — Emily loves it and would hate to leave. But, says her mother, 'I think a lot of the teachers don't quite know what design and technology is about. I think particularly that applies to women teachers who never learned it at school themselves, and are perplexed by it. I have a feeling that Emily, like other children of high potential, wants to absorb as much as possible of her own particular subject as soon as possible. Her feeling is that if she waits until she gets to college to specialize, the boys will get ahead. Emily has been doing this sort of work since she was about four or five years old. There has always been a corner of the room where she was cutting or pasting and I am supportive, particularly since her father died. But she is not the sort of girl to be pushed in any direction that she doesn't want to take.

Emily has a strong Yorkshire streak in her. She is a very determined young lady. She suffers setbacks like any twelve-year-old, and she does despair from time to time, but she has a very strong vein of humour running through her character, so that stands her in good stead.'

'I would be wary of using the word gifted,' adds Mrs Holt, 'because it implies that everything is being handed to the child on a plate, and that isn't so. She is very hard-working, I think she has a talent – she is practical, and I think she has a high potential.' One of the advantages of her personal crusade, Mrs Holt believes, is that she has learned a lot from the exercise itself. 'Making contact with the outside world in this way has made it an education, so she is not suffering. Progress is coming little by little.'

Making Better Babies

In 1983, according to a recent report in *The Observer* newspaper, 89,000 out of 640,000 pregnancies in Britain ended in miscarriage, perinatal death, or a malformed or underweight baby; one child in ten has asthma, one in eight eczema and one in ten, learning difficulties. Some doctors in Britain believe that these sad, though not uniquely British, figures could be improved if only mothers *and* fathers paid more attention to looking after themselves not just during pregnancy but actually before conception.

The kind of theory that should typically emerge from southern California turns out to have its very respectable supporters in such solid and sensible places as Surrey, Leeds and North Devon. Geoffrey Chamberlain, professor of obstetrics and gynaecology at St George's Hospital Medical School in London feels that pre-pregnancy care should be taught in schools; John McGarry, consultant obstetrician at North Devon District Hospital, says there should be a Ministry for the Unconceived. 'Not-yet-conceived members of our society have no say in how they're being poisoned. They are defenceless and need protection.'

The kind of toxins Mr McGarry is referring to are principally alcohol, smoking, junk foods. Many women try to cut down while pregnant, but few have previously considered that such substances should be avoided during the months before a couple plan to start a baby. 'Unhealthy couples produce unhealthy babies; fit and healthy people don't,' says McGarry. 'You can't change your genes, and many birth defects are genetic – Down's Syndrome, Turner's Syndrome and cystic fibrosis, for example. But I would say ninety five per cent of birth defects are environmental.'

Dr Paul Moxon, a Leeds GP, says 'I maintain that it's what parents eat in the six months before conception that determines pregnancy outcome and birthweight, and our clinical experience supports this. But this message hasn't got across to most people.'

Professor Chamberlain is particularly interested in the timing of conception, the aim being to match the freshest possible egg with sperm whose owner has not been drinking alcohol. The egg shed on the fourteenth day of a woman's cycle lives around thirty six hours, he says; 'If the egg is at the end of its effective life when it is fertilized, there is some evidence that there may be an increased risk of congenital abnormality.'

Research from the University of Washington suggests that men who have two drinks a day *or* five or more drinks in any *one* day during the month of conception tend to father babies whose birth weight is an average of six ounces less than the children of lighter drinkers.

In Britain there is a thriving charity promoting these ideas outside the health service. Foresight, the Association for the Promotion of Pre-conceptual Care, run by Mr Nim Barnes from Witley, Surrey, funds research and is in touch with interested doctors. Foresight babies, it is claimed, are heavier by eight and a half ounces, 'exceptionally bright' with alert personalities and fine physiques. In one in four couples paying the £20 to £40 consultation fee, the woman is over thirty eight. A large number are also apparently infertile or have suffered miscarriages.

Foresight diverges from more conventional medicine by promoting the method of hair mineral analysis – testing hair as a guide to levels of metals and trace elements in the body – as a way of assessing the nutritional state of pre-conceptual couples. The analysis might typically recommend that one of you has an unsafe lead level, and suggest extra zinc, garlic and vitamin C. Claims Mr Barnes, 'Many defects reputed to be genetic can be ironed out with good nutrition. We seem to be able to control not only many malformations, but also to encourage optimum development of intelligence, behaviour and emotions.'

But, it has to be said, British hot housing, as it exists, is primarily done some considerable time *after* conception. One of hot housing's main British proponents is Dr Edward de Bono and his Cognitive Research Trust, based in Cambridge. CORT, as it is known, publishes 'thinking materials' which are an important part of national hot housing efforts in Venezuela. CORT is aimed at everyone; it is meant to teach 'thinking skills' – and is a means of problem-solving based more on applying a method – or model. It does not rely on formal academic qualifications. De Bono's 'thinking lessons' involve identifying, breaking down and assessing ideas, and are occasionally used in British schools. Dulwich Village Primary School, in a solid and fashionable area of South London, for example, organizes 'brainstorming sessions', where pupils might typically explore possible ways of dispersing an oil slick or floating a brick across a swimming pool.

Under the banner of pre-school education, many less economically well-endowed areas in Britain (the left-wing London Borough of Waltham Forest is one) employ educational visitors to help children, particularly those from deprived homes, acclimatize to school. The work involves, for example, taking educational toys into homes where they are not in evidence.

It is an interesting point that whilst often diligent in helping deprived children in various ways, it is the Labour-controlled boroughs in Britain that are particularly loath to make provision for the gifted, largely, their critics would say, because 'giftedness' smacks of yuppiedom, ambition, middle-classness and, essentially, vulgarity. A left-wing councillor in the borough of Islington was forced to resign when his 'exceptionally talented' daughter won an assisted place at the renowned St Paul's Girls' School. 'I often wonder whether those who still mock or ignore giftedness do so out of petty prejudice or out of envy, masquerading as egalitarianism,' says one leading campaigner for the rights of gifted children.

Recognizing perhaps that general educational standards were in need of some improvement, the Inner London Education Authority announced a 'blitz' early in 1986 and stressed the importance of the three Rs, particularly reading, as a key to other learning. At around the same time, in France, the left wing education minister, Jean-Pierre Chevenement, shocked his fellow radicals in France by putting his considerable intellectual weight behind a return to basic fact-learning, and the classic French values of merit, scholarship and patriotism. Chevenement, a graduate of the ultra-élite hot house, the Ecole Normale d'Administration, said of this formal farewell to the carefree classroom days that followed the 1968 student revolution: 'I am in favour of conserving the values which have been the strength of the state school system – a taste for knowledge, intellectual curiosity, the effort and work needed to learn.'

Think-Ins

Too often in Britain, teaching thinking as a separate subject is done for remedial reasons. Because the CORT methods do not demand high standards of literacy, they can be used with people who have few academic skills. At an Ethnic Minorities Training Centre in Bath, attempts are made, funded by the Manpower Services Commission, to help young black people aged eighteen to twenty five, who have slipped through every hole in the educational net. It is a well-intentioned and hopeful, but rather forlorn salvage operation. Some progress is made, but all the participants are without jobs and often have difficulty with the most basic verbal skills. When asked to give the opposite of the word 'plus', not a single one could do so. Some have children of their own.

'By helping these eighteen- to twenty five-year-olds we are setting a precedent for the younger ones who may still be at school, and who enjoy copying their elders,' says the Centre's simply duplicated leaflet. 'In this way, we are helping youngsters to help themselves in a positive way, which in turn will stand out as an example to the under seventeen-year-olds . . . Such a project will not only help to alleviate unemployment, but also give them a sense of purpose in life and society; at the moment they have got nothing meaningful to do, and there are signs that suggest that if as adults we do not lift them up today, then tomorrow they will drag us down.' Truer words . . .

Gifted children are equally capable of 'dragging down' their colleagues when their talents go unrecognized and they resort to anti-social behaviour. Interestingly, however, the official educational line of the National Association for Gifted Children is not in favour of placing gifted children in separate units like Hunter in New York.

Former teacher John Welsh, the association's director was a bright boy from a poor family – 'the lowest working class,' he describes his background. He scoffs at the notion that the bright and gifted typically come from the middle class. Now in his late fifties and politically inclined towards the left-of-centre, Welsh would prefer to see gifted streams emerge within the existing state system. He declares himself committed to the comprehensive system, whilst admitting that it serves the gifted poorly. 'The gifted are a national resource. They have an enormous contribution to make to the welfare of society,' he insists. 'I firmly believe in the notion of noblesse oblige!'

> I am opposed to divisive forms of education, [he says]. I would take the systems that exist and persuade teachers so to modify those systems that they make adequate provision, in the same way that they tend at the moment to make adequate provision for children who have learning difficulties. The comprehensive system can only, I believe, survive in a serious way if children of all abilities are sent to these schools. If some are removed, then the word comprehensive ceases to mean anything. It is important to foster the abilities of all children including the gifted for their own intrinsic worth, and, as an offshoot, for the advantage of our society. I should say that if the teaching climate (catering) for the needs of the gifted were to be radically altered, then we would have every reason to suggest that children from the lowest working class might eventually start going to universities in sizeable numbers.
>
> It destroys the comprehensive systems when parents take away bright children at great expense to themselves, have them educated in independent fee-paying schools. In attempting to foster the own aim of egalitarianism, equal opportunities for all, the system is actually destroying the comprehensive idea. Comprehensive schools can only survive in a serious way if children of all abilities are sent to them.'

What is the most important change needed in the state school system? 'First, I would like teachers' attitudes towards the importance of supplying the individual needs of all children to be changed, and notably for them to be concerned about satisfying the potential of gifted children' he says. Mr Welsh explains that, as things stand, his association funds 'Saturday 'clubs' for children hungry for more learning – and some of the clubs are in troubled areas like Brixton, Handsworth and Liverpool's Toxteth. Even this modest, part-time provision is so sensitive that local education authorities do not generally publicise the existence of such clubs. Equally, the NAGC keeps a very low profile on the subject. Facilities are lent by local authorities of many political complexions, often on the tacit understanding that such largesse will not be trumpeted too loudly.

But how can you raise educational standards for disadvantaged youths in a social wasteland like that served by the Ethnic Minorities Training Centre? Would early hot housing make a difference to these young people? Do 'disadvantaged' young people from the inner cities need a British version of Head Start or the Missouri Project? Or are we seriously to deny them such a scheme on the grounds that it is of un*proven* value, or explicitly reinforces 'middle class white values'?

Like Edward de Bono, another champion of the teaching of thinking skills in Britain is the teacher and writer Tony Buzan, a good populist presenter of new ideas. 'I think historically we are positioned astoundingly well in this coming war of intelligence,' says Buzan. 'But functionally, we are really way behind in the field. For example, we are amongst the most literate of nations, we have a higher video-watching group than any other country, and yet the use we make of these things at the moment is lagging behind third world countries like Venezuela.'

Buzan argues that IQ is not constant throughout life, but can be systematically improved. 'We now realize that you can raise IQ and you can raise creativity in children. You can raise memory ability, all the brain's fundamental capacities, and we have to do that. In England there are isolated groups of people working in this area, and people within the government who are starting to get interested.' And indeed a new policy of creating a group of inner city super-schools, half private and

174 Hot House People

half publicly-funded was announced by the Thatcher government in late 1986 — with the Prime Minister's personal backing. (Another innovation, perhaps, was her insistence that banks, insurance companies and stockbrokers help to endow the schools following the example of Elizabethan merchants who founded the ancient grammar schools.)

'Training anyone to use their brain,' Buzan goes on, 'is not only a good idea, it is essential. The problem with the British and other school systems is that they haven't yet focused on learning *how* to learn. Hot housing can be interpreted to mean forcing people to grow too quickly — which I would not encourage; but what I would say we do is allow children, you might say, to breathe. What we have been doing is putting kids in a dark environment with virtually no light, no space to grow, infertile soil and occasionally throwing on some poison. What we need to do is to take the roof off, say "Here's some sun," which is love and information; the soil is an environment which is encouraging to them, and the knowledge is how they grow.'

Education seems to invite horticultural metaphor; 'Education in Britain is preoccupied with and divided by very narrowly defined scholastic values,' the Opposition leader Neil Kinnock has written. 'In too many respects it is little more than a great weeding-out process organized to exclude large proportions of succeeding generations at each stage of educational provision. That may work wonders for roses and cattle. As a method of discovering and nurturing human abilities, it is wasteful, arbitrary and incompetent.'

9

I'm Gonna Live for Ever

'Nobody's ever got out of this world alive yet' (Elderly resident of Sun City, American suburb built for the elderly)

There's much talk these days of the 'Greying Trend'. What is meant is that a demographic shift is taking place – the population of the western hemisphere is getting older. As medical care and nutrition improve, as the birth rate falls and life expectancy rises, the number of older citizens is expected to increase steadily. By the turn of the millennium, it is forecast that one fifth of the population of Britain and America will be aged sixty five or over – that is approximately twelve million Britons and fifty million Americans – virtually double the present number of pensioners.

The Greying Trend has implications in every area of life, from voting patterns to consumer trends. We can expect, in the near future, to see profound changes in attitude and expectation – perhaps initiated by the 'new' elderly themselves, but certainly reflected throughout society. One conclusion seems inescapable in a civilized world: if people are going to live *longer* (and it seems that they are) they must also live *better*. The old must be helped to remain healthy, active and alert – or the burden of care may soon grow too great to sustain.

Life expectancy and life span are two often confused terms, and are worthy of an early explanation. Average life expec-

175

tancy has increased steadily since the turn of the last century. It is at present about seventy three for men and seventy eight for women; the figures have almost doubled since Roman times. Life span, however, has hardly changed since that time. The ceiling for human life remains obstinately at 120. True, there are more centenarians about today, i.e. more individuals are living longer, but no one, it seems, can break the 120 barrier. There are, of course, complex reasons why human beings appear to 'wear out' and die – and which scientists and gerontologists are just beginning to understand. In the last five years, there has been real progress in discovering how cells age – and what possibility there may be of intervening in that process, perhaps by manipulating the gene (or genes) implicated in human ageing.

Until gene therapy is available, however, the most reliable and best advice on offer for hanging onto your faculties is summed up by the slick but accurate old saying 'use it or lose it.'

Using It

The music is loud and funky, the coloured lights, strobes and the mirrored ball are flashing all round the home basement gymnasium, with its jazzy carpet and full-length mirrors. The athlete working out grimly and professionally on an array of floor equipment – a universal gym, a Monark stationary bicycle, a slant board for sit ups, a punch bag and a Real Runner – is formidable behind his steel-rimmed spectacles. The skin tone is not perhaps up to Jane Fonda standards, however, and most fitness freaks do not wear a deaf-aid neatly tucked behind one ear. There again, at seventy four, it is something George Braceland need not be too self-conscious about. Braceland, lying face down and pushing his feet back against the Real Runner pedals to develop muscles for explosive bursts off the starting blocks, is as serious an athlete as they come.

Lydia Bragger is ten years older, fourteen times a great-grandmother, though she hardly looks it in her smart pin-striped suit and businesslike white winged collar. Lydia, who worked for many years as a church council public relations director, is one of the founders of an extraordinary pressure group called the Grey Panthers. She is the scourge of Madison Avenue advertising agencies; just when advertisers thought there was at least *one* social grouping left that they could safely patronize, stereotype, trivialize and generally exploit, Lydia Bragger came along in her relentless, tireless rooting out of the latest 'ism' – age-ism.

Granny is no longer content to sit quietly in the corner; grandpa is through with whistling on the front porch. The last and least likely group to seek liberation is on the march, and a startled American business world is taking notice for the very best of reasons – ignoring the elderly costs money. The consumer society has discovered a new mother lode – that passive quarter of the population for years perceived as victims. But now industry is taking note: cornflakes come in small packets; the airlines offer special 'senior citizens' rates to encourage the leisured elderly to get up, up, and away.

In Britain, the old at the moment are largely poor and neglected, and seem forced to be pathetically grateful for a meagre state pension. They are a non-issue in the marketplace. Grannies appear in the media in four situations, as: (i) 'battling grannies'; (ii) victims of muggers; (iii) knitting booties for a Royal baby who doesn't need them, or (iv) suffering from hypothermia. The situation is little better either in the model welfare state of West Germany or in Catholic countries like Italy. In the USA, however, a larger proportion of old people than ever before are well off and have decent expectations of life. They have political and commercial clout (not to mention condominiums in Florida). As the idea of hot housing spreads in the US, the old see no reason why they too should not be trying to maximize and preserve their mental and physical potential. Eighty year-olds work out with weights, sign up for tennis lessons and eat plenty of bran. Death, they are beginning to feel, is optional.

In the Soviet Union too which, like China, and latterly the USA, has been run by a succession of gerontocrats, there is a rapacious interest in the old. This is perhaps fueled by a cultural predisposition to value the 'wisdom' of the elderly. Of thirty three articles in a 1982 journal of the International Association for the Artificial Prolongation of Human Specific Lifespan, thirty two are by Russian researchers. In Japan, facing the oldest population (as well as the most 'intelligent') in the world, scientists are working on a 'welfare robot' which will be capable of such tasks as serving meals and drawing baths. In Britain too, a London company is developing a nursing home robot to save staff back-breaking jobs such as turning old people in bed. So far, only its mechanical arm is functional. Already installed in nursing homes in the USA, it can pour a perfect cup of coffee or save arthritic hands the task of opening stubborn jar tops.

The Granny Boomers

Demographers calculate that by the year 2030, eighteen per cent of Americans will be over sixty five. In Britain, where thirty years ago there were 200 centenarians, there are now well over 2,000. The shift is only partially explained by improvements in medical care and nutrition. The director of the Royal College of Physicians' research unit into the phenomenon even speculates that it could have something to do with religion; the will to live has a lot to do with longevity, and a century ago, it is reasoned, more people believed in the hereafter. Now they are more inclined to hang on to as much of the herebefore as possible. The effects of the demographic shift are already being felt.

Businesses such as baby food and clothing manufacturers may be forced to move into older markets or face hard times. In Japan, film manufacturers are blaming a dip in sales on a drop in births and weddings, the occasions that traditionally call for a barrage of snapshots. Companies are starting to market everything from shampoo for older hair to single-serving portions of frozen and tinned food to magazines, travel clubs and resorts for what is being called the Third Age. Levi Strauss & Co introduced roomy Actionwear slacks for middle-aged men in 1979. Sears Roebuck brought out a moderately-priced Fashioncare line for the elderly 'and handicapped', with deeper arm holes, bigger pockets and Velcro instead of buttons for people with arthritis. Wilson Sporting Goods, aware that one in four golfers is over fifty five, has designed a golf club weighted for 'the mature swing'.

'Older people in TV ads,' commented the *Wall Street Journal*'s marketing page in 1981, 'are recognizable by their stereotypes: half-dead codgers, meddling biddies, grand-fatherly authority figures or nostalgic endorsers of products that claim to be just as high-quality as they were in the good old days. Rarely are older people shown just as ordinary con-sumers.' Their consumer needs however, do not end at denture cleaner and laxatives. Older customers also spend more than other adults on decaffeinated coffee, wine, travel, ski equip-ment and luxury cars – forty eight per cent of which are bought by drivers over fifty five. (Not every commercial exploitation of the new old works, it must be said. Heinz Foods went badly wrong with a range of Senior Food products similar to baby foods. The product offended the sensibilities of many older Americans who have found the presidency of Ronald Reagan, who is well advanced into his eighth decade, an enormous inspiration.)

Lydia Bragger says she will kill the next person that calls her 'spry', and spits at the euphemism 'Senior Citizens'. She was a high school dropout at sixteen, and eloped with her husband Albert at eighteen; the couple spent their first honeymoon night under a canoe on a Rhode Island beach. Now she lives in a Upper West Side apartment, hosts a talk show on independent New York radio on WBAI-FM, and conducts workshops for groups from TV directors to medical students. Her business card announces her as a 'media consultant on ageing'. Mrs Bragger has done a lot already to change the elderly image from helpless and passive to confident and assertive. 'Old people were always shown then as being in the way, a bother, dishevelled, dragging their feet, all the negative images you can think of. Commercials carry a subtle message. One had a young couple and an old couple eating yogurt. The young couple were eating strawberry. What did the old couple get? That's right. Prune! So it affected young people's behaviour patterns and their attitude towards older people. They didn't treat them with the respect that they should, and middle-aged people were scared of getting old. They said, "This is the way I'm going to be", so we decided something had to be done.'

Advertising agencies are staffed largely by young people, she points out, having life-crises about turning thirty. 'I say "show the older people – in diverse ways, because they are just as diverse in their activities as younger people. When you must show impairments, do it in a sensitive way that will create understanding rather than being made the brunt of a joke. And why should young people be used as models in all the clothing advertisements? I want to know what a suit or dress will look like on someone of my age. I'd like to model in commercials.' The Gray Panthers, she explains are into more than just consumerism. Health care is the big issue; so is world peace; 'Right now, we have a good thing going with peace,' says Mrs Bragger. We've established links with the Russians, a Russian delegation. We hope to go over there for talks. 'I really have broken out since I got older,' Mrs Bragger comments. 'I was very repressed as a young person, and I've made up for it in the last twenty years, doing a lot of things I always wanted to do. You don't have anyone depending on you, so you're free, to do what you want, say what you say and act the way you want to act. It's good. When you feel confident and good about yourself, you're going to be involved, you're going to be active. It makes all the difference in the world. It's the beginning of going out there and living a much better life.'

The campaign is busy 'raising awareness' among street advertisers and the media – such as the magazine that in one instance rejected an advertisement for incontinence pads as 'an aesthetic downer'. Madison Avenue is gradually starting to glamourize the old, one way at least of approaching the problem. ('As soon as they heard that older people represent a sixty billion dollar market, their ears pricked up,' laughs Mrs Bragger.) Exemplifying the new/old look is Kaylan Pickford, a fifty seven-year-old model who has appeared on camera to extol such products as De Beers diamonds and Clairol's Silk and Silver hair colouring. She has yet to do an ad for incontinence pads. And there was Clara Peller, the eighty five-year-old star of the 'Where's The Beef?' commercial for Wendy's hamburgers, (effectively) adapted as a political catch-phrase in the 1984 Presidential campaign.

TV producers are now prepared to push ahead with series like the successful *Golden Girls* situation comedy, about a group of ladies in their sixties; the programme might do a lot to dispel some of the image abroad of older American women being mutton dressed as Crimplene and facelifts all round. The film *Cocoon*, a delightful fable about life beginning at (at least) sixty, was another small breakthrough for the elderly. Set in 'God's Waiting Room' – otherwise known as Florida – it tells of a real fountain of youth, a swimming pool, inhabited by aliens and discovered by three mischievous old buffers out trespassing one day. The film's stars, Don Ameche, Wilford Brimley, Hume Cronyn, Jack Gilford, Maureen Stapleton,

Jessica Tandy and Gwen Verdon had a combined age of over 500 years; and forced Hollywood producers (sharply focused on the 'Brat Pack') to conclude that the elderly are now 'box office'.

In Britain, the Victoria and Albert Museum's Boilerhouse has staged an exhibition of products for the elderly by fasionable designers from all over the world. The brief designers were given was to produce ideas that were not like crude pieces of surgical equipment, driving a wedge between old and middle-aged consumers. 'There is no reason why people shouldn't be able to grow old stylishly,' insisted Helen Hamlyn who organized the show. The prototype exhibits included clothes by Marimekko's chief designer, with easy fastenings for the semi-disabled, and a new type of combined spoon and fork by David Mellor for those who can only manage one piece of cutlery.

Equally on the political front, the once quiescent elderly have begun to take a higher profile. Grey Power lobbying efforts in the US have so far resulted in some gains and concessions, such as special public transport discounts. The University of Oklahoma has started arranging grants for the over sixty fives to return to college. But the elderly lobbyists are also beginning to direct public consciousness towards the big economic issues, notably healthcare and pensions. In Britain John Allfrey, director of the registered charity Age Research, lobbies with the help of influential elderly patrons like the Queen Mother and (until his death in late 1986) the late Lord Stockton, former prime minister Harold MacMillan, who remained politically active in his late eighties. Allfrey demands to know why a developed country like the UK is not doing more for the old. Why has Britain got the worst rate of heart disease in western Europe? Why is Britain not doing more to come to grips with the obvious implications of a ageing population? The elderly, he says, claim the *right* to be the best and the brightest, regardless of age. Three score years and ten is no longer enough, he says; his personal motto is 'three score years *and then*'. Besides, he reminds us, the already strapped National Health Service will surely seize up in years to come unless older people are healthy people. Deterioration, John Allfrey insists, is a luxury Britain cannot afford.

Perhaps it is no wonder that after so many years as the Cinderella branch of medicine, geriatrics is at last taking its place in the sun. The old – and that includes you, or will do shortly – demand better quality and longer lives . . . plus a chance to exorcise a few popular stereotypes. For example, senility is not as common as people think. When Ronald Reagan stood for President, he had to stress in a press conference that he was not suffering from memory loss or any other aging disability. He even went so far as to promise that if the White House physician ever determined that he had become senile, 'I would walk away'. In point of fact, only one in five people *over* the age of eighty suffer from what might be termed 'senile dementia' – but the phrase has become a virtual synonym for 'old.' Also, it is becoming increasingly understood that a person can be several ages at once – mentally, physically, creatively and emotionally. And, as a refreshing change from arguments about hot housing embryos, foetuses, babies and children, there is very little in the way of moral dilemma to dog the steps of scientists trying to make things better for the old. It is an opportunity for less chat and more do.

George Braceland is a perfect example of the new elderly; today, at seventy four, he runs hurdles in record time and pole vaults with the best of them. But until the age of fifty he was too busy running his Philadelphia printing business to run two hundred metre dashes as well. Now his sons, in their twenties have a hard job beating him. 'I was doing very well,' he explains. 'But when I reached fifty I realized that unless I exercised I might not live to enjoy it. So I started all my exercising – running, rowing, karate, tennis and any sport I can find. It dropped my weight primarily and gave me more confidence in myself. I started competing, and you have a lot of peace of mind when you win races, I can guarantee you that. And in things like javelin and discus, I'm throwing further now than when I was in my fifties. You learn as you get older more about style and how to pace yourself. I work out every day and try to average an hour and a half to two hours of exercise a day. If you don't use it, you will lose it.'

Helping the old to use it in 1987 is a new exercise video for the over fifties presented by a Florida group called the Silver Foxes; the personnel line-up on the tape is worthy of note. There's Jacqueline Stallone, aged sixty five, who tapdances every day; then there is seventy three-year-old Pauline Fawcett – Farrah bought her an exercise bike for Christmas. Harry Hoffman is seventy nine and 'jazzercises' three times a week before an hour's work-out; Sal Pacino, sixty four, dances most of his nights away with his thirty eight year-old girlfriend – 'Al thinks of me as a middle-aged person,' he says.

Athletics for the elderly are known in the US as Masters events, and there is even a 'hothouse Olympics' each year run by the National Masters Association at San Diego. Athletes between forty and eighty compete there. Masters – or 'verterans' as they're sometimes known – are running, pole vaulting and hurdling in other countries too. In Britain the best runner in the *Sunday Times* Fun Run series is Dr Joan Franklin-Adams, a pencil slim lady in her late seventies.

Old Dogs, New Tricks

Is there any medical proof that 'use it or lose it' is a valid principle, a real method of somehow delaying old age? No, according to Dr Richard Greulich of the National Institute of Ageing. 'I've no medical proof,' he said, 'but I have a feeling that it has an effect. What everybody agrees is that once the rot sets in, the effects of dementia cannot be reversed. So, when we say "use it or lose it" we're talking about prevention rather than cure.'

The principle which frequently motivates elderly Olympians has even more parallels in the brain function. Dr Warner Shaie, an eminent researcher on the elderly in Seattle, feels that the old adage may well have some basis in medical truth. 'The principle applies not only to the maintenance of muscular flexibility, but to the maintenance of a high level of intellectual performance as well.' The hot housing implications of what Shaie says are enormous. Thousands of patients rocking away quietly in nursing homes suspected of being well on the path towards senile dementia may have very little wrong with them at all, he and several other investigators of ageing now believe. In fact the fundamental belief that we by definition 'slow up' mentally as we age appears to be false. Researchers can now demonstrate that large areas of human intelligence do not decline in old age at all, among people who are generally healthy.

Some aspects of intelligence may fade very early in life, such as the quick-thinking abstract abilities of the mathematician or the chess player. But, crucially, some other important forms of intellectual growth now appear to continue well into the eighties. The belief that the brain cells die off with age and with every alcoholic drink and that this 'brain shrinking' necessarily leads to a lowering of mental capacity, is viewed by many scientists now as highly questionable. For example at UCLA, Dr Arnold Schiebel's work on dendrites – the branching arms of nerve endings thought to correlate with much intellectual function – seems to show that they continue to grow in elderly rats as long as the creatures are kept mentally stimulated. When stimulation decreases, the rats' dendrites shrivel.

'The expectation of a decline is a self-fulfilling prophecy,' asserts Dr Shaie in Seattle. 'Those who don't accept the stereotype of a helples old age, but instead feel they can do as well in old age as they have at other times in their lives, do not become

prematurely ineffective.' He says there are now thought to be
two types of intelligence; the first is the 'fluid' type, that is
involved in abstract patterns and relationships, and is vulner-
able to ageing changes in the nervous system. The second type
is described as 'crystallized intelligence,' a person's ability to
use accumulated information to make judgements and solve
problems – the sort of intelligence required to understand
arguments, or deal with problems for which there is no black
and white answer, only the proverbial shades of grey, the
better and worse options.

It is that form of intelligence, the researchers now think, that
actually builds and develops in the older person. There is
nothing new in the notion; the Ancients called it wisdom and
revered it. But it is a salutary lesson for the entire generation
brought up in the 1960s onwards and now in its prime, confident that youth, and all youth said and did, was superior to
anything that could be produced by the old. 'Never trust
anyone over thirty,' said Jerry Rubin. Chances are he's
changed his mind.

The defects found in the healthy aged are in a minor range,'
says Dr Jerry Avorn of Harvard Medical School's Division on
Ageing. 'At worst they are a nuisance, like not being able to
remember names or phone numbers as well as before – but
they present no real problem for daily living.' Psychologist
John Horn of the University of Denver says: 'The ability to
bring to mind and entertain many different facets of information improves in many people over their vital years. One
way this shows up is in the ability of older people to "wax
eloquent" – they have a rich, evocative fluency . . . they can
say the same thing in five different ways. In our research,
they're better than the young people we see.' 'The fluid intelligence drop has some impact, but people learn to compensate,
even in later life,' says another psychologist, Martha Storandt.
'You can still learn what you want; it just takes a little longer.'

Ironically, it now seems that much of the folklore about the old 'losing their marbles' was derived from cognition tests that in fact tended to prove the opposite. According to Leonard Poon, a Harvard Medical School psychologist, 'Many tests that were used to assess the cognitive abilities of the elderly are biased in favour of younger people. One test involved remembering pairs of nonsense words. College students are motivated to try their best on such tests. But older people just don't care about nonsense words. What looks like a diminished ability in the elderly may partly be lack of interest.' Actual brain scans performed by the National Institute of Ageing on men from twenty-one to eighty-three have found, in fact, that 'the healthy aged brain is as active and efficient as the healthy young brain.'

Other flaws in the battery of studies 'proving' that there was no fool like an old fool have emerged. Many of the elderly test subjects were using medication that blurred their perceptions; uneducated people in their seventies, unused to the conventions of test-taking were often compared with young college students.

Being mentally active is clearly a vital part of maintaining or increasing mental capacity late in life. Having a 'flexible personality' is thought by some researchers to be equally crucial. People most able to tolerate ambiguity and enjoy new experiences in middle age have been found to best maintain their mental alertness in old age. But most important of all, it appears, is staying socially involved. Old people who decline, it is noted, are frequently those who withdraw from life. Elderly people who live with their families and are actively engaged in life frequently test better than those who live alone. Of those who 'withdraw' or abandon old interests, the greatest decline is observed in widowed housewives – and especially those who never had a career.

Using Even More Of It

No one can have 'used it' more in his life than the patriarch of behavioural psychology, B. F. Skinner. Skinner, inventor of the Skinner Box used for the rat experiments beloved of undergraduate psychology students, is now eighty three, and lives and works in Cambridge, Massachussets on books about 'how to ward off the decay and rot of old age.'

Skinner hot houses himself as he almost literally once did his daughter Debbie who was brought up in a glass box, the Skinner Baby Tender. Boxes have played a great part in B. F. Skinner's prodigious life. In this temperature-controlled environment, Debbie could romp around naked. Her father claims this advanced her neurological development, and helped her stand up, walk and talk more quickly than the average baby. These days, he can often be seen working in his study at five in the morning, or walking two miles from home to his office at Harvard University. His house bristles with self-help gadgets to replace the diminishing 'fluid intelligence'; buzzers to alert him to phone calls and timers to turn his stereo off in case he forgets. He has a tape recorder on the wall by his bed for ideas he may get in the middle of the night. They are rarer in old age, he feels, and he doesn't want to waste any. On his desk stands a home-made coffee warmer which uses a light bulb to keep his drink hot for up to two hours. He believes in conserving his remaining mental energy by allowing himself periods of rest between heavy bouts of cerebral exertion. Skinner has produced eight of his eighteen books in the past ten years. 'I tell myself that I have five good years left in which to get things done,' he jokes, 'and I'll keep saying that until it's no longer so.'

Skinner is best known for his controversial theory that human behaviour is controlled not by free will but by what he calls positive or negative reinforcement supplied by the environment. He has been described as a fascist for suggesting that societies could improve human behaviour by reinforcement, much as his laboratory rats and pigeons could be trained to perform tasks by reward and punishment systems. (His unpopularity in some quarters led to ugly rumours; there are people who still swear today that Debbie committed suicide because of Skinner's 'ill treatment' of her – in fact, she works as a landscape artist and lives in North London.) But when he talks about reinforcement as he practices it today on himself, it sounds like an ingenious, if eccentric, method of staving off old age's ravages. B. F. Skinner is not only a gadget enthusiast but a crafty strategist.

'I practise a very strict circadian rhythm,' he says. 'I go to bed very early, seven thirty or eight o'clock. It sounds ridiculous, but I then sleep one three-hour rapid eye movement cycle and get up and work for one hour. That is often my best hour of the day, but then I go back for another rapid eye movement period, and then I get up. I get up at four forty and work from five to seven, the hours when no one ever interrupts with the phone. And those are my three good hours for the day.' He spends the rest of the day on chores, but keeps noting down odd thoughts on a series of tactically positioned tape recorders and notebooks with the next clear page marked, because he forgets what he was going to write if he has to hunt for a blank page. If he hears on the weather forecast that rain is due, he hangs his umbrella by the front door to avoid leaving it behind.

The entire secret, he claims, to growing old cleverly is in creating a stimulating environment, devising little memory tricks and working fewer hours. 'Leisure should be relaxing,' Skinner told a fascinated audience of fellow psychologists in Washington recently. 'Possibly you like complicated puzzles, or chess, or other demanding intellectual games. Give them up. If you want to continue to be intellectually productive, you must risk the contempt of your younger acquaintances and freely admit that you read detective stories or watch Archie Bunker on TV.' Foods can be highly flavoured to make up for less sensitive taste buds; pornography should be used to extend sexuality into old age; those who cannot read should listen to book recordings.

Aging scholars must be wary of repeating themselves, he said. 'One of the more distressing experiences is discovering that a point you have just made, so significant, so beautifully expressed, was made by you in something you published a long time ago.' He recommends never recounting personal experiences going back more than a decade unless you are asked. And he warned colleagues against academic flattery; 'If you have been very successful, the most sententious stupidities will be received as pearls of wisdom, and your standards will instantly fall,' he said. 'Are you still thinking and writing as well as ever, or can you notice a decline?' we asked. 'I think I'm doing those things as well as before,' he said, 'But you can never be entirely sure about yourself.' His attitude to old age is curiously practical and unemotional. He lists his impairments with no trace of feeling or self-pity. Old age feels, he says, like seeing the world through smeared glasses, wearing thick leather gloves and ear muffs. Then he adds: 'I'm sure old age is an emotional experience, because people have told me it is. But I'm happier now, and enjoy myself more than ever before in my life.'

In a *People* magazine question and answer session, Skinner elaborated:

Do everything you can to make the rest of your life interesting. I've improved my audio equipment [he has a Compact Disc system with four mighty speakers] so that it's a pleasure now to listen to music. I've deliberately explored new areas of reading, such as historical biographies. I no longer drive, but it has taken me a long time to learn to stop looking straight ahead at the road and to look out of the window. Now I'm seeing how the seasons change. When the things you used to do no longer pay off, it is time to start doing something else.

Change your surroundings with new wallpaper or inexpensive art reproductions. Learn something new in an adult education course or by watching educational TV programmes. Revive an old hobby, see different people by going to different places. You must accept the fact that you are old. Then enjoy it.'

The one time age hurts him, Skinner says, is when passing an attractive woman; 'At one time, there would have been a second look from her. When there was no second look, I realized that I was changing.'

And if finally he is struck down by a debilitating illness, B. F. Skinner plans to apply the ultimate negative reinforcement – he says he will kill himself, if he can, rather than submit to an undignified old age.

The President's Brain
is Missing!

Not long ago, Gloria Steinem, the well-known feminist, held a press party to celebrate her 50th birthday. 'Look at me,' she said to the assembled company, 'this is what fifty looks like!' Ms Steinem was echoing herself. When she was forty, she held a similar party and announced, 'This is what forty looks like.'

The search for eternal youth lost credibility at some stage in history, but an interest in prolonging old age a little longer remains keen and transcends all national and cultural boundaries. 'Everyone wants to live longer,' says the National Institute of Ageing, 'but nobody wants to grow old. This is the human dilemma.'

Why is it that some people of eighty-five look and behave like sixty year olds while some people not yet eligible for retirement look decades older than they are? Researchers have always been baffled as to why some people age better and live longer. The pervasive system of creative accounting has probably given them more grey hairs than the other problems of medical research.

Consider the case of the renowned Dr Alexander Leaf, professor of clinical medicine at Harvard Medical School and chief of medical services at Massachusetts General Hospital in Boston. In 1971, on sabbatical leave, he set off for three areas of the world where great longevity had been reported, hoping to find common denominators that might account for it. He went to the Abkhazia region of the Caucasus in the USSR, to the province of Hunza in the Karakoram mountains of Kashmir and to the mountain village of Vilcabamba in the far south of Ecuador, which was experiencing an avalanche of tourists eager to check out reports that the locals were routinely living to 140 and 150 years of age.

The only common factor Dr Leaf could identify was the rather disappointing one that all these people shared a simple, pastoral life. The recent census in Vilcabamba had indeed revealed truly extraordinary results. Of 819 residents of the town, nine were over 100 – a rate considerably better than that of the US. Dr Leaf met one relative youngster in Vilcabamba of 122. Imagine his surprise three years later, when he met the same man again, except that now he was 134.

Dr Leaf and subsequent researchers discovered that the Ecuadorians were simply cheating. Although, as Roman Catholics, they had good baptismal records, the people of Vilcabamba confused things by using identical names. There was, it was true, a high proportion of elderly in the village, but this was because most of the younger people locally had migrated into larger towns. The fact was that, quiet pastoral life or not, individual longevity in Vilcabamba was pretty much the same as everywhere else. The *New York Times* summed the studies up in a headline worth columns of type: 'Very Old People in the Andes Are Found to be Merely Old'.

How we grow old

Such an entertaining sideshow could not distract doctors from the basic question, however. Why are some people alert and active at eighty five, others bent, decrepit and ga-ga at sixty five? Does high-quality, long life rely upon what we eat and what we do during our lives, or on some inherited genetic propensity to age at a certain point? Is it, so to speak, a re-run of the 'nature versus nurture' debate at the opposite end of the age scale? Or do bodies and minds simply 'wear out', even if the elderly are free of the diseases commonly associated with old age? Is there such a thing as a 'death gene', released at a predetermined moment by an individual's biological clock? If that were the case, it could rather blunt the point of finding cures for the diseases of old age – cancer, arthritis, and the dreaded Alzheimer's, a disease of largely unknown cause, marked by its progressive, devastating effects on the mind. (Alzheimer's Disease is a controversial topic in itself. Doctors seem divided about whether the problem is simply another name for a terrible but logical consequence of getting old – a continuum of the ageing process – or is a completely separate pathology, a disease in its own right.)

But there is now, for the first time in fifty years, a mood of optimism amongst biological researchers in the area of ageing. There is a confidence that they are finally beginning to understand how cells work and break down, which is the key to understanding the ageing process. Some of the most fascinating experiments actually involve observing and hot housing test groups of elderly volunteers for extended periods. In Mill Hill, north London, Dr Robin Holiday heads a medical research unit looking at cell growth and breakdown. His conclusions, from working on tissue cultures (though not on live volunteers) reflect much American research in the area; cells, he explains, renew themselves and repair damage countless times in a lifetime; but, with the exception of cancer cells, which appear immortal, at some unpredictable point they break down. Why does this happen at different times in different people? Can artificial substances maintain regeneration?

The 'death gene' notion is troubling and a little eerie: yet why, researchers ask, would nature bother to conceive a gene for growing old, since growing old confers no reproductive advantage – the only ultimate biological imperative? The answer, reported *Newsweek* magazine in June 1986, is that rather than the phenomenon being a 'death gene', it could perversely be a 'longevity gene' – with ultimately deadly consequences.

Leonard Hayflick of the University of Florida, one of the most famous names in gerontology, known for his work on cell reproduction is now suggesting that the human body is 'over-designed', like a space probe targeted only on Mars that manages to reach Jupiter and send back pictures in excess of requirements. No longevity genes have been found in people, but Thomas Johnson, at the University of California, has found a gene mutation in the roundworm that appears to postpone death and increase longevity by sixty per cent. If this process also takes place in humans, it may allow them to live long beyond their reproductive years, until the body becomes victim to the law of nature that systems become more chaotic as time goes on. The increasing disorder, or entropy, appears in many forms, such as enzymes not doing their job and DNA malfunctioning (i.e. not keeping up its necessary repair rate) – a law remarkably parallel in concept to the wear and tear familiar in machinery.

One of the most intriguing (and fashionable) current ideas is called Free Radical theory. It has attracted wide support. Certain molecules, it seems, natural by-products of body cells' use of oxygen, react with every other molecule they encounter, including those in the cell's DNA. The floating malevolent molecules, known as 'free radicals', do slight damage to the cell's functions; the accumulation over years of this damage constitutes, according to this theory the process of ageing. Free radicals are thought to be particularly linked with atherosclerosis (where they transform a benign form of cholesterol into the plaque that clogs arteries) and are thought to contribute to the development of cancer and Alzheimer's.

If free radicals are so damaging, it should follow that creatures able to produce chemicals that attack or neutralize them will live longer; however, feeding a free radical killer such as vitamin E into laboratory animals did not seem to help them to live longer. It is, in fact, thought that cells can only contain a certain number of naturally occurring free radical scavengers; so that any attempt at an artificial increase would subsequently be balanced by the body. The mysterious mechanism of the 'logevity gene' nevertheless, it is speculated, may simply be that it is especially efficient at producing free radical scavengers. But free radicals are not thought to be the only danger to cells; young cells are capable of repairing themselves by breaking down harmful proteins but this ability declines in old age. A second defence against these substances seems to grow in later years — but this works at the expense of other beneficial enzymes in the cell. By encouraging the early-life defences against these proteins — method yet to be determined — it may one day be possible to postpone the diseases of old age. It is also known that in old age the immune system breaks down; it may be that research into a cure for AIDS, may also be of use in arresting old age.

Yet whatever the chemistry of the human cell, there remains compelling evidence that using your mind is the best known way of maximizing longevity here and now. Remember how the Terman life study of bright youngsters in California showed them to be exceedingly vigorous and long lived. 'They just go on and on,' says the present study director, seventy nine-year-old Professor Robert Sears. 'Whereas in the American population in general, large numbers of people expect to retire by age sixty two, we only had three people who had retired by sixty two — three people out of 1,500! One woman, for example, aged seventy eight is the active editor of a weekly newspaper and making good money out of it, too. Another man is a lawyer who is not only still practising law about a third of his time, but is spending a third as chairman of the board of quite a good-sized corporation. And they are quite typical. If you look among the women who have been homemakers, you find that a very large number of them in their seventies are volunteer workers for one, two, three days a week in hospitals, or with musical societies, art galleries or theatres. I think "use it or lose it" is an excellent statement.'

At the Jewish Home for the Aged in Miami, the motive is by no means to create geniuses. Yet the home is the scene of an attempt to make certain that the *institutionalized* elderly are hot housed, too, and not simply left to deteriorate. The building and its interiors are planned to keep residents alert. There are bright and pretty colour schemes. All windowsills are kept low so patients can always see out from wheelchair or bed level. There are books, videos, lectures and screenings. Floor layouts and surfaces encourage mobility, and robots are used to help the disabled to perform routine tasks. Anything is done to keep patients stimulated and prevent them from getting 'dreamy'.

Don't have a physical, have a mental!

All mankind's attempts to investigate the brain and its function rely on something of a hands-off approach. The heart or the stomach can be examined physically and engineered, but the intangibility of what goes on in the brain accounts for its mystery, and the great difficulty we have in agreeing on almost anything about it.

Intelligence tests of all kinds rely in principle on what we *say* is going on in our mind, so its workings appear through several screens – the physical fact of the skull, the limiting nature of language and so on. Yet there have been noteworthy advances in a more physical examination of the brain, not only of use in theoretical research into the mechanism of thinking, but in examining brain diseases and malfunctions such as depression, Parkinson's, strokes and Alzheimer's.

In America, if not in Britain, older people have long accepted the notion of a yearly physical – a check up – but now it is

possible for them to take a 'mental' too. At the Cognitive
Research Center of New York University they start with the
old methods, such as memory tests on everyday things such as
phone numbers, to measure any decline in cognitive function,
but then move on with the help of sophisticated new
machinery to look inside the brain in a far more complex
manner than conventional X-rays. The latest system in brain
scanning is called PET – Positron Emission Tomography – and
it allows doctors actually to see the brain at work – and most
significantly, what changes take place when functions break
down.

The PET scan is a computer-reconstructed image of planes
within the brain, which can depict in vivid colour not the
anatomy of the brain, but biochemical changes within it.
Patients are injected with a positron-emitting radionuclide in
glucose, which gives doctors a picture of the rate at which
glucose is metabolized – burned up – in the brain. And what
neurobiologist Mony de Leon and his team of investigators are
finding is that glucose metabolism is substantially and consistently reduced in the brains of Alzheimer's Disease patients.
What is still uncertain, of course, is whether they are observing
cause or effect.

Their tests have shown that in a group of normal young
people, normal elderly and elderly Alzheimer's sufferers,
glucose utilization is equal for both normal types, but eighteen
to twenty seven per cent *down* in the Alzheimer's sample.
Alzheimer's disease has always been difficult to detect in its
early stages, and the new PET scan is proving far more accurate
than the conventional battery of psychological and neurological tests. Many Alzheimer's patients display so little structural change in their brains that the disease cannot even be
detected by standard methods of brain scanning. By combining
the older CAT method (more like an X-ray) with PET (which
shows a process), the De Leon team have achieved a high
degree of accuracy in diagnosing Alzheimer's.

The method is still experimental, and the million dollar machines also need the availability of a nearby cyclotron to produce the short-lived radionuclides (only one such exists in the UK, at Aberdeen), but it is showing more than a mere diagnosis of the condition. Most significantly, it is indicating that Alzheimer's is not, as previously assumed, a simple extension or acceleration of the normal ageing process, but something entirely different – a biochemical disease.

What can de done to reverse, arrest or prevent the disease is still not certain. There are no drugs in existence, though the team talk hopefully of the possibility of offering patients a cocktail of neurotransmitters – chemicals which relay messages from one nerve cell to the other – within the next ten years. About ten per cent of Alzheimer's patients are thought to have inherited the disease. Early in 1987, Dr Peter St George-Hyslop of Massachusetts General Hospital was principal author of an article in the journal *Science*, claiming to have found evidence of inherited Alzheimer's being caused by a defective gene on chromosome twenty one. (Humans have around 100,000 genes on their twenty three pairs of chromosomes – a gene is a segment of DNA.) The discovery, found with the help of researchers elsewhere in the US, Canada and Europe, does not yet hold out hope of a cure, but will be of great help in predicting and diagnosing the disease.

Old Rats, New Tricks

In Los Angeles, at UCLA, Dr Arnold Schiebel has devoted his scientific life to examining brains, and is coming to the conclusion that both the notion that children should be hot housed at a very early age, and the idea that the elderly should 'use it or lose it' – that you *can* teach an old dog new tricks – have firm foundation in the actual physical structure and development of the brain.

Part of Dr Schiebel's investigations have rested on the some-what Frankensteinian fact that he located bits of Albert Einstein's brain kept in bell jars at the home of a pathologist in Missouri, (where they had been for thirty years) and shipped them out west. His discoveries from this proud and rare acquisition have been fascinating. It must be remembered that it is very hard to investigate the link between brain structure and intellect. To do that, you would have to know that autopsy brains had come from known geniuses; this is why most brain research in this area relies much more frequently on animal studies.

Dr Schiebel is an advocate of what is known as dendritic branching theory. Dendrites, he explains, are branching arms of nerve endings, extensions from nerve cells that spread out in the space around them like the antennae on a TV set, picking up information from fibres coming into them and carrying it to the nerve cell, which then processes it and sends it out. 'Every nerve cell dendrite complex,' he says, 'is a little information collating system.'

'At one level at least, the more dendrites you have, the more information you can bring in. Cells in the cortex, in the brain hemispheres themselves, which are responsible for what we call intelligence and higher cognitive function, for them dendritic input is their lifeblood.' Dr Schiebel and his wife Dr Miriam Diamond, have done a great deal of work on colonies of rats to determine whether dendrite growth is possible as the animal ages, or whether increased growth is typical only of a younger and more active animal. They set out to establish possible links between the structure of the brain and the quality of its function. Schiebel and his wife took two groups of rats. Those in the first group were simply shut into their cages with nothing to do. Those in the second were given a selection of rat toys, which were changed once a day. When the rats died, they were examined and their dendrites counted. The stimulated rats had far richer dendrite growth than the bored ones.

'There is clear evidence now that the dendrites remain grow-able or plastic throughout the life of the individual,' says Dr Schiebel. 'The data on the rat are very clear; what it comes down to is the more you use your dendrites, the more growth you get. And in periods when you don't use your dendrites, there apparently is retraction, or the negative of growth. This is based on rat data, but it does seem to be true in the human.'

Unfortunately, he has no hard data on that – except for the brain of Einstein. 'It is very difficult to get brain tissue from the kinds of people who would represent the most intelligent,' Dr Schiebel says. 'In this laboratory, we are just beginning to look at such material, and the data suggest that those parts of the brain that deal with higher level – you might say "more intel-lectual"– functions, have cells with greater dendrite com-plexity, and those parts which have computationally a simpler task to perform, have fewer dendrites, less complex branching.

We heard actually through chance that Albert Einstein's brain was still available. We had always thought about trying to find something like this because we had been interested for a number of years in the possible structural basis for giftedness, or extreme intelligence. My wife and I were able to get small amounts of this tissue, already thirty years old, since Einstein died in 1955, and although there were limits to what we could do on this old tissue, we found that in certain parts of the brain of Einstein, where imagery and higher conceptual functions are known to take place, there were certain structural changes which made it rather dif-ferent from the brains of a number of control individuals, smart enough individuals who were not otherwise unusual. And we could count these differences, in terms of little metabolically supportive "helper" cells, that support the neurone. And this to us suggests that related to the kind of gift he had, there are demon-strable, visible structural changes.

It was not possible for Dr Schiebel to examine the number of dendrites in Einstein's brain, he regrets. After thirty years, its condition was not good enough. Dr Schiebel is also anxious to qualify his findings; 'You must realize that it's not clear even from counts of this sort whether these changes were there originally, via the genetic component, or whether they were there secondarily, because for some reason or other, he used these parts of the brain more effectively or more richly than non-gifted contemporaries. But it is quite clear, at least from rats, that dendritic growth is a possibility right up until the end of life. The structures may grow more slowly in the later phases of life, but they grow. That is the most important and optimistic message that we can give any of our people.'

Is genius inborn – or created? 'My own hunch' says Dr Schiebel, 'is that geniuses are born different, because they show their differences, their gifts, their flair, so early in life. I am thinking of a Mozart, a Beethoven, thinking of a young genius that I have got to know about only last year, who at one year was speaking three or four languages. The ordinary child is not able to do this.'

So what of hot housing, of creating youthful genius? Dr Schiebel believes most parents' hopes are misplaced – but, (bearing in mind that he also supports the notion of the continual growth of dendrites and their relationship to intelligence) he believes at the same time that an enriched (but not overloaded) background for a baby may help, if only in a limited way, and that it certainly can't hurt. 'The more we enrich the environment during the critical first three, five or six years of its life,' he says, 'I think the more we leave with the child, the more we lead it in a sense to higher levels of good cognitive function. But I hate to be bound into any statement of this sort, because the data are so tenuous.'

If our dendrites do correlate with intelligence, and continue to grow all our lives if exercised, then are there steps we could take to stave off senile dementia? Dr Schiebel believes (a little depressingly) that once a disease like Alzheimer's has taken hold, there is no cure – but that preventative work may have an effect. In the same way as B. F. Skinner (but using his brain structure theory rather than the psychologist's approach) Dr

Schiebel maps out a strategy for active old age: 'Fill your life intellectually and emotionally. The fact that you are a specialist in whatever you do is fine, but by the time you are forty or forty five or fifty, you should add new interests, learning things that make you struggle in a sense to pick up new techniques. It's like building muscle; the brain in that sense is a muscle. And the more you challenge your brain, the better chance you have of developing further dendritic growth and alertness as you get older.'

Building up the brain as if it were a biceps muscle is a fairly contentious (though actually rather commonsensical) idea; the newer notion of brain transplants seems more like a grizzly borrowing from science fiction. But no such transplants, already attempted, are expected to be more commonplace in a matter of a few years, though, it must be said, not quite in the sense of extracting entire brains and installing them in vacant heads. The (partial) brain transplant (i.e. of brain tissue) could soon be routine therapy for Alzheimer's Disease, Parkinson's and possibly even Down's Syndrome. Even the Pentagon is said to be interested in the subject, reported Andrew Veitch of *The Guardian* in January 1987, as a possible method of treating brain damage caused by radiation.

Alzheimer's, described by one researcher as 'the extinction of the mind' involves the physical shrinking of the brain, and the widespread degeneration of brain cells (neurones). One way of treating the disease, proposed by Dr Susan Iversen, director of behavioural pharmacology at the Merck Sharp and Dohme neuroscience research centre in Harlow, Essex, is simply to transplant young, healthy neurones into the brains of Alzheimer's patients. The cells, she explains could come from human or animal foetuses. Early experiments have shown that transplanted cells succeed in producing a neurotransmitter called acetycholine that is lacking in Alzheimer sufferers. Down's (which has similarities to Alzheimer's) may also be affected by the treatment, but it is in helping Parkinson's sufferers that brain transplants offer the most hope.

In Parkinson's, the missing neurotransmitter is called dopamine. Cells from the adrenal gland, which lives above the kidneys, produce dopamine when they are implanted into the brain. A team at the Karolinska Institute in Stockholm and Lund University, led by Dr Anders Bjorklund, implanted these tissues into four Parkinson's patients. The first, a fifty five-year-old man who had had the disease for eight years, had pieces of his adrenal gland chopped finely and injected through a metal tube into his brain; it worked to a limited extent. For a week, they produced dopamine, and the patient's movement improved. The next three patients showed similar improvements, and the Swedish team is widely felt to have made an important step.

The US National Institute of Mental Health hopes to start transplants for Parkinson's patients immediately, and are looking at methods of getting dopamine-producing cells both from the brains of aborted foetuses and from some laboratory-manufactured cancer cells, as well as from adrenal glands. American scientists at Yale and Rochester University, New York, have already reported repairing monkey brains by transplanting monkey foetus cells. The cancer-based transplant material is the most promising, partly because it has fewer ethical pitfalls.

Predictably, such research is never far from the ethical borderline. A neuro-surgeon, Dr Robert White of Cleveland's Metropolitan General Hospital, was heavily criticised by British and American medical associations in 1985 when he revealed that four years earlier, he had swapped entire heads and bodies on fifty apes. The experiment was not fatuous; if a terminal cancer patient could have his head connected to the body of someone whose brain had been crushed in a car crash – a body transplant, rather than a brain swap, perhaps – we might all be the better for it. Such a prospect is unlikely at present, however. Half the heads, Dr White discovered, continued to function after they had been connected by tubes to their new bodies. Yes, eyes moved, mouths chewed, and the monkeys felt pain, he reported. Unfortunately, Dr White could not connect the spinal chords, so he was left with a set of paraplegic apes, all of whom died. What Dr White's critics were most concerned about was why he needed as many as fifty monkeys for the experiment. It is perhaps a good thing for humanity in general that at that stage, it was Dr Schiebel rather than Dr White who heard of the existence in some glassware down in Missouri of the late Dr Albert Einstein's late brain.

---11---

Finally, We Bring You the Secrets of Life . . . or You Are What You Eat

It's Official

Thirty miles west of Boston, in Massachusetts, is the town of Framingham – population 50,000. It has a primarily white, middle class and blue collar population. This is the home of the 'Framingham Heart Study' – one of medical science's longest-running investigations. Framingham was chosen because its population is mixed, but relatively static. It looks, at first glance, like a typical New England town. Yet this is a living laboratory – human experiment on a grand scale. And inside the neat white frame houses beat 6,000 of the most famous – and most closely scrutinized – hearts in America.

It may seem an odd place for a study of heart disease; the town has so many steak houses, pizza parlours, ice cream bars, burger palaces and spaghetti joints that locals call its main street Alka Seltzer Row. Yet Framingham is largely responsible for the dramatic drop in heart disease which the USA (and Canada and Australia) are experiencing – the National Heart, Lung and Blood Institute say the drop was a staggering thirty per cent between 1963 and 1980. Framingham's residents are at this point remarkable for their high degree of health awareness; they are able to discuss their systolic and diastolic blood pressures with as much easy familiarity as they talk about football.

Framingham was first used as a human laboratory in 1918,

when researchers were looking into an epidemic of TB; the townspeople seemed to react well to being part of a medical experiment. In 1949, when a new epidemic – this time of heart disease – was causing concern, Framingham was the natural choice. The townspeople are now the most informed medical consumers anywhere.

The project has been running from an unpretentious white wooden house for thirty eight years. In 1949, a population sample of half the townsfolk, then aged between thirty and sixty was chosen. 5,600 volunteers were culled at random from the local phone book and many are still alive (though their average age is now in the late seventies). They were observed, and data have been collected for two main studies; firstly, who developed heart disease – and what were the links between cardio-vascular ailments, diet, exercise and ageing. The second strand of the investigation was the social problems which people experience as they age. Director of the study, the well-known cardiologist Dr William Castelli explains: 'We look at people who are really sharp in their eighties and try to see what they were like thirty five years ago. On that basis, we can begin to *predict* how certain groups of people will age – what factors are present when people age well.' Again, volunteers regularly submit to a battery of exhaustive tests. And to help establish the role of heredity in the development of heart disease, children and grandchildren of the original cohort are added to the study as they reach thirty.

The great significance of the Framingham study has been that it has firmly established the link between the four main risk factors – high blood pressure, smoking, overweight and high cholesterol – and heart disease. The results have been straightforward and virtually conclusive; the higher your cholesterol count, the greater your risk of heart attack – but if you lower your blood cholesterol level, you will probably live longer. Dr Castelli says he has quite simply *never seen* a heart attack in anyone with a cholesterol level of 150 or less. Castelli has already been responsible for making Americans aware of the dangers of high blood pressure, and is about to do the same again, by launching a 'Know Your Cholesterol Count' crusade across America. He is aided and abetted by a neat new piece of medical technology – a portable computer which analyses a drop of blood taken from a finger, and comes up with a cholesterol reading in two minutes flat. Like an old-fashioned travelling medicine man, he sets up his life-saving machine on a stall on street corners.

Families like the de Collibuses in Framingham hardly need any more crusading. A typical 'Framingham family', John de Collibus, now sixty seven, was an original subject of the study. His son, Paul, is thirty seven and works with his father in his TV shop. Paul has his own portable blood-pressure gauge and checks his reading twice a day. They have been aware for years that high blood pressure is a family problem. John de Collibus says he watches his diet and has cut down very carefully on fats; he is one of the subjects who developed heart trouble. On the day Paul's wife had twins he was so nervous that he suffered a minor attack – and ended up in the same hospital as his new grandchildren. He says the attack would have been worse had Dr Castelli not warned him to change his ways – and his diet – years earlier.

The Framingham study has also drawn attention to the effect of substances called lipo-proteins on heart disease. The best known of these lipo-proteins, High Density – HDL – is the most effective at preventing cholesterol from being deposited in the blood vessels. Dr Castelli thinks HDL levels are as important as cholesterol level readings and should be tested more readily than they are now. 'The American diet,' says Castelli, 'and especially things like fast food hamburgers and hot dogs, is fit only for three animals – cats, dogs and rats – all of whom have very high levels of HDL.'

Probably the longest running 'conventional' research pro- gramme on ageing in the world is the Baltimore Longitudinal

Study, now in its thirtieth year and scheduled to continue for another twenty five. The Baltimore study is a federally-funded attempt to centralize and coordinate all age research in the USA, and is unquestionably the biggest databank in the world on the ageing process. Doctors in Baltimore have been tracking the progress of more than 800 men and women, who now range in age from twenty seven to over one hundred. They are not a random or representative sample, as is the case in Framingham. Subjects are self-selected and mostly educated, health conscious and middle class – but the study is considered a virtually unique information resource for all kinds of satellite studies – biological and behavioural. Every two or three days, a selection of ten to twenty volunteers check into the Baltimore City Hospital, where they remain for three days of intensive physical and mental testing. There are tests of strength, coordination and memory, treadmill and stress tests. There are even 'sensory deprivation' chambers.

The idea is to allow scientists to see how each person is faring in the losing battle against time; why some deteriorate while others do not; why some score high in problem-solving ability even at ninety; why some retain memory and others forget. Skin and tissue cultures are periodically collected and frozen for ten or twenty years so that, as the volunteers grow older, younger cell samples in 'suspended animation' can be thawed and compared with older, contemporary cells. It is like confronting a middle-aged person with him or herself in youth, and will, it is hoped, give new insights into the ageing process.

Director of the Baltimore project is Dr Richard C. Greulich, who says confidently that the data shows beyond reasonable doubt that senility is *not* inevitable. All the testing, he adds, appears to have done the volunteers some good; diseases and problems are identified early, and the group is in top mental and physical shape. Dr Greulich stresses that the study does not attempt to prolong human life, but to investigate how it might be improved – he foresees no likelihood of average lifespan being increased beyond seventy eight for men and eighty four for women in the next century. Dr Greulich says he is more interested in the quality of life than its quantity.

The Baltimore study has established firstly that many systems in the body do not deteriorate with age. Most intriguingly, perhaps, the human personality appears to be totally stable from age twenty onwards – and that means that significant changes in behaviour, far from being a natural concomitant of the ageing process, are a more serious indicator of physical or mental ill health than had previously been thought. Even the heart does not seem necessarily to lose its ability to function. It changes its method of operation in older people, however, which ensures, Greulich says, that many old people have as efficient a circulatory system in practice as people of twenty. The Baltimore cohort has now been extended to include women, in the hope of solving the age-old question of why they live longer than men and have statistically fewer heart attacks. 'When we find out, I promise to get men to live longer, not to shorten the female lifespan,' jokes Dr Greulich.

Another contribution of the project has been to observe and note the extent to which the ageing process varies. As yet, Baltimore doctors can offer no explanation for this. Dr Greulich tends to think longevity is largely a genetic ability. Actual age in years is, he says 'a terribly imprecise way of judging at what stage in ageing an individual may be.' We are far from establishing just what the biological markers of age are.' And his formula for longer life? 'The use it or lose it adage is appropriate,' he says, reflecting the fact that the study has clearly shown that, for example, in tests of problem-solving ability, old people who have spent their lives solving problems do best. 'I would only amend it by saying, "Do things in moderation." In today's faddish society when jogging is a popular pastime, if you've not jogged before, it's probably questionable whether you should jog like a professional right away. Don't do things in extremes because of guilt that you have not done right by yourself.'

The Oranges of Anxiety

In the balmy, if slightly polluted, air of southern California they have a rather clever saying these days. 'It used to be *The Grapes of Wrath*, out here,' they tell you; 'now it's more *The Oranges of Anxiety*'. Life here is (at least for the reasonably affluent population) lived at an extraordinarily high standard. Convenience and comfort are worked at assiduously and frequently achieved. But if wrath is manifestly lacking for most people, there is anxiety aplenty. It comes as no great surprise, then, to discover, beautifully situated on the beach at Santa Monica in west Los Angeles, a phenomenon called the Pritikin Centre, established in 1976 to improve the 'quality of life' for aged Americans.

This is no mere fat farm. The Pritikin is where you go if you are determined, or compelled for health reasons, to make total lifestyle changes. The centre is placed symbolically, it would seem, on the edge of the continent; this is the last resort – literally – for people who have run out of excuses and have their backs to the sea.

The improvement in Pritikin patients' quality of life is achieved by encouraging fairly Draconian changes in both diet and lifestyle, complete with comprehensive medical testing and lessons in stress management. There is an unspoken suggestion – generally understood by the clientele – that the Pritikin programme, if strictly applied, may even *prolong* life. The Pritikin Center is, in effect, a hothouse experiment, the crux of which is the assertion that changes in nutrition, especially the drastic lowering of fat intake, can prevent or even reverse heart disease, certain forms of cancer, diabetes and senile dementia. The Pritikin literature cites many cases of people with heart disease who have been able to bypass surgery, and diabetes sufferers who, after retreat at Pritikin, have returned home practically drug-free, their condition controlled by diet alone.

While the Center is careful to avoid making claims it cannot substantiate, the message is clear. Pritikin helps you to beat the clock. Four weeks in residence can mean a metamorphosis for people who have spent a lifetime killing themselves. Some – especially those with chronic health problems – have exhausted all other possibilities. Pritikin is one last chance – and failure here is simply not an option. But this life-or-death treatment is so radical that people need the reinforcement of a residential programme to make the total lifestyle changes required.

They can choose the thirteen- or twenty six-day programme. Both provide the perfect hot house environment needed to reeducate people and prepare them to make fundamental changes in their habits. Addicts all, they must be reprogrammed to forever eschew pastrami-on-rye in favour of raw cauliflower, steamed, salt-free vegetables and assorted pulses. Only three ounces of animal protein are allowed each day. The diet is largely, though not exclusively, vegetarian. Eating between meals is encouraged – as long as inmates stick to raw vegetables. This means that there is food available most of the time; Pritikin doctors claim that weight and cholesterol are better controlled with a series of small meals than two or three large ones. The hot house people insist that they don't so much eat as graze.

Pritikin is basically an adult reeducation centre which, for the considerable price of a temporary residency ($3000 for a thirteen day course and $6000 for the full four weeks) will at least radically alter an old person's way of life – and not-so-old either. Men and women as young as forty, and even a few overweight teenagers with a family history of high blood pressure, enroll for a 'preventative 'course. The establishment's proprietor, Robert Pritikin, son of the late founder, Nathan, boasts his most impressive results with elderly people, up to eighty, entering with some form of pathology – angina pectoris, hypertension or adult-onset diabetes.

Independently corroborated statistics show astonishingly

that eighty five per cent of those who enter Pritikin dependent upon medication for high blood pressure leave after the twenty six day course with lowered pressure. They are also drug-free. Over ninety per cent of diabetics using oral drugs were also able to stop taking all forms of regular medication. The results seem to last as long as the programme is strictly adhered to at home. Success of this kind has meant that many of the medical costs of attending the centre are covered by health insurance. The hotel section of the centre is expensive, but elderly Americans of all colours and backgrounds seem to regard it as a very worthwhile investment.

The late Nat Pritikin, founder of the Center for Longevity, was best categorized as an enthusiastic amateur with, as his public relations handout says, 'a life-goal of changing the whole country's health'. He was an inventor with nearly fifty patents to his name in chemistry, physics and electronics. He read voraciously about medicine from earliest childhood, and formed an interest in nutrition when he developed heart disease at the age of forty. 'I thought I was immune, since I followed what everyone considered the "good American diet",' he said. 'Eggs every morning, lobster Newburg every Friday, a pint of ice cream every night, cheese every day. At that time, in 1955, physicians weren't aware of the relationship between nutrition and disease. I was instructed to cut out all activity and take medications, and I only got worse. It took me two years of research to convince myself my diet was at fault.'

For twenty five years, he followed his own principles, eating mainly fresh and cooked fruits and vegetables, whole grains and small amounts of fish and poultry, all coupled with an exercise regimen of walking and jogging. He reduced his cholesterol level late in life to a virtuous 100, compared with 300 at its height, and ran a vigorous twenty five miles a week.

Deliberately increasing lifespan is far from easy. During the programme, residents are virtually 're-born', learning to eat, live, exercise and even think differently. New recruits at Pritikin are exhaustively screened for possible medical problems; doctors, wires and electrodes are everywhere as a battery of tests assesses the customer's state of health and exercise-tolerance levels. Heart function, blood pressure and sugar level are carefully monitored, while elderly entrants undergo rigorous treadmill exercise tests. New Pritikin computer programmes can measure blood flow or calculate the internal tissue-fat level for the entire body. When all the tests are complete, ageing participants know precisely what their capabilities and problems are, and what their cholestrol and exertion levels ought to be. Individual diets and exercise routines are then custom-designed for them. As they exercise, roving members of staff take pulse-rates, and blood pressure. The patients wear tags indicating how far they can be pushed. Some are told they are overdoing things, others are encouraged to work harder. The Pritikin courses also deal with the psychological problems of ageing and living with chronic health problems, and aim to reduce the fear and pessimism which can accompany old age.

But it is in the dining room that a truly cosmic struggle for the soul takes place. This leads to a kind of euphoria. Although they have to break the habits of a lifetime and do without many of the things they enjoy, far from feeling miserable or deprived, many Pritikin residents seem to be relieved and exhilarated. Suddenly, they feel 'in control' and begin to realise that there is much more in life to look forward to than regular cheese-burgers. Pritikin doctors speak of extending life from its western average of seventy five years to what they regard as its theoretical maximum of 110 to 120 years. Seventy-year-young inmates trot along the beach and work out on treadmills. Participants in stress reduction classes learn from psychologists social skills such as the knack of saying 'no' at dinner parties. They are taught to beware the 'friend' proferring forbidden food, or relatives determined to sabotage their rigorous

The Secrets of Life, or You Are What You Eat 215

effort, and role play in order to learn to handle the situation with tact and finesse.

True, there is no tea, coffee, ice cream, nor hamburgers in a Pritikin-ordered world, no butter nor margarine *on* the bread, no salt nor shortening *in* it. Yet the centre is full of fat-free food which inmates *can* eat – and much of it tastes remarkably good if bland. What is important is that they feel so much better, more alert and more confident. All day, they sit through classes and lectures planned to reinforce new habits.

Pritikin-style cookery isn't quite as grim or monastic as you might expect. It means beet borscht (no soured cream); tuna and dill salad, pasta salmon salad; perhaps some banana and peach 'ice cream' – well, ice anyway. Menus are imaginative. Breakfast may be pitta bread, oatmeal cereal, half a banana or papaya. Lunch is typically some broccoli bisque soup (vegetable stock, no salt), squash pie baked in a hollow orange with curry sauce, cabbage, carrots and cauliflower. In the afternoon there is a snack, often steamed artichokes or baked potatoes (no butter, no salt). A randomly chosen dinner may be asparagus pudding with parsnips and a fruity dessert. And there is a light evening snack. This is starvation de luxe! After 'graduation', reports Dr William Manchester, medical director of the centre, eighty per cent of Pritikin inmates stick to the diet for eighty per cent of the time – and ten to fifteen per cent adhere rigidly to the régime for ever.

Despite already being thin, Dr Steve Inkless, the head nutritionist at Pritikin, lives on the Centre's diet and says he loves it. 'One of the misconceptions about being thin,' he says, 'is that it indicates that one has a good blood cholesterol level or is otherwise in good health. I eat this way because I want to keep my blood cholesterol at an optimum range, and being thin is no guarantee of having an optimum level'. He says the average American or Briton should restrict his animal protein intake to no more than three to three and a half ounces of fish, chicken or lean meat per day. This, in addition to eliminating the added fats of the typical diet would soon be enough to accomplish an ideal blood cholesterol level.

All this talk of cholesterol may lead sceptics to wonder if saturated fat is in fact a proven killer. Many doctors still express doubt, but the vast weight of evidence is that a high cholesterol level is a major risk factor in the development of cardiovascular disease. As corroboration, the large-scale re-education of the American, Canadian and Australian public, the process of prying them away from their twelve-ounce steaks, appears to have led to a dramatic thirty per cent reduction in heart disease in those countries in the past fifteen years. Yet curiously, and to the horrified fascination of Professor Philip James, one of Britain's leading heart specialists, the British people and their successive governments seem as ready to believe in the importance of low cholesterol levels as they are to believe in the Tooth Fairy. Britain has the highest rate of cardiovascular disease and cancer in Western Europe; Glasgow is the heart attack capital of the world, and yet still even the over-eighties scoff sausage rolls which would cause their New World counterparts to choke.

It was Professor James who, in 1983, produced an official report (the NACNE report) concluding that the average British diet was in need of radical change, and that people should be eating twenty five per cent less fat, cutting back further on the dangerous saturated fats and so on — the standard international advice for avoiding heart and circulatory disease. The report was castigated and Professor James pilloried by many of his medical colleagues. 'There is this marvellous British tendency to say "let's gamble on it", "why worry, you have got to die some time." I get that also from experts,' says the bemused professor. 'But what we are talking about are premature, preventable deaths, not immortality, but living to a ripe old age in a healthy, functional, enjoyable state.'

Perhaps it is part of that cultural resistance to change that typifies the British, but this country appears to be deliberately ignoring the simplest, cheapest and most effective form of longevity hot housing that exists. And two of the greatest, though unwitting enemies of good health, according to Professor James, are your friendly, whistling milkman and his accomplice, your jolly local butcher — 'I'll give you some extra strips of fat to lard it, luv.' The problem, as Professor James sees it, is terribly clear; Britain has one of the worst diets in the world, high in fat, sugar and salt, which accounts for high rates of cardiovascular disease and strokes. 'I think we have a bizarre diet,' he says, 'one that is certainly not very appetizing as far as I am concerned, and indeed not particularly appetizing if you have been around the world and seen other options. People do go in for sausage rolls and very fatty things, and this reflects a major problem which in some way we are going to have to tackle on a national basis. But we do not have as part of our culture a highly flexible, responsive approach to almost anything.'

So while door-to-door milk deliveries may be a convenience, there is a school of thought which suggests that lonely, housebound OAPs who rely heavily on a diet of full-cream milk are being done no favours. (In fact, the professor says he has nothing against the milkman, if only people would order skimmed milk from him — and some of the big dairies are at last beginning to promote the low fat alternative.) The problem with butchers, he says, is that, 'they and the marketing men between them still have this idea that you don't get a luscious joint or piece of meat unless it is absolutely swathed in fat, and that actually, scientifically, is not true. It has been shown very clearly that it is not true, but the butchers still believe that their fifty year-old ideas are the right ones.'

Government figures released in 1987 showed that the healthy eating message is beginning, if in a very limited way, to get through to Britons. Consumption of low fat milk rose by fifty per cent in 1986 over 1985; butter intake was twelve per cent down, sugar seven per cent; people were eating less beef, and more poultry and fish.

Professor James says he understands why some experts say the heart disease reduction rate in the US (and Belgium, Finland and Australia among other countries) need not necessarily be due to low-fat diet. They say other changes have occurred, particularly a reduction in smoking; but he says, 'One can spend hours nit-picking over the evidence, and that is what the British love doing, I think it is very clear that if one has a low cholestrol count, then that is associated with a low death rate. There is no absolute proof in proper, strict, scientific terms that dietary change will, without any question, reduce the heart attack rate. The point is that all the evidence when put together suggests that this is a very reasonable thing to do.'

A disturbing part of the British reluctance to make necessary changes is that the accepted cholesterol 'danger level' at which doctors are prepared to intervene and treat is much higher in Britain than in other developed countries. It is known that ninety five per cent of people with a cholesterol count of over 300 *will* (not *may*) go on to have heart attacks. On the other hand, heart attacks in people showing a level of 150 or below are very rare indeed. 'Doctors would regard 300 in Britain as a level at which they should treat, but what we ought to recognize is that the "average" level of, say, 225, is also a problem,' Professor James says. 'And in fact most enlightened experts would consider that 200 milligrammes of cholesterol or more should be treated. The majority of deaths in Britain actually occur in people having so-called average levels, which in the past we always thought of as normal. They are not normal – they are the average, the very high average, of the British population.'

Much of the official anger at Professor James's 1983 report came from what some regarded as the unhealthy alliance between the Conservative government and the food processing industry. Yet the mass of criticism directed against Conservative junior health minister, Mrs Edwina Currie, when she criticised the unhealthy eating of the northern British working class in early 1987, came from the political left, who appeared to be the sudden defenders of saturated fat, in so far, at least, as it was a proletarian phenomenon. (This is perhaps unfair; many Labour MPs defended 'working class food' on the grounds that it was all many people could afford, thanks to the unenlightened British food industry.)

One of the many aspects of the food debate that puzzles Professor James is that the measure that he proposes – reducing fat in the British diet, – is not necessarily a threat to the food industry. 'In the last two years,' he says, 'there has been a very striking increase in low fat milk production, and sales. In fact, may food companies have done extremely well from changing their milk systems to low fat products. It is actually a marvellous opportunity, and I cannot understand why the food industry is not jumping on this fantastic band-wagon, to make millions in profits, which is perfectly right and reasonable, from this new concept.'

Tufts: Where Table Manners Are Suspended

A major examination of ageing in the USA takes place at a combination of hotel and laboratory in downtown Boston where volunteers are cloistered for months at a time while scientists feed them with painstaking care. Every crumb is counted, every drop of food and drink weighed and measured. All excrement is collected and analysed. Volunteers' showers have no drains – the dirty water is trapped and the perspiration traces and bodily wastes examined. The idea is to discover how *diet alone* affects the process of growing old. If the research succeeds, scientists are hopeful that they can help people to preserve healthy minds and bodies well into the later years – just by watching what they eat.

The effect of the diet on health has long interested researchers but it is hard to collect facts unless people can be persuaded to live in confinement for long periods, while doctors control, measure and record everything they eat. So the Tufts University Research Centre is home to fourteen to twenty eight live-in volunteers. Some stay for only a few days, some check in for six to nine months. They have pleasant private rooms, a swimming pool, a games room and a good library. The study pays special attention to post-menopausal women.

Lunchtime in Boston is something to behold. Milk is measured out with an eyedropper. A roving nurse urges a woman to wipe the remnants of food from her plate with her fingers. You *have* to lick your plate clean whether you like your food or not. Your drinking glass has to be rinsed repeatedly, so that you get the last molecule into your system; inmates attest that the most revolting sight in the world is a milk glass on its second rinse, the contents taking on the hue and taste of used dishwater. If a crumb of food is dropped on the floor by accident, it is painstakingly retrieved and weighed so that the calculations should not go askew.

The centre arranges outings to the theatre, the cinema and the beach. But the 'patients' cannot leave the building alone, and since some are in for three months or more, a term at the centre is a considerable commitment. Everywhere the hothouse people go, a chaperone goes too . . . to make sure no one, in a moment of human weakness, spoils the experiment with a quick beer and pizza. 'A single potato chip could throw off an entire month-long study,' says the centre's director, Dr Jeffrey Blumberg. But the restrictions don't prevent one eighty-year-old woman saying, 'It's like staying in the best hotel in town.' The food? 'Perfection is my word for it,' says another willing prisoner. 'I don't have to cook it!'

There are frequent tests to check the effects of diet on blood, bones and organs. There is a fascinating machine called a 'whole body counter' which encloses the body and measures naturally-occurring radiation. Already strides are being made in preventing osteoporosis (brittle bones) and cataracts by controlling diet.

The osteoporosis can be delayed by dietary calcium and calcium supplements; and, in tests, vitamin C has shown encouraging signs of preventing or delaying cataracts. Salt is proven to lead to increases in blood pressure; and good diet has been found to contribute to mental alertness in old age. Vitamin E is showing promise in preventing the ageing immune system from breaking down. (But don't overdose on the vitamin in the hopes of either staying young or staving off AIDS, as its long-term side effects are not yet known.)

'I think we're still a long way from understanding the secrets of ageing,' Dr Blumberg admits, 'but we are very close and clearly coming up with practical information on how appropriate diets can intervene in the ageing process, and prevent or at least delay some of those conditions we associate with ageing. I think we're also beginning to learn that dietary patterns and habits are developed in childhood, and that if you develop good eating habits then, you are likely to do much better than if you wait until you're seventy years old and then say "What can I do to improve my life?" ' Tufts scientists are working now to perfect gene probes able to identify people at risk from, say, high blood pressure. Within the next few years, doctors should be able to take a sample of umbilical cord fluid and present a newborn baby with a life diet plan to help it avoid the diseases to which it is predisposed.

Live Longer, Eat Even Less

Professor Roy L. Walford, the UCLA Professor of Gerontology, has no connection with the Pritikin centre, but lives and works close to it, on the beach at Venice, California. Most days, sixty three-year-old Professor Walford can be seen jogging along the famous boardwalk, dodging the Walkman-wired rollerskaters and breakdancers. A highly respected scientist, indeed one of the world's leading experts in the science of ageing, he fully intends doing the same thing for the next fifty years.

The long-distance jogger is noted for his work on 'under-nutrition,' and is the author of a book called *Maximum Life-span*. Walford firmly believes that humans should be enjoying a natural life span of approximately 110 to 120 years, and is exploring ways of prolonging the lives of animals – notably mice – in his UCLA lab. He has demonstrated that he can reliably extend the life of the average mouse by thirty to fifty per cent by underfeeding it – giving it a high quality, calorie-restricted diet which eliminates some one third of its body weight. Not only do the mice fed in this way live longer, but they stay alert longer and develop fewer cancers than the normally-fed control group. Professor Walford held up two elderly mice by their tails for us to see; one had been systematically underfed, the other fed normally. The underfed mouse was bigger, as it had not shrivelled in old age. It also had a glossier coat. If a mouse can look good, there was little doubt about it; this was a goodlooking mouse.

No one is really sure why diet restriction prolongs life, but it does. Theories are that underfeeding may increase the rate of DNA repair in the cells; it may in some way keep the body's immune response capacity young and active, or increase the supply of free radical scavengers (the natural chemicals that fight malign ageing substances in the cells), or it may affect the hormonal system. Whatever it does, Walford believes that underfeeding slows the rate at which the animal matures physically. If you do that, he reasons, you can postpone puberty, deterioration, and finally death. Professor Walford says that you can start underfeeding a mouse late in the creature's life – as late as the equivalent of sixty in human years – and still see the benefit in terms of increased longevity. Furthermore, he maintains, by doing so, you do not simply prolong the animal's period of *old* age. Underfeeding seems somehow to stretch out youth and middle-age, but leave the animal with a relatively short period of actual old age.

But does all this apply to humans? Roy Walford believes so; humans, he argues, are simply another species of mammal. To help demonstrate the theory, Walford is following an under-feeding way of life himself; he has reduced his calorie intake to about 1,600 a day (plus supplementary vitamins and minerals) and virtually eliminated fats. He also fasts occasionally for a day, and, of course, exercises. He fully expects to live for 120 to 130 years, and wants to do so (actually, he says he would rather live to 220) because, he says, 'There are so many things that are going on that are interesting. One lifetime is just not enough!' Early in 1987 he published a new book called '*The 120 Year Diet*.'

Is this kind of life fun? Walford emphasizes that he advo-cates a *high-quality*, low-calorie diet. He also contends that underfeeding yourself need not take the enjoyment out of life – as shown by those who fast (as he did at the outset of his régime, when he was in his late fifties) and experience an energetic, clear-minded high. Underfeeding apparently has the same effect apparently on rats, worms, flies and one-cell organisms as it does on Walford's mice. There is also some evidence that it will prolong the life of chickens and cattle; and as far as people are concerned, Dr Walford is running his life on the basis that humans *should* fit into the same pattern; other scientists are less inclined to agree.

'About half of them protest that they have to *wait* until it is proven in humans before underfeeding can be generally recom-mended,' he says. 'Of course, medicine recommends very many things to humans that are not formally proven, such as low salt, increasing the fibre in your diet and the benefits of exercise. None of these are confirmed in the pure biological, scientific sense, but with a high order of probability, they work, and so they are recommended by physicians. Caloric restriction is in the same category. But because it deals with ageing, and because there is a kind of inbuilt ageism even in the medical profession, some doctors exhibit a reluctance to think about extending lifespan.'

'Man has had a problem since the beginning of his history, in accepting the inevitablity of physical death. We have invented all sorts of ways of evading the issue. Religion has arisen to answer the problem – after all, if there is life after death, then physical death is unimportant and you don't have to worry about it. Philosophers deal with this problem and evade it in different ways. So when you ask doctors, you also confront an issue that's not involved in other medical questions.'

Professor Walford regards underfeeding as so clearly effective that it is already an 'established' concept, and is now looking to other methods of prolonging life. With genetic and hormone manipulation (he is working on both), he believes the rigours of a calorie-restricted diet could eventually be modified, or even rendered unnecessary. 'My view is that we will certainly have breakthroughs in these non-caloric restriction areas before the end of the century,' he says. 'Prediction of this sort is always difficult. I am reminded of the fact that C. P. Snow, in his book *The New Physicist*, tells us that in 1933, Einstein, Lord Rutherford and Niels Bohr all predicted that we would never get power from the atom – and of course, in 1945, we had power from the atom.'

At the Wolfson Institute of Hull University, in Yorkshire, endocrinologist and age specialist Dr Brian Merry has added credence to Walford's theory by increasing the lifespan of his colony of 5,000 rats – the world's largest – by deliberately underfeeding them. He has also made the experiment work on insects and fish. Merry says he is finally in a position to begin extracting the bio-chemical and molecular information needed to reach conclusions about the links between nutrition and ageing. One thing is certain, he says: the British have their diet all wrong, which accounts for the highest rate of cardio-vascular illness and cancer in Europe.

There is a fighting chance that four-year-old Kyle Holford from Hampstead will never suffer from senile dementia. While Roy Walford started his ultra-diet late in life, and his life span is therefore limited (he admits) to 120 years, Kyle's parents, Patrick and Lizzie, started him on healthy food at birth, if not before. He has still never tasted meat or sugar, and Mr and Mrs Holford predict he should make at least 110 – Dr Walford would say that starting as young as Kyle did, he could see 150.

The Holfords, who are in their late twenties and have a health food shop, also run a non-profit organization called the Institute for Optimum Nutrition. For £100, they will draw up a personal health programme to prevent premature ageing, reduce the risk of degenerative diseases and improve physical and mental performance. 'I want to promote nutrition for the masses,' says Mr Holford, a psychology graduate of York University. 'We have got to get the message across. My feeling is that there is nothing better to do than to serve people. I have the knowledge, and I know it works.'

Turning Back the Clock

Does any reputable doctor claim to have a 'cure' for old age? Dr Ward Dean comes close. A disturbingly young-looking fortyish gerontologist who runs a full time life-extension clinic on Sunset Boulevard, Los Angeles, Dr Dean says he can turn back the clock and actually reverse the ageing process. And, even in the world of human hot housing, that is a considerable claim to make.

The Centre for Bio-Gerontology is a saucer-shaped building which looks remarkably like the Starship Enterprise, and Dr Dean (a former flight surgeon for Delta Force, the top-secret

American counter-terrorist unit) has a mission – to boldly go where no (reputable) doctor has had the nerve to go before.

Ageing, the doctor argues, is a terminal illness, and everybody over thirty has caught it. 'No one knows if intervention is doing any good, so we need a way to "diagnose" people's ages.' Chronological age, Dean asserts, means little; everyone knows eighty-year-olds who behave as if they are sixty five and people in their fifties who seem prematurely aged. The important question is, how old a person's vital functions are – heart, kidneys, lungs, eyesight, and so on. So Dr Dean has invented his own system of biological age measurement. 'Patients undergo a battery of biochemical and psychological tests, then we assign a number, which stands for the biological age of each organ. By testing at regular intervals, we can determine whether our programme is helping patients to win the battle against time. They are human guinea pigs – that's what I tell them. We can, for example, identify reduced kidney function, and come up with changes in diet and exercise, but also with *drugs*, which may prove helpful. This is, until genetic engineering allows us to reprogramme their genes.'

A typically prematurely-aged patient of Dr Ward Dean is a thirty five-year-old woman who, after undergoing his repertoire of tests – sedimentation, haemoglobin, alkaline phosphates, cholesterol, kidney function are amongst them – was told that her biological age was fifty five. So what now?

'After a complete analysis of the woman's lifestyle and diet, we try to eliminate bad habits which accelerate ageing, such as excessive smoking, drinking, sedentary lifestyle. We put her on a good healthy diet, we start a nutritional supplementation programme and an exercise régime. These are all standard public health measures; then we will go beyond that to incorporate some potential age-retarding substances, one of which is Hydergine, which is a drug indicated in Alzheimer's Disease, but is actually very beneficial for those who just want to improve memory, alleviate depression, or reduce the ageing pigment – liver spots – on their hands.'

This, he insists, is not the principle of using a sledgehammer to crack a nut – doctors prescribe 'creatively' all the time. Dr Dean, it must be said, specifies that this and other controversial drugs, like L-Dopa and Minoxidil (for hair growth) are *potentially* anti-ageing or age-retarding, adding that for 'normal' people (whose chronological age tallies closely with their biological age) 'nothing has yet been found to reverse the ageing process except exercise.'

Particularly controversial – some would say a little dangerous because of the possible risk of kidney damage – is his use of the process of chelation – intravenous chemical therapy which literally claws arterial plaque out of the bloodstream. Yet hope springs eternal, and Dr Dean attracts patients: 'I'm going to be beautiful, I'm going to be twenty nine again,' says Jock O'Mahoney, a sixty seven-year-old in a cowboy-style string tie, his left arm linked to a drip, having his system chelated. On shelves in the background stand rows of plastic jars containing Dr Dean's specially patented anti-ageing formula diets, Weighless (With the Rich, Natural Flavor) and Eatless (supplement and homeopathic Eating Reduction Medicine in Natural Cherry Flavor).

Jock O'Mahoney is only half joking when he talks of being twenty nine again. A former Hollywood stuntman, he played the title rôle in a series of Tarzan films (such as *Tarzan Goes to India*) and could swing through the trees with the best of them. Once an athletic sixteen stone, six feet four, with a fifty-inch chest, he knows all about feeling fit. But in his fifties he suffered a series of strokes. His fees at Dr Dean's clinic are being paid by the Screen Actors' Guild, and he expects to 'ride hell out of his horse' again with the help of Dr Dean's chelation therapy.

'Everything that's good for you is in there,' he said, looking up admiringly at his drip. 'It makes you feel younger, it makes you feel peppier, gives you more energy. Now I'm sticking my neck out, going into a field I know absolutely nothing about, but I think chelation will literally help get rid of cancer. It's taking the plaque out of my blood, out of my veins, eliminating all of the rotten stuff. The body is nothing but a series of pipes. You think about it and you realize all of a sudden that all the veins and arteries and capillaries and everything are just pipes — pipes, pipes, pipes. And like any pipe, if you put anything through it, including water, it gets clogged. By the time people are twenty years old, they've usually, because of fast foods, lost up to fifty per cent of the volume that can possibly go through the pipes. So, you heard it first from Jock O'Mahoney, OK?' he says with a wink, 'and I pray to God I'm right.'

Tell Me, Mr Methuselah, to what do you attribute your advanced years?

Everybody knows of someone who reputedly lived to a ripe old age taking out their everyday frustrations with therapeutic hard work of the chopping wood, or kneading bread variety. Interestingly, today's joggers and exercisers are thought to achieve relaxation by the release in their brains of the naturally occurring morphine-like tranquillizer endorphin. The substance accounts for the irritating (to non-exercisers) 'runner's high' — the pleasant, relaxed feelings following an intense workout.

But you needn't work up sweat in order to reduce stress. A Boston cardiologist, Dr Herbert Benson of Harvard Medical School and the city's Beth Israel Hospital, has a slightly more off-beat method, which in more than one sense bears thinking about. Following the very widely accepted view that stress reduction is a great aid to preventing heart attack, Dr Benson prescribes a form of meditation to patients with high blood pressure, or as he calls the approach, a 'demystified' route to 'the relaxation response.'

Dr Benson suggests finding a quiet room where you are

unlikely to be disturbed for at least twenty minutes. Make sure it is at least two hours since you last ate. Sit comfortably, close your eyes, let your muscles relax, and concentrate on breathing, he says. Every time you breathe out, say a word of your choice silently to yourself; concentrate on the word and block out distracting thoughts. Continue this for ten to twenty minutes. When you have finished, open your eyes, but sit quietly for a few more minutes. And repeat the dose twice a day for best results. So effective does Dr Benson consider this exercise that he tells patients taking drugs for high blood pressure to tell their doctor before starting it – it could, he claims, change the way their bodies use the drugs.

Stress reduction is, in fact, the longevity factor most commonly ascribed by the very old themselves to their achievement. This is perhaps hardly surprising, because few people over 100 are ever likely to have heard of cholesterol before they were already very old.

'If I can do anything about it, I'll do it. If I can't, I just forget it. Take things as they come, and don't worry about it,' said one centenarian in a 1981 book, *Living To Be 100: 1,200 Who Did It And How They Did It*, by Osborn Segerberg Jnr,. Typically, personal testimony from the elderly and anecdotal evidence are of limited use, and not as enlightening as might be hoped. Schigechiyo Izumi, 120 when interviewed by Oliver Gillie of the *Sunday Times* on a remote Japanese coral island in 1985, did not really know why he was the oldest man in the world. He smoked until he was 116, and at seventy took up drinking a local white rum, *shochu*. For most of his life, he lived on vegetables from his own farm (freedom from chemical fertilizers?); they were stir fried in pork fat, but then the pigs had been fed on fresh vegetables rather than concentrates, as most British pigs are. (Did this make a difference?) True enough, exercise had played a large role in Mr Izumi's life – he was once a champion Sumo wrestler. He died in early 1986. Other Japanese researchers, in a country which is hardly stress-

free but is achieving amazing longevity records, put the phenomenon down to daily helpings of fresh, particularly green or
yellow, vegetables.

The vegetable theme was repeated in Wales, incidentally one
of Britain's worst health blackspots, where Anna Williams
became the oldest-ever Briton at 112 in 1985. She too had
eaten a great number of greens from her own allotment – and
like Mr Izumi, had taken a lot of exercise growing them. Near
Mrs Williams, however lives John Evans, 109 in 1986 who has
done little that could be described as archetypally healthy,
apart from always wearing a wetted handkerchief over his
mouth to keep out the dust of the coalmine where he worked
for sixty years. He had led a hard life as a miner, and his
favourite food was bread and lard with salt sprinkled on it. To
what does Mr Evans attribute his longevity? No alcohol, no
bad language and 'a mugful of boiling water with a little honey
in it to take the taste of the boiling out.'

Life Extension: The Chemical Solution

John Evans, still going strong at the time of writing, would
probably regard the lifestyle of Durk Pearson and Sandy Shaw
as distinctly odd, even though one day (well, perhaps) they
may share an entry in the record books. Pearson and Shaw,
both in their forties, have made an industry out of their 'Life
Extension' products and books. They live in Los Angeles, have
undergraduate degrees in physics and chemistry respectively,
and confidently expect to toast in the twenty-second century
with their favourite vitamin cocktail. The couple are walking
encyclopaedias of the latest research on nutrition, drug intervention and lifespan, and quaff age-retardant chemical substances known as 'nucleotides'; they also sniff (often a little
disconcertingly during meals) regular doses of a nasal spray
called Diapid, which contains a synthetic hormone similar to

one produced by the pituitary gland, and apparently makes you alert and intelligent. Both habitually take a few whiffs before TV interviews.

The couple believe devoutly in the effectiveness of modern medicine. They believe chemical substances have reached such an advanced stage that they can do everything for you. You need not jog, or diet, or really do anything very much to live to a great age. The couple's fridge is so packed with promising substances that when you open the door, an avalanche of bottles and packets cascades out. Durk and Sandy each down twenty eight drugs every day, and spend their stress-free hours and days reclining on their waterbeds, working and writing on computers suspended over them at arm's length.

Desperate people are (the couple say) terribly keen to see them; one cancer patient tried to bribe a highway patrolman into divulging their address. Another hired a private detective. The address turns out to be two adjacent houses along the Pacific. One is entirely converted to use as a library, and contains almost every book and periodical ever published on the all-important subject of beating the clock. Life Extension, as advocated by Pearson and Shaw, is a curious mix of a kind of hippy culture and considerable medical research. The couple are not loved by the Federal Drug Administration. One Life Extension devotee, in a letter of support, offered to bump off the FDA's chief. 'I just sent him a letter back saying, "No thank you, they'd only replace him with somebody equally bad. Please don't bump anybody off," ' says M.I.T. graduate Pearson.

Pearson and Shaw's 858-page book *The Life Extension Companion* is a constant fixture on the bestseller lists – yet still they are out of step even with the more eccentric characters in the California scientific community. They confidently believe that their massive doses of drugs and vitamins and relaxed West Coast lifestyle are worth between 115 and 150 years of high-quality life. Death before that time could be caused only by murder, suicide or accident. An average day's sustenance for them, on top of a relatively routine food diet, includes niacin, RPM powder compound, beto-carotene, amino acids, minerals, prescription drugs such as L-DOPA (used to treat Parkinson's disease), lashings of monsodoium glutamate meat preservative ('The body is like a piece of steak, and many of the same ageing mechanisms apply to it,' they say) and more than a soupçon of that Diapid nasal spray. Scoff if you will – but seven major league baseball teams take regular doses of the couple's best-selling powder fructose energy drink. Furthermore, health conscious, high-income young professionals are reported to be spending up to $150 a month on other life-extension elixirs like Long Life, Brain Power, Maxi Life and BHT, a food preservative that Pearson and Shaw say can not only cure herpes but inhibit cancer and remove fat deposits from the arteries – all this despite warnings from more orthodox experts that Life Extension routines can damage kidneys, and cause headaches and intestinal problems. There is even a persistent rumour that at least one well-known Hollywood tough-guy is among the high-income Life Extenders.

It goes without saying that pills and potions designed to extend life are frequently a big business proposition long before they are formally proven effective – and it is not merely a fringe group of the desperate, the cranky and the hopeful who use them. Over half the doctors in Nevada – a state with a large number of retired people – until recently wrote regular prescriptions for a drug developed in Romania called Gerovital. They no longer need to prescribe it because it is available, in Nevada only, across the chemist's counter.

Gerovital – known as the 'feelgood pill' because it is said to relieve many of the discomforts of old age, and even reverse the ageing process – is made by a firm called Rom-Amer Pharmaceuticals (the name is an amalgamation of Romania and America) in Las Vegas. It is reported that tests have shown

Gerovital to be free from negative side effects. In fact, its opponents in the state and federal authorities maintain that it is free of *any* effects at all. Rom-Amer won permission to make the drug and sell it in Nevada only after a series of legal battles.

Gerovital was developed nearly thirty years ago by the Romanian gerontologist Dr Ana Aslan. Rom-Amer sensibly dissociates itself from Fountain-of-Youth claims, saying that Gerovital simply ameliorates the effects of ageing. Widely known for many years before its acceptance in the state of Nevada, the drug was regularly bought in Europe (where it is available over the counter) and smuggled back into the US in smart suitcases by clued-up elderly Americans, who claimed it make them feel clear-headed, fit and alert. Drugs of this nature have always been open to charges of 'placebo effect'. American baby boomers may remember the IQ Tablet made by a New York firm and sold over the counter in the early 1970s. One a day was recommended during school term, with an extra dose at major exam time. The Consumer Fraud Bureau discovered the pills were nothing more than chewable multi-vitamin and mineral tablets.

In China, sales of age-retarding concoctions are booming among the nouveau-riche peasantry. A bestseller, reportedly, is Ching Chun Bao, an anti-ageing liquid distilled from ginseng and royal jelly. Perhaps there is more incentive in China to seek long life, since the elderly are revered, and often run the country. Ching Chun Bao is thought to be a staple of China's elderly leaders, according to Mr Feng Hangzhou, manager of the computerized factory where it is made. Mr Feng's factory also makes such old favourites as donkey skin gelatin, buffalo horn tablets, rhinoceros horn, musk deer glands, tiger bones, extract of gecko, turtle essence, various bits of snake and lizard and a sexual potency elixir made of powdered deer antlers. Mr Feng insists that Ching Chun Bao has been tested in clinical trials on 10,000 guinea pigs, mice, rabbits and dogs. The guinea pigs, he says, outlived their usual two year lifespan, and twenty per cent survived for two and a half years – a twenty five per cent increase, equivalent to nearly twenty extra years in human terms. Ching Chun Bao is also a useful foreign exchange earner – a ten day supply retails for $15 in the US, five times the price in China.

The University Genetics company of Norwalk, Connecticut, which develops university-based inventions by either licensing them to industry or by setting up new companies to make them, recently sponsored the development of a bovine substance that – in the test tube at least – slows the metabolism and ageing of human skin cells. The work on 'Tissue Control Factor' was done at Case Western Reserve University in Cleveland, Ohio. The idea now is to produce it in the form of a face-cream. The prospect of a balm which could one day could give middle-aged people the faces of twenty five-year-olds – a biogenetic cosmetic moisturizer – is a cosmetic-maker's dream. Zanadu Laboratories of Ronkonkomar, Long Island has already leapt into action with their new 'Essence de Vie' skin cream, with TCF. Other drug companies are looking at TCF with a view to using it either as a skin preparation, or as a drug (either systematic or subcutaneous).

University Genetics' British-born chemist and molecular biologist Dr Alan Walton, who trained at Birmingham and Nottingham Universities, (one of the British brains who was drained) was instrumental in the discovery of TCF. He had observed that some children developed the disease progeria, involving rapid ageing and premature death, after brain damage. He also noted that progeria victims suffered damage to the pineal gland, a small organ in the brain. 'Could the pineal be the source of a "youth hormone", secreted into the bloodstream and used to slow cellular ageing?' he wondered. During a decade of research, Walton's team at Case Western laboriously isolated over a hundred factors secreted by cow pineal glands, and screened them for their ability to retard the growth of human cells designed to mature the skin cells. Only one of these pineal secretions had the desired growth-inhibiting qualities, and was christened TCF.

In laboratory tests on primitive (chick) and human skin cells, TCF stops cell division and growth entirely. While cells are exposed to TCF, they are said to remain in a state of suspended animation. After the removal of TCF, they resume their normal growth pattern, apparently unharmed. The factor seems, Dr Walton says, to penetrate to the nucleus of the cell and cling to the DNA. He believes TCF may act as some form of 'gene switch', in the sense of 'switching off' part of the activity of the cell. The results of his tests suggest that by retarding the metabolism and ageing of mature skin cells, and slowing their replacement with new cells, a youthful appearance may be preserved. Better news still – TCF in its moisturizing base has been investigated successfully for inflammatory character, toxicity and immunogenic response. There seem to be no signs of adverse effects on skin or open wounds, and the substance is hypoallergenic.

Cows are not the only possible source of youth in a tube. In Switzerland, Professor Paul Niehans, who died aged eighty nine in 1971, pioneered the use of fresh glandular cells from young black sheep to revitalize the failing tissues of ageing human beings. Black sheep are said to be particularly strong, healthy and disease-resistant. Treatment at La Prairie clinic in Switzerland is expensive – $5,500 a time, but that was not too much of a problem for fifty-ish Princess Elizabeth of Yugoslavia, (cousin of The Queen and mother of the Dynasty star Catherine Oxenburg) who recently endured ten painful injections in as many minutes – five in each buttock – in the quest to remain as young as possible. 'I felt as though I had sat on an extremely large hairbrush,' she announced. Such faith has she had in the treatment, however – 'Six weeks later,' she said, 'there was a huge difference. I felt fantastic' – that the clinic has asked her to act as one of its spokespersons. 'I feel younger, I have more energy. I need less sleep.'

But, if mysterious ointments from Switzerland, China and Connecticut ultimately fail the elderly self-hot houser, researchers from the University of Oklahoma may provide the real answer to turning back the biological clock, for men at least. In a sober and statistical way, Laurel Klinger-Vartabedian, Dorothy Foster and Lauren Wispe have discovered the life-enhancing property of a younger wife.

The death rate for men aged fifty to seventy nine and married to women one to twenty four years their junior is, they assert, thirteen per cent lower than the average for their age; men with older wives, on the other hand, suffer a twenty per cent *higher* death rate than average. According to Ms Klinger-Vartabedian, the team only set out to examine the folklore and myth of the older man with the younger woman, to answer people's curiosity about whether men like Fred Astaire and Cary Grant owed their youthful looks and long lives to living with young women – or whether, as the other popular myth has it, marrying a younger woman simply kills a chap. The Oklahoma survey, no explanation of which has yet been reached, attracted the instant wrath, as might be expected, of the Gray Panthers' 'older citizens' advocacy group'. The results, they announced, were 'a little silly – and pretty degrading to the ageing process, because it's the old maxim that older women are detrimental to your health'.

Space Travel: The Final Frontier

Dr Ralph Pelligra of NASA, who has studied the effect of absence of gravity on the ageing process, believes that older people will make marvellous space travellers. Stress on brittle bones may be alleviated in zero Gs, and ageing circulatory systems may function more efficiently than on Earth, with the heart requiring less effort to pump blood to the brain.

The film *Cocoon*, in which the final solution for the problems of old age turns out to reside in outer space, where there is no time and no death, speculates on whether old people would, if offered the chance, actually *want* to live forever. It is only fiction, of course, but two thirds of the elderly folk in the story plumped for eternal life, even though, to their earth-bound grandchildren, this effectively meant death, as the oldies would never be able to return to their planet.

In his futurology extravaganza *July 21, 2019*, published in 1987, Arthur C. Clarke boldly suggests that hot housed elderly astronauts will be commonplace in the space stations of the twenty first century.

The notion of geriatric skywalkers still seems odd today, when Exlax and Steradent sound like anything but the Right Stuff. But stranger things have happened. And one thing that unites hot house people – both young and old – is their common and over-whelming desire to reach for the stars.

Bibliography

Doman, Glenn *Teach Your Baby to Read*, Cape, 1965, Pan, 1975
―――― *How to Multiply Your Baby's Intelligence*,
―――― *Teach Your Baby Maths*, Jonathan Cape, 1979
―――― *How to Give Your Baby Encyclopaedic Knowledge*,
Elkind, David *The Hurried Child*, Addison Wesley, 1981
Hardyment, Christina *Dream Babies: Childcare from Locke to Spock*, Cape, 1983
Kamin, Leon *The Science and Politics of IQ*
Lewis, David *How to be a Gifted Parent*, Souvenir Press, 1979
Painter, Frieda *Living with a Gifted Child*, Souvenir Press, 1984
Pearson, Durk and Shaw, Sandy *The Life Extension Companion*
Rosenthal, R. and Jacobson, B. *Pygmalion in the Classroom: Teacher Expectations and Pupils' Intellectual Development*, 1986
Stott, Denis *The Parent as Teacher*, University of London Press, 1974
Terman, Lewis *The Measurement of Intelligence*, 1916
White, Burton, L. *The First Three Years of Life*, Star Books, 1979

Index